Newsmakers®

The People Behind Today's Headlines

Louise Mooney
Editor

1992
Issue 2

Includes Nationality, Occupation,
Subject and Newsmaker Indexes

Gale Research Inc. · *DETROIT* · *LONDON*

STAFF

Louise Mooney, *Editor*
Suzanne M. Bourgoin, *Associate Editor*
Marilyn O'Connell Allen, *Editorial Assistant*
Barbara Carlisle Bigelow, Victoria France Charabati, Kevin Conley, John P. Cortez, Ellen Creager, Harvey Dickson, Simon Glickman, Joan Goldsworthy, Christine Ferran, Anne Janette Johnson, Virginia Curtin Knight, Mark Kram, Michael L. LaBlanc, Jeanne M. Lesinski, Glen Macnow, Nancy Rampson, Sharon Rose, Isaac Rosen, Julia M. Rubiner, Susan Salter, Robert F. Scott, and Patricia Strnad, *Contributing Editors*

Peter M. Gareffa, *Senior Editor, Newsmakers*

Jeanne Gough, *Permissions and Production Manager*
Margaret A. Chamberlain, *Permissions Supervisor (Pictures)*
Pamela A. Hayes, *Permissions Associate*
Amy Lynn Emrich, Karla Kulkis, Nancy Rattenbury, and Keith Reed, *Permissions Assistants*

Mary Beth Trimper, *Production Director*
Shanna Philpott Heilveil, *Production Assistant*
Arthur Chartow, *Art Director*
Nicholas Jacubiak and C. J. Jonik, *Keyliners*

Victoria B. Cariappa, *Research Manager*
Mary Rose Bonk, *Research Supervisor*
Reginald A. Carlton, Clare Collins, Andrew Guy Malonis, and Norma Sawaya, *Editorial Associates*
Mike Avolio, Patricia Bowen, Rachel A. Dixon, Shirley Gates, Sharon McGilvray, and Devra M. Sladics, *Editorial Assistants*

Cover Photos: Mario Cuomo and Barbra Streisand (both AP/Wide World photos)

⊚™ The paper used in this publication meets the minimum requirements of the American National Standard for Information Sciences—Permanence Paper for Printed Library Materials, ANSI Z39.48-1984.

ISBN 0-8103-2247-1 (this volume)
ISBN 0-8103-2245-5 (complete 1992 set)
ISSN 0899-0417

Printed in the United States of America

Published simultaneously in the United Kingdom
by Gale Research International Limited
(An affiliated company of Gale Research Inc.)

Contents

Obituaries

Introduction

Newsmakers provides informative profiles of the world's most interesting people in a crisp, concise, contemporary format. Make *Newsmakers* the first place you look for biographical information on the people making today's headlines.

Important Features

- **Attractive, modern page design** pleases the eye while making it easy to locate the information you need.

- **Coverage of all the newsmakers** you want to know about—people in business, education, technology, law, politics, religion, entertainment, labor, sports, medicine, and other fields.

- **Clearly labeled data sections** allow quick access to vital personal statistics, career information, major awards, and mailing addresses.

- **Informative sidelights essays** include the kind of in-depth analysis you're looking for.

- **Sources for additional information** provide lists of books, magazines, and newspapers where you can find out even more about *Newsmakers* listees.

- **Enlightening photographs** are specially selected to further enhance your knowledge of the subject.

- **Separate obituaries section** provides you with concise profiles of recently deceased newsmakers.

- **Publication schedule and price** fit your budget. *Newsmakers* is published in three paperback issues per year, each containing approximately 50 entries, and a hardcover cumulation, containing approximately 200 entries (those from the preceding three paperback issues *plus* an additional 50 entries), *all at a price you can afford!*

- And much, much more!

Indexes Provide Easy Access

Familiar and indispensable: The *Newsmakers* indexes! You can easily locate entries in a variety of ways through our four versatile, comprehensive indexes. The Nationality, Occupation, and Subject Indexes list names from the current year's *Newsmakers* issues. These are cumulated in the annual hardbound volume to include all names from the entire *Contemporary Newsmakers* and *Newsmakers* series. The Newsmakers Index is cumulated in all issues as well as the hardbound annuals to pro vide concise coverage of the entire series.

- **Cumulative Newsmaker Index**—Listee names, along with birth and death dates, when available, are arranged alphabetically followed by the year and issue number in which their entries appear.

- **Nationality Index**—Names of newsmakers are arranged alphabetically under their respective nationalities.

- **Occupation Index**—Names are listed alphabetically under broad occupational categories.

- **Subject Index**—Includes key subjects, topical issues, company names, products, organizations, etc., that are discussed in *Newsmakers*. Under each subject heading are listed names of newsmakers associated with that topic. So the unique Subject Index provides access to the information in *Newsmakers* even when readers are unable to connect a name with a particular topic. This index also invites browsing, allowing *Newsmakers* users to discover topics they may wish to explore further.

Suggestions Are Appreciated

The editors welcome your comments and suggestions. In fact, many popular *Newsmakers* features were implemented as a result of readers' suggestions. We will continue to shape the series to best meet the needs of the greatest number of users. Send comments or suggestions to:

The Editor
Newsmakers
Gale Research Inc.
835 Penobscot Bldg.
Detroit, MI 48226-4094

Or, call toll-free at 1-800-347-GALE

Newsmakers®

Roone Arledge

AP/Wide World Photos

Television executive

Full name, Roone Pinckney Arledge, Jr.; born July 8, 1931, in Forest Hills, NY; son of Roone (a lawyer) and Gertrude (Stritmater) Arledge; married Joan Heise, December 27, 1953 (divorced in 1971); children: Roone Pinckney III, Elizabeth Ann, Susan Lee, Patricia Lu. *Education:* Columbia College, B.B.A., 1952; attended Columbia University's School of International Affairs.

Addresses: *Office*—ABC, 1330 Avenue of the Americas, New York, NY 10019.

Career

Joined the Dumont television network, 1952; produced and directed public relations radio spots for the U.S. Army, beginning in 1953; joined NBC-TV in 1955, produced and directed public affairs and children's programs, including Shari Lewis's *Hi, Mom*, a TV puppet show; joined ABC-TV in 1960 as producer of network sports, including *NCAA Football* and telecasts of American Football League games; created *ABC's Wide World of Sports*, April, 1961; became vice-president in charge of sports, 1963; became president of ABC Sports, 1968; created *NFL Monday Night Football*, 1970; became president of ABC News in 1977, while retaining his post as president of ABC Sports; creator of *20/20*, 1978, *Nightline*, 1980, and *This Week With David Brinkley*, 1981; promoted to group president of ABC News and Sports, 1985; creator of *PrimeTime Live*, 1989.

Awards: Won dozens of Emmys over the years, including one in 1958 for *Hi, Mom* and several others from 1966 through 1974 for ABC Sports; *TV Guide* award, 1964; Cannes Film Festival grand prize, 1965 and 1966; three George Foster Peabody awards for promoting international understanding; National Headliners Award, 1968; Distinguished Service Award, New York chapter of the Broadcast Pioneers, 1968; Kennedy Family award, 1972; named Man of the Year by the National Association of TV Program Executives, Philadelphia Advertising and Sales Club, *Football News*, Ohio State University, and the *Gallagher Report*; named to the Academy of Television Arts and Sciences Hall of Fame, 1990.

Sidelights

Roone Arledge has earned many bragging rights since joining ABC-TV in 1960. But he is perhaps most praised, especially by sports fans, for bringing professional football to the prime time airwaves. Arledge is the architect of *NFL Monday Night Football*, the show responsible for turning sportscaster Howard Cosell's name into a household word. In addition, Arledge is widely revered as one who revolutionized TV coverage of the Olympics and other sports events. His innovative techniques, now employed routinely by television broadcasters, include the use of instant replays, isolated cameras, slow motion, and stop action. His telecasts were the first to provide a more intimate, personal focus on the athletes.

Also the creator of several popular and enduring ABC programs, including *20/20, Nightline,* and *PrimeTime Live,* Arledge is credited with propelling ABC into the major leagues of network TV, permanently changing the face of TV sports coverage and turning the network's once-fledgling news division into a successful, top-rated organization.

Roone Arledge was born on July 8, 1931, in Forest Hills, New York, the son of Roone, an affluent attorney, and Gertrude Arledge. After graduating from Mepham High School in 1948, he attended Columbia College. There he served as president of

---

"If you asked me the secret to Roone's success, I'd say it is his considerable intellect, his tenacity, his personal charm and, at some moments, some ruthlessness."
—Ted Koppel

Phi Gamma Delta fraternity and was a member of the wrestling team. He graduated in 1952 with a degree in business administration and subsequently attended Columbia University's School of International Affairs. He left the school after a short time to join the Dumont television network, but was drafted by the U.S. Army in 1953. During his two-year stint in the service, he produced many public relations radio commercials.

In 1955, Arledge joined NBC, where he eventually served as a producer and director public affairs and children's programming. He won his first Emmy in 1958 for *Hi, Mom,* a popular TV puppet show hosted by Shari Lewis. Arledge—who "had already acquired a maverick's reputation" at a time when "mavericks were not welcome at NBC and CBS," as *Sport* magazine noted in 1986—moved to ABC in 1960. Thus began the legacy that, according to the *New York Times Magazine,* "put ABC on the map."

At the time ABC hired Arledge, rival stations CBS and NBC were much stronger in news and entertainment, dominating audiences and forcing ABC "into a survival mode as the network of audacity," *Sport* reported. Within weeks of joining ABC, Arledge sent a memo to his boss, Ed Scherick, regarding college football. The memo, according to *Sport,* read: "Heretofore, television has done a remarkable job of bringing the game to the viewer—now we are going to take the viewer to the game! We will utilize every production technique that has been learned in producing variety shows, in covering political conventions, in shooting travel and adventure series...we will have cameras mounted in jeeps, on mike booms, in risers of helicopters, anything necessary....In short—we are going to add show business to sports!'"

Arledge soon began covering sports events for ABC using what were then groundbreaking techniques, including instant replays, handheld cameras, and multiple cameras. He also utilized methods common in documentary filmmaking in order to "personalize" athletes. In the early 1960s, noted *Sport,* Scherick had an idea that sent Arledge "flying around the country and the world, buying up rights to obscure and oddball forms of competitions." The anthology series featuring footage of these little-known sports events eventually became known as *ABC's Wide World of Sports.* "The idea was to travel to the world's greatest events and try to capture whatever it is that makes these events fascinating," Arledge explained in *Playboy* in 1976. The show became a regular, airing on Saturday afternoons, beginning in January of 1962.

Once Arledge's programs began creating a huge market for sports, he turned his attention and talents to other sporting events, including the Olympics. Arledge became ABC's vice-president in charge of sports in 1963 and was promoted to president of ABC Sports in 1968. As executive producer of the Olympic Games in 1964, 1968, and 1972, he helped turn Olympics telecasts, which once had a small following, into programs that appealed to the masses. Meanwhile, he was earning himself a reputation as a risk-taker and a big spender, continually outbidding ABC's rivals for the rights to the Olympics and other sporting events.

In 1970, Arledge tapped the talents of Howard Cosell and introduced the immensely popular *NFL Monday Night Football* to prime time. According to *Sport,* "Howard Cosell was a played-out minor curiosity, a strident, nasal, noisome journeyman in his forties when Arledge rescued him from limbo and made him into a star—and a ratings gold mine for nearly two decades."

Two years later, ABC's Olympics coverage received much attention, when Palestinian terrorists killed two Israeli athletes and took nine hostages during the games in Munich, Germany. Arledge oversaw the station's more than 18 hours of eyewitness coverage of the tragic event, and ABC's national ratings soared. But it would be the 1976 Olympics—which ABC aired along with its prime time lineup—that helped the network achieve its first Number One ratings finish in its history.

With the popularity of its sports programming boosted, ABC turned its attention to the news division. Arledge's success with ABC Sports won him the post of ABC News president in 1977; he accepted the position while retaining his presidency of the sports division. According to *USA Today*, ABC's weak news programming had contributed to the network's nickname, the "Almost Broadcasting Company." *Channels* reported in March of 1989 that before ABC's successful 1976 season, an old Milton Berle joke "best characterized ABC's mood: 'If you want to end the Vietnam War, book it on ABC and it will be cancelled in 13 weeks.'"

The network, however, had little money to spend on news coverage, had fewer affiliate stations than its competitors, and lacked a half-hour network newscast until 1967, four years after NBC and CBS had expanded their news programming. In other words, it was lagging far behind the competition. "We needed a different approach to news," Frederick Pierce, network president, recalled in *Channels*. "Roone had demonstrated abilities, especially with events like the 1972 Olympics."

But TV critics and ABC staffers were aghast at Arledge's new post. Many were worried that the notorious "showman" would turn the news into a gimmicky, theatrical production and that he didn't understand the gravity of the news. "Our reaction when Roone came on was hostility, suspicion," ABC anchor Ted Koppel remarked in *Channels*. "We saw Roone as something of an interloper. While he had a distinguished sports career, we believed unless you grew up cutting teeth on news, the transition was impossible."

In addition, Koppel was quoted by the *Los Angeles Times* in 1992 as saying: "I thought he would be doing *Wide World of News*." Arledge himself told the *Los Angeles Times* that he was surprised by the negative reception to his promotion. "I felt that my whole emphasis in sports had been to elevate it,

getting rid of announcer approval, introducing journalism to it." He continued, "I turned down a lot of offers at the time to do movies and entertainment because I loved the news, and I thought ABC News was a wasted institution."

Arledge, a lavish spender holding clout with ABC management, quickly reshaped the news; he implemented showmanship, glitzy graphics, and what was then the revolutionary technique of split-screen interviews. He also expanded the network's news coverage, adding programs like *20/20*, *Nightline*, and *PrimeTime Live*. Don Hewitt of CBS's news program *60 Minutes* commented in *Channels*, "[TV news] is not a pure journalism medium like newspapers. Roone understands that. A fine line divides news and show business. The trick is to go up to that line, touch it, but don't cross it." Arledge raided other networks for news talent and big names, offering high salaries for both on-air and behind-the-scenes personnel. He told the *Los Angeles Times*, "When I came [to ABC News] nobody wanted to work here. It was the same way it had been when I took over ABC Sports and found out that the organization was considered below zero because they'd reneged on half their contracts. We were so far behind in the news that I felt we had to make a fairly big splash to tell people we were serious."

ABC's cast of talent as of the early 1990s included such popular figures as Peter Jennings, Ted Koppel, David Brinkley, Barbara Walters, Sam Donaldson, Diane Sawyer, and Hugh Downs. Arledge is often credited—and sometimes blamed—for creating the "star system," in which networks vie for the most popular newscasters by offering exorbitant salaries. He tried to lure anchor Tom Brokaw from NBC and when he "went after [CBS News anchor] Dan Rather, he ended up giving Rather the tools for winning a $35 million, 10-year contract from CBS," *Channels* reported.

In 1978, Arledge made a controversial staff change, replacing Barbara Walters and Harry Reasoner, the evening news anchor team, with the trio of Peter Jennings in London, Frank Reynolds in New York and Max Robinson in Chicago. Arledge told the *Los Angeles Times* that he felt Walters and Reasoner "looked like a bickering married couple on the air because Reasoner resented his high-paid female co-anchor." In 1983, after Reynolds's death, Arledge made Jennings the sole anchor of *World News Tonight*, which in 1989 became the top-rated network news program, a position it has held through the early nineties.

But acceptance of Arledge as a newsman by TV critics and staffers didn't come immediately. One obstacle was ABC's assignment of Geraldo Rivera, a reporter for the affiliate WABC, to cover the arraignment of New York serial killer "Son of Sam," David Berkowitz. Rivera—who went on to host a talk show centering on such controversial topics as incest and white supremacy—"had no less a reputation for the sensational than he has today," *Channels* reported in 1989. "That assignment outraged ABC correspondents, especially after Rivera seemed to convict Berkowitz in one report."

Arledge's next move was the launching of *20/20* in 1978. The premiere episode contributed to the show's initial flop; it featured a doll modeled after former U.S. president Jimmy Carter singing "Georgia" and a disturbing Rivera segment on rabbits being used as live bait to train greyhounds. The *New York Times*'s review read, "In addition to being pointless, the new ABC News magazine is dizzyingly absurd." The poor reception of the show prompted Arledge to replace the hosts—Robert Hughes, an art critic for *Time*, and Harold Hayes, a former editor of *Esquire*—with Hugh Downs and to change *20/20*'s format. Barbara Walters joined Downs as co-anchor in 1984, and the show has since enjoyed success, surviving what could have been a disastrous programming move from Thursday to Friday night in 1987.

In 1980, Arledge secured a late-night time slot for news bulletins on the Iran hostage crisis. Koppel, then the network's chief diplomatic correspondent, was anchor. "When he interviewed various people around the world at the same time, that struck me as the nucleus for a new program," Arledge recalled in the *Los Angeles Times*. That series evolved into another popular and innovative program, *Nightline*. "I'm prouder of that show than of almost anything I've ever done," Arledge said in an interview with *Newsweek*. "It gives us a dimension no other network has ever had."

In another move that strengthened the reputation of ABC's new division, Arledge hired NBC anchor David Brinkley in 1981 to rejuvenate its Sunday morning talk show, renaming it *This Week With David Brinkley*. *Newsweek* characterized the show as "the product of Arledge's relish for risks .... Many TV executives regarded ... Brinkley as a sour, burnt-out has-been. But Arledge believed that the stimulus of a political round table was all Brinkley needed to recharge his glow."

With the Capital Cities Communications purchase of ABC in 1985, Arledge's future with the network was unclear. Capital Cities was known as a frugal company, and by then Arledge had become renown for being a big spender. But Arledge adapted and presided over cutbacks at ABC News without disrupting the network's operations. In 1986, he was made group president for news and sports; he was eventually stripped of his sports responsibilities. Concentrating on news, Arledge made few changes, encouraging the division to produce more shows.

ABC's *PrimeTime Live* premiered in 1989, co-hosted by the network's former White House correspondent, Sam Donaldson, and former *60 Minutes* reporter Diane Sawyer. As with the first episode of *20/20*, the program—which featured a studio audience—got off on the wrong foot. The first show "was an embarrassment from the lack of chemistry between Donaldson and Sawyer to an embarrassing interview with [actress/comedienne] Roseanne Barr and a live studio audience whose silence was deafening," according to the *Los Angeles Times*. With such negative feedback about *PrimeTime Live*'s format, ABC decided to drop the "live" aspect of the show, and the program's popularity increased.

Having established a successful news division, Arledge began what *Channels* described as a "new approach" to network news, "an integration of journalistic standards with good TV, and an emphasis on profitability with an acceptance of the new economics of TV." The approach, Arledge told the magazine, "is consistent with the great news organizations—[the *New York Times*], the *Los Angeles Times*, the *Washington Post,* all are financially sound organizations. The old idea that if a news division made money it would be the end of the world because of the pressures is just not pertinent today."

Arledge's raw energy and enthusiasm for television has earned him the praise of many colleagues and peers. Former CBS News president Richard Salant was quoted in *Channels* as saying, "I find it very ironic that the newcomer in the business is now the veteran, the industry statesman. I wouldn't have given a plumb nickel to be an admirer of Roone Arledge. Now I'm a guy who has an enormous respect for him. He's overcome enormous obstacles." And Ted Koppel declared in the *Los Angeles Times:* "If you asked me the secret to Roone's success, I'd say it is his considerable intellect, his tenacity, his personal charm and, at some moments, some ruthlessness. Anyone who has succeeded as he has has that."

Sources

Channels, March 1989.
Los Angeles Times, January 5, 1992.
Newsweek, February 6, 1984; June 15, 1987.
New York Times Magazine, July 28, 1991.
Playboy, October 1976.
Sport, December 1986
USA Today, January 8, 1991.
U.S. News & World Report, February 8, 1988.

—Patricia G. Peabody

Bobby Bonilla

Professional baseball player

Born Roberto Martin Antonio Bonilla, February 23, 1963, in Bronx, NY; son of Roberto (an electrician) and Regina (a social worker) Bonilla; married Millie Quinones, c. 1985; children: Danielle. *Education:* Graduate of Lehman High School, New York City, 1981.

Career

Professional baseball player, 1981—. Signed with Pittsburgh Pirates organization, 1981; played for Bradenton (Florida) Pirates, 1981-82, Alexandria Pirates, 1983, Nashua Pirates, 1984, Prince William (Virginia) Pirates, 1985. Traded to Chicago White Sox, 1986; returned to Pirates the same year. Member of Pittsburgh Pirates, 1986-91. Joined New York Mets as free agent, 1991.

Awards: Named to the National League All-Star team, 1988-91.

Sidelights

At the tender age of 28, Bobby Bonilla has become the highest paid player in all of professional baseball. The switch-hitting Bonilla achieved stardom during his years with the Pittsburgh Pirates, but he has since moved to the New York Mets, who offered him a phenomenal $29 million in salary and promotional endorsements in a five-year contract. Bonilla is expected to become a team leader with the Mets, both on and off the field. "The first year is going to be tough; you don't have to be Einstein to

figure that out," he told the *New York Times*. "I think the Mets want to make something happen. [But] I'm here to have fun. If you can't play the game like you did when you were in high school, you're in trouble."

Bonilla helped guide the Pirates to two National League East championships and was voted a member of the National League All-Star team every year since 1988. With a batting average hovering around .300 and fine defensive skills at third base, he was considered a mainstay of the Pittsburgh squad. Unfortunately for the Pirates, Bonilla became a free agent after the 1991 season, and other teams in bigger cities deluged him with lucrative contract proposals. The Mets won the bidding, and Bonilla has returned to the city in which he was born. "The [Mets] organization has asked me to be myself, to do what I've done elsewhere and not to try and do more," the player told the *New York Times*. "And I feel that if I put up the numbers that have appeared on my bubble gum card for the last six seasons, I'm not going to have a problem."

Bobby Bonilla is not a stranger to the Mets' home of Shea Stadium. He once attended an open Mets tryout when he was only 15. On that occasion he scooped up a fistful of dirt to take home to his girlfriend as a souvenir. Many times he wondered if that was the closest he ever would get to becoming a major league baseball player.

Bonilla grew up in the South Bronx, one of New York's toughest, most crime-plagued regions. A *Chicago Tribune* reporter described young Bonilla's environs as follows: "The drugs are out of control, the crime rate is as high as the unemployment rate and the banks send out for extra cash when the welfare checks come rolling in at the first of the month. It's not safe at night, and not much safer by day. There are more homicides in a couple of months than many big U.S. cities have in a year." Growing up in the South Bronx, Bonilla witnessed shootings, drug sales and use, gang violence, and the hopelessness poverty can bring. "It's worse now than it used to be," Bonilla told the *Pittsburgh Press* of his old neighborhood. "When it got bad where I lived, we moved. We must have had seven or eight places."

Even in such desperate circumstances, Bonilla remained a "good kid," devoted not to trouble-making but to sports, especially baseball. As a child he even took his bat to bed with him, in case he wanted to take a few practice swings in the middle of the night. He spent many hours on the playgrounds in his various neighborhoods, playing sandlot baseball or more organized games for school teams. Still, even getting to the playground could be a dangerous experience. One morning, he told *Sports Illustrated,* "I walked out the door at 7 a.m. and there went a guy chasing somebody down the street with a .22 [rifle]. We were all ducking under cars to stay out of the line of fire." Bonilla added: "I always looked out the peephole before I went outside, and one day I saw people in the hallway. When I opened the door a crack, I could see they were shooting heroin. When you see people injecting themselves with a needle, you know something is wrong. I was just 10 years old, but that made me realize that was not where I wanted my life to lead. But it's very hard to get out of."

One factor in Bonilla's favor was his relationship with his father, Roberto, who worked as an electrician. Even though Bonilla's parents divorced when he was eight, his father continued to take an active role in the lives of the children. "Kids today are looking for idols, but sometimes they look too far," the player told the *Chicago Tribune.* "When I was growing up, my idol was right there . . . my father. I didn't have to look any farther. The neighborhood was bad, but my home life wasn't bad." Bonilla's father encouraged him to excel in sports and spent time with his son by taking him to the abandoned

buildings where wiring needed to be done. "My father would go up into these old buildings where the wires all look the same, so you couldn't tell negative from positive," Bonilla said. "Sometimes he'd get knocked off the ladder by the shocks, but he always got right back up there. Every time some kid tells me I'm his idol, I say, 'No, no, your parents should be your idols.'"

By virtue of his good grades and behavior, Bonilla qualified to attend Lehman High, a predominantly white, middle-class school in another district. Bonilla had to ride two different city buses to get to the school, and he remembered in *Sports Illustrated* that he wasn't necessarily welcome there when he arrived. "I didn't really know about racism and had never given it much thought until I got to high school," he said. "There were always a couple of guys there saying, 'You don't belong here, we're going to blow your head off.'"

> *"Every time some kid tells me I'm his idol, I say, 'No, no, your parents should be your idols."*

Fortunately for Bonilla, baseball coach Joe Levine did not share that attitude. Levine detected greatness in Bonilla while the youngster was at Lehman, but because the school was in the inner city, no scouts ever visited. Nor did the team get to play a heavy schedule; one year Bonilla only played in 33 games. Nevertheless, after Bonilla graduated in 1981, Levine was able to find him a position on an Eastern U.S. high school stars' tour of Scandinavia. *Sports Illustrated* correspondent Bruce Newman noted: "After growing up in the shadow of Yankee Stadium, Bonilla had to go to Europe to get discovered."

One of the other players on the Eastern all-star team was Jim Thrift, whose father, Syd, was a part-time scout for the Pirates. Syd Thrift—who has since become something of a legend in Pittsburgh—heartily recommended that the Pirates sign Bonilla, and promptly. The phone call came to Bonilla's home in the Bronx. "When they called me and asked me if I wanted to play, I thought, 'What a stupid question.' Of course I wanted to play," Bonilla told the *Chicago Tribune.* Right out of high school in 1981, the future superstar reported to Bradenton, Florida, where the Pirates had a farm team.

Bonilla did not burst upon the scene at Bradenton with all the talents he has now. He had far less experience than most of the other rookies, but he had the maturity to realize that the minor leagues existed to help him develop his talent. During his first two seasons in Bradenton, he batted only .217 and .228, but he was tutored by former Pirate great Willie Stargell and other batting and fielding instructors. By 1983 he had raised his average to .256 for the more challenging Alexandria team. Still, Bonilla realized that many minor leaguers never make the big leagues. In the off season he attended a technical college to learn repair work.

During a season of winter baseball in Puerto Rico, Bonilla's high school girlfriend, Millie Quinones, visited him on the island. The two of them decided to marry, and Bonilla had to borrow the money for the wedding license. The marriage has endured through some hard times—in 1985 Bonilla was a good prospect to make the Pirates when he broke his leg in spring training. The break was severe, taking months to mend, and when it did heal Bonilla was shipped back to the low minors. "I don't think they thought I

Bobby Bonilla practices batting during the New York Mets' spring training in Port St. Lucie, Florida, in February of 1992. AP/Wide World Photos.

would ever play again," Bonilla told *Sports Illustrated.*

In the winter of 1985-86, Bonilla was left off the Pirates' 40-man roster. The omission made him eligible to sign with another team, and the Chicago White Sox hired him. He was there only a few months, however. Syd Thrift persuaded the Pirates to trade for him, and he returned to Pittsburgh in exchange for pitcher Jose DeLeon. He joined the Pirates permanently in 1986 and became a starter in mid-1987.

Reflecting on Bonilla's contribution to the Pirates organization in early 1988, manager Jim Leyland told the *Washington Post:* "Bobby's big and has great power from both sides of the plate. He's got a great arm. He's quick. His foot speed is okay and he's a pretty good base runner. He's always been kind of laid-back [off the field] but he plays pretty gutsy. If I were him, I wouldn't worry. I'd go ahead and buy a house here in Pittsburgh." The following year, when the Pirates reversed their fortunes and contended for the pennant, Leyland told the *Chicago Tribune:* "If we hadn't had Bobby Bonilla, you might have needed a flashlight to find us. We might have been 40 games out. He's a switch-hitting third baseman who hit 24 homers and knocked in 100 runs [in 1988].... How many teams do you think would like to have Bobby Bonilla?"

Leyland's question was answered soon enough. Although he rarely complained during the season, Bonilla became increasingly disenchanted with the Pirates organization. He wanted to stay in Pittsburgh, but the ownership there offered him little incentive to do so, challenging him when he asked for salary arbitration. Even as he finished third in the voting for league Most Valuable Player and helped the Pirates to advance to the National League Championship Series in 1991, Bonilla let it be known that he would become a free agent at the end of the season and peddle his wares elsewhere.

Offers poured in, especially from the Philadelphia Phillies and the New York Mets. The Mets finally won the bidding war for Bonilla with a $29 million plan that will pay the player $5.8 million over the next five years. Facing an army of reporters with an easy smile, Bonilla said that he will enjoy playing in New York, that the city feels like home to him, and that he has many family members and friends there. "I was a free agent, and I had the right to talk to everyone," he told the *New York Times.* "People say I ran to the money, but I would have been the highest-paid player in baseball with any of the deals I could have signed. After I lost at arbitration in the past, people said I was underpaid. Now they say I'm overpaid. Hey, I'm home. I'm happy to be here. I have my smile, and it's going to be hard to knock it off."

The Mets are looking for greatness from Bonilla, who may very well develop even further as a hitter and fielder. The pressure to excel is immense for the 6'3", 230-pound superstar, but he is not a man who has been coddled throughout his life. "You talk about pressure in baseball?" Bonilla asked the *Chicago Tribune.* "There is no pressure in baseball. Pressure is growing up in the South Bronx." Bonilla stresses, however, that he does not necessarily want to be considered a "hero," no matter how well he does for the Mets. "If kids are looking for a hero," he said, "they don't have to look any farther than their home, because those are the people that really love you. They are the real heroes."

Sources

Chicago Tribune, June 18, 1989.
New York Times, December 6, 1991.
Pittsburgh Press, April 28, 1991; August 8, 1991; November 19, 1991; December 3, 1991.
Sports Illustrated, October 14, 1991.
Washington Post, May 18, 1988.

—Mark Kram

Sonny Bono

AP/Wide World Photos

Entertainer and mayor of Palm Springs, California

Born Salvatore Philip Bono, February 16, 1935, in Detroit, MI; son of Santo and Jean Bono; married first wife in the mid-1950s (divorced, 1962); married Cherilyn LaPiere (singer and actress known as Cher), October 27, 1964 (divorced, 1974); married Susie Coelhoe (a model), December 31, 1982 (divorced); married Mary Whittaker; children: (first marriage) Christy; (with Cher) Chastity; (with Whittaker) Chesare Elan (son). *Politics:* Republican. *Religion:* Scientologist.

Addresses: *Office*—Office of the Mayor, Palm Springs, CA.

Career

Worked various jobs while writing songs, 1951-57; during the late 1950s served as assistant producer, staff producer, and recording artist (under name Don Christy) for Specialty Records; assistant to Phil Spector at Phillies Records during the late 1950s and early 1960s; part of singing duo Sonny and Cher, 1964-74; creator and co-host of *The Sonny and Cher Comedy Hour*, CBS-TV, 1971-74; creator and host of *The Sonny Comedy Revue*, 1974; mayor of Palm Springs, CA, 1988—. Producer of records, including *The Two of Us, Look At Us, Sonny and Cher,* and *Bittersweet White Light*. Solo recording artist of album *Inner Views*, Atco. Producer of films, including *Good Times*, Columbia, 1967, and *Chastity*, American International, 1969. Actor in television movies, including *Murder in Music City* and *The Top of the Hill*.

Sidelights

Few people in show business have experienced such extreme highs and lows as those that have marked the career of Sonny Bono. He and his now-ex-wife Cher, today a mega-star of films and music, went from obscurity to national stardom almost overnight in the mid-1960s, only to see their success fade within a few years. The duo were outcasts of the entertainment world for a time, but canny business moves by Sonny eventually took them to an even higher level of success than they'd enjoyed the first time around. Their divorce and the subsequent breakup of their act in the mid-1970s then plunged Sonny into another low. For a time he seemed destined to be remembered only as the luckless ex-husband of Cher, yet he reemerged as a winner in the political arena, becoming mayor of Palm Springs, California, and a possible candidate for state legislature.

Born in Detroit, Michigan, to Sicilian immigrants, Sonny moved with his family to Los Angeles when he was seven years old. Home life was difficult; his parents eventually split in a painful divorce that Bono recalled years later in his composition "You'd Better Sit Down Kids," which became a hit song when it was recorded by Cher. From an early age, he was preoccupied with breaking into the music business. School was certainly not his focus; after years of poor grades he dropped out at age 16. There followed a period in which he supported himself working a variety of jobs, including delivery boy, waiter, butcher's assistant, construction worker, and truck driver—all while writing and attempting to sell his songs. After years of striving, he got his first break in 1957 when one of his compositions, "High School Dance," was released as the B side of Larry Williams's "Short Fat Fanny" and went to Number 90 on the charts.

On the strength of "High School Dance," Bono landed a position at Specialty Records. It was an invaluable learning experience. He worked as an assistant producer, did a little recording under the name Don Christy, and eventually became a staff producer, working with the likes of Sam Cooke and Little Richard. The knowledge he gained at Specialty led him to found his own record company, but it quickly collapsed. Bono then worked as a record promoter for a time before being hired as an assistant to legendary producer Phil Spector. Once again Bono had a hand in all aspects of the business—arranging, engineering, and producing records, continuing to write (his "Needles and Pins" was a big hit for the Searchers, as was "Koko Joe" for the Righteous Brothers), and singing backup for many groups, including the Crystals, the Ronettes, and the Righteous Brothers. During the late 1950s he married and in 1959 his wife gave birth to a daughter, Christy; but by 1962 the union had ended in divorce.

Bono met Cherilyn LaPiere in 1963 at a vocal backup session for the Ronettes. She was a 16-year-old runaway who was hungry for fame and looking for some kind of break into the recording industry. "As a producer, I thought Cher was a natural star, immediately," Bono told *New York Times* interviewer Digby Diehl. The two quickly gravitated toward one another, and in October of 1964 they were married in Tijuana, Mexico. "Maybe I was kind of naive, but I really saw us as a couple who were going to last forever," Bono told Eric Sherman in *Redbook*. "I don't think either of us has ever had as much fun with anyone else as we had together . . . . Cher knew what I was thinking and I knew what she was thinking." Back in the States after their wedding, the couple returned to singing backup, but "the real strong message from Cher was, 'Make me a star,'" Bono told Sherman. "That took a lot of energy and I went at it with tremendous intensity. I was aware of my job, and I didn't want to let Cher down. I promised myself and her that I would pull that off—and I did."

Giving up the security of working under Spector's wing, Bono devoted his time to writing songs especially for himself and Cher to perform. Billing themselves as "Caesar and Cleo," the duo recorded a couple of unmemorable songs for Vault and Reprise labels before reverting to their own nicknames and signing with Atco in 1965. In June of that year "I Got You, Babe" was released to become an immediate hit, racing to the very top of the pop charts. Cher had her wish, and Sonny had the payoff for his years of hard work; they were at the time the most popular singers in the country. Their success continued with their followup release, "Baby, Don't Go," and a solo release by Sonny titled "Laugh at Me" also reached the top ten that year. Their gross income in 1965 was $3 million—approximately a thousand times more than they had earned in 1964.

More hits, such as "Bang Bang," "All I Really Want to Do," "What Now, My Love," and "The Beat Goes

> *"I was thinking, 'All right! I've delivered. I've made Cher a star.' That's why our breakup was such a surprise. It literally came overnight. I never saw it coming."*

On" kept Sonny and Cher at the top of the pop world for the next two years. Bono described the intense pressure he felt at the time to Arnold Shaw of *BMI* magazine: "It was too demanding. Getting a hit record constantly was on my mind. It gave you three more months of survival as a star . . . . When the three months were up, the panic was on. I had to get to the piano and come up with another hit." Although Sonny was indeed a seasoned veteran of the music business, and both he and Cher were ambitious— even driven—to maintain their popularity, they presented a very different image to their fans. Their public personas were those of two kooky flower children in an advanced stage of puppy love. That's how they protrayed themselves in *Good Times*, a 1967 film release with music arranged and conducted by Sonny. In it, they flew in the face of convention and confounded record company executives with their hippie clothes and attitudes, acting as though their fame was a total surprise and of little concern to them.

By the time *Good Times* hit the theaters the duo had sold 40 million records internationally—yet the movie itself was a box-office flop. The simple sounds of folk-pop were giving way to harder-edged music as the mood of the times turned darker and more political. Sonny and Cher suddenly seemed out of date, and the pair saw their good fortune leave them almost as quickly as it had come. Deciding that they needed to give the public more gritty reality, Sonny conceived of a nonmusical, dramatic film that would serve as a star vehicle for his wife. He wrote and produced *Chastity*, a loosely plotted tale of a teenage runaway who hitchhikes through the Southwest and Mexico. "I wanted to be a part of show business, and they wouldn't have me," Bono recalled in a *Good Housekeeping* article. "So I invested everything I had—emotionally and financially—in that movie. I was trying to say, 'We're solid entertainers. You've got to accept us.'" Neither the public nor the critics responded to that plea, however. Upon its release in 1969, *Chastity* was panned as a pretentious, superficial, and ultimately boring attempt to cash in on the youth culture of the day. Bono, who'd mortgaged his house to finance the project, lost over half a million dollars. Even worse, he and Cher had become the laughingstocks of the entertainment industry.

Despite the humiliation and financial hardship brought on by *Chastity*, Sonny vowed to Cher that within five years he would have them on top once again. In planning his strategy for accomplishing that goal, he decided that they should try to appeal to a more stable, mature audience than the fickle youth market that had been their mainstay thus far. The first step on their road back was to begin working the nightclub circuit with a more sophisticated, adult act. Gone were the bell bottom pants and love beads; Sonny now wore a tuxedo, and Cher began appearing in the revealing costumes that would become her trademark. They sang a mix of their old hits, club standards, and contemporary favorites. Along with the music, they featured a stand-up comedy routine in which Sonny played straight man, delivering monologues to Cher. She would stand there silently, her expression one of profound boredom, as she tossed her waist-length hair over her shoulders. Finally she would speak—devastating her husband with a one-line putdown. No matter how many barbs and off-color remarks the couple exchanged, the act always ended on a happy note as they sang their signature song, "I Got You, Babe."

Audiences loved the act, and in 1971 the revamped Sonny and Cher were back in the top ten with the song "All I Ever Need is You." In the summer of that year, executives from the CBS television network invited the pair to host a six-week summer replacement series of hour-long variety shows. Once again Sonny took personal responsibility for creating just the right format, blending elements of their nightclub act with elaborate production numbers, spectacular costumes for Cher, and comedy skits with their guest stars. Response from the viewing public was most enthusiastic, leading CBS to make the show a regular offering beginning in the winter of 1971. *The Sonny and Cher Comedy Hour* drew consistently high ratings, which the Bonos backed up with continued live appearances. Once again they were selling out concert halls.

The show was still going strong early in 1974 when Cher announced unexpectedly that she was leaving her husband. "I thought we loved each other," Sonny told Eric Sherman. "I guess what was going on in her head and what was going on in mine were two totally different things. I was thinking, 'All right! I've delivered. I've made Cher a star.' That's why our breakup was such a surprise. It literally came overnight. I never saw it coming." Almost as stunned as Bono were the CBS executives, who were unsure of how to market a husband-and-wife comedy team in the throes of a divorce. The network continued the show for a brief time, but by mid-1974 it was off the air. The ex-spouses each resurfaced with new variety shows, but both *The Sonny Comedy Revue* and *Cher* were short-lived. "It was hard . . . . One day, you're on top of the world, but the next, you not only lose your career, but your wife and your kid. Just *everything* . . . everything went at once. The breakup made me comatose for awhile," Bono told Sherman.

Eventually the songwriter-performer began struggling to win acceptance in his own right. He took acting lessons, appeared on the dinner-theater circuit, made a few television movies, and was a frequent guest on the popular TV shows *The Love Boat* and *Fantasy Island*. Any measure of success he may have had was certainly dwarfed by Cher's, for she had gone on to become an Academy Award-winning actress. Bono opened a restaurant; it failed. In 1982 he married model Susie Coelhoe, but before long they were divorced. More than ten years passed before his fate took a turn for the better. In 1985 he left Los Angeles to take up residence in Palm Springs. There he married his fourth wife, Mary Whittaker, and opened a second restaurant that became a profitable business grossing $2.7 million a year. In 1987 he faced up to the past by reuniting with Cher on the set of *Late Night With David Letterman*, an experience he described to Sherman as "strange. There was tension, there was anxiety, there was mystery, there was magic . . . . It was bittersweet. Part of it was fun, but there was also sadness over the fact that the old Sonny and Cher days were gone forever."

Early in 1988 Bono became entangled in an ongoing dispute with the Palm Springs planning board concerning the remodeling of his Spanish-style mansion. His dealings with the town fathers convinced him that they were blocking not only the construction work on his house, but also the economic progress of Palm Springs. The city has long been known as a playground for the rich and famous, yet it has gradually changed into a sedate retirement community, with one-third of its 83,000 residents being of retirement age. That demographic shift, combined with economic competition from new resort areas like nearby Palm Desert, has caused Palm Springs's mean income to sink to half that of some of its neighboring communities. In 1988 the city posted a $2.5 million budget deficit.

Bono was convinced that if Palm Springs would recognize the importance of tourism, make an investment in restoring its faded glamour, and promote itself aggressively, its economy would be revitalized. He declared himself a candidate for the mayor's office, running on a platform of "growth through glitz." Retiring mayor Frank Bogert called him "everything from a hippie to a squirrel," reported a *People* magazine contributor, but despite the insults, Bono defeated six opponents in a surprise landslide. He began following through on his campaign promises soon after taking office by bringing several new events to his city and increasing the appeal and visibility of others. Under his leadership, Palm Springs hosted the Miss Hollywood pageant, rock concerts, and an international film festival. A vintage Grand Prix auto race held annually in the town drew three times the spectators that it had before he assumed office. He also convinced the city council to approve plans for a multi-million-dollar complex that would include an amphitheater, a championship golf course, and a horse racing track.

Controversy accompanied his achievements, however. The increased bustle didn't please all residents; some objected to the disruption of Palm Springs's tranquility. Other factions accused Mayor Bono of using his station as a means of putting himself in the public eye in order to revive his entertainment career.

They pointed to his use of $4,500 of city funds for publicity photos of himself as an abuse of power. The fact that Bono had performed at a New York City nightclub, filmed a television pilot, played a major role in John Waters's film *Hairspray*, and made a Miller Lite beer commercial indicated to some groups that he was not devoting enough time to his public responsibilities. Bono garnered additional bad press when he fired three longstanding members of the Visitors and Promotion Board and tried to silence public comment on the issue. "That elicited cries of 'Mayor Bonehead' and 'Sonny Bonaparte,'" Todd Gold commented in *People*.

When Bono backed out of an AIDS benefit walkathon with the excuse that he needed to spend time with his family, Bill Gordon—owner of the local gay publication *Bottom Line*—was spurred to launch a mayoral recall movement. After a long meeting with Bono, however, Gordon backed down, satisfied that the mayor had become more aware of his shortcomings. Without Gordon's support the recall movement lost steam, and Bono continued unchallenged as mayor. As his term draws to a close, he is considering running for state-level office, having seen encouraging poll response to that proposition. Bono, who told his story in the autobiography *The Beat Goes On*, has ambitious plans for his future, but at the same time, he is philosophical about the elusive nature of fame and success. He told Sherman: "I could say to my wife tomorrow, 'OK, Mary, let's sell everything, move to the Caribbean and sell sandals on the beach.' I'm spontaneous. That's the way I've lived my life—and that's just how I like it."

Selected writings

The Beat Goes On, 1991.

Sources

BMI, April 1972.
Business Week, May 1972.
New York Times, July 9, 1967; December 14, 1988.
People, January 18, 1982; February 28, 1983; March 21, 1988; October 2, 1989.
Redbook, September 1988.

—Joan Goldsworthy

Kenneth Branagh

Actor, writer, and director

Born Kenneth Charles Branagh, December 10, 1960, in Belfast, Ireland; son of William (a carpenter) and Frances (a housewife; maiden name Harper) Branagh; married Emma Thompson (an actress), August, 1989. *Education:* Graduated from Royal Academy of Dramatic Art. *Religion:* Protestant.

Career

Actor, director, and playwright. Has appeared in numerous stage productions, including *Three Sisters, Hamlet, Another Country, Francis, Henry V,* and *Golden Girls;* has appeared in feature films, including *High Season, Henry V,* and *Dead Again;* television credits include play *Too Late to Talk to Billy* and the BBC series *Fortunes of War;* directorial credits include films *Henry V* and *Dead Again.* Co-founder of the Renaissance Theater Company, 1987.

Awards: Bancroft Gold Medal from the Royal Academy of Dramatic Arts, c. 1982; named SWET "Best Newcomer," 1982; Academy Award nominations for best director and best actor, both 1989, both for *Henry V;* named best new director by the New York Film Critics Circle, c. 1989.

Sidelights

After several years of remarkable success as a stage actor and playwright, Kenneth Branagh took the movie industry by storm with his 1989 film of William Shakespeare's *Henry V.* The picture garnered an Academy Award for costumes, and nominations for acting and directing. At the age of 28, Branagh was laughing off the scores of critics who compared him to his most famous predecessors—actor-director geniuses Sir Laurence Olivier and Orson Welles—figures to whom most artists only dream of being likened. For his next film project, 1991's *Dead Again,* he flouted expectations by directing and playing two roles in a mainstream romantic thriller. Of course, before this time he had already written an autobiography and formed an independent theater company that broke records for advance ticket sales. Branagh's energy and ambition as an artist—and artistic entrepreneur—raised expectations in the press that he must be arrogant and difficult. Yet he capped his other achievements by charming his interviewers completely. No wonder audiences were able to accept Branagh as Shakespeare's unstoppable and charismatic young king.

Branagh's early life was humble enough: He was born to a lower-middle-class family in Belfast, Ireland, in 1960. The family's residence was in the same neighborhood where the two sets of grandparents had lived; Branagh's grandfathers worked on the docks and spent the balance of their lives—and their wages—in the pubs. His father had escaped a life of work at a textile mill by becoming an apprentice joiner; according to Branagh's autobiography *Begin-*

ning, Bill Branagh—whose own father did some work as a "handy man" when not on the docks—fully expected his son to carry on the trade.

Young Kenneth, however, had taken an early shine to movies and books. In *Beginning* he recalled seeing the film *The Birdman of Alcatraz* as a boy; the naturalistic performances of star Burt Lancaster and the supporting cast made a huge impression on him. "No one appeared to be 'acting,'" Branagh wrote. The first play he saw was a production of Charles Dickens's *A Christmas Carol;* the force of this experience surpassed anything Kenneth had seen at the movies. "They were there, actually in front of me," he recollected. "There was no other word for it. Magic."

Sectarian violence between Protestants and Catholics had become so bad in Belfast during Branagh's adolescence that his family moved to Reading, England. His father had a good job opportunity there, so the family began the uncomfortable process of adjusting to life in a London suburb. Kenneth's Belfast accent gave way to what the English call "received pronunciation," and his guilt and ambivalence about his cultural identity would follow him well into his adult life. "I was acutely aware of my speech at a school where it seemed to me everyone spoke like BBC newsreaders," he recalled in his autobiography.

At school Branagh landed his first acting part, playing Dougal the dog in the play *The Magic Roundabout.* Shortly thereafter, he wrote a short play for a festival; it told the story of Lord Ponsonby-Smythe, who improves conditions for his laborers when he discovers the difficulty of their lives. More roles in school plays followed, but young Branagh's path to small-scale stardom was interrupted by another change of family domicile. A new house meant a new school, and Kenneth had to face another adjustment ordeal. He became captain of the rugby and football teams, "more, I suspect, for my innate sense of drama—I loved shouting theatrically butch [macho] encouragment to 'my lads'—than for any real sporting skill." These speeches may have served as preparation for Henry V's "encouragement" of the English troops at Agincourt in Shakespeare's play.

By age 16, Branagh knew he wanted to be a professional actor. Parts in school plays were coming fast and furious, so much so that his parents worried about his schoolwork. Meanwhile, the young aspiring actor buried himself in drama magazines and actors' memoirs, dreaming of a career on the stage. Family, friends, and career counselors did their best

to talk him out of such flighty pursuits, but he was implacable. After a few unsuccessful tries, he landed a part with Reading's Progress Theater group, appearing in a melodrama called *The Drunkard, or Down With Demon Drink.* His parents began—albeit slowly—to accept Branagh's chosen path, and he snapped up parts in all kinds of local productions. An important milestone during these early years was his first trip to Stratford-on-Avon, Shakespeare's home and center of the Royal Shakespeare Company (RSC). In *Beginning*, Branagh described his hitchhiking trip to the town, his drink in the actors' pub, and his attendance of several Shakespeare plays, as a virtual religious pilgrimage. He began to attend more Shakespeare productions, and was particularly thrilled by famed actor Derek Jacobi's performance in *Hamlet*, which he saw in Oxford.

Branagh's schoolwork suffered as he acted in more plays, but before finishing school he'd applied to

> *"The first two terms at RADA let me see that I was gifted in particular ways—good at sight reading, good at accents, quick in most ways—but that this was not always a help."*

both the Central School of Speech and Drama and the Royal Academy of Dramatic Art (RADA). His auditions were sufficiently strong to land him a place at both schools, and he chose the more prestigious RADA. His audition there led to an introduction to someone who would influence him tremendously: director and teacher Hugh Crutwell. Crutwell taught Branagh a great deal almost immediately; in the space of an audition the teacher managed to change the young actor's focus from "presenting" a part to letting the part play the performer. This experience marked the beginning of Branagh's maturation as an actor.

There was one catch to Branagh's starting at RADA in the fall of 1979: funding. His family couldn't possibly afford tuition at the Royal Academy, so Branagh applied for assistance from the Berkshire County Council. He auditioned for the council, and had to wait in agony before hearing, to his joy and surprise, that they would provide the necessary money. It was the first of many hurdles for an ambitious artist in search of various levels of financial assistance. He bid farewell to his parents and went to live in London; his life as an actor had truly begun.

Branagh remembers his earliest work at RADA as a "breaking down" of his amateur habits before his "building up" as a real actor. Thus he endured the minuscule criticisms of voice teachers, movement teachers, acting and music teachers. His early confidence gave way to deep insecurity, but he retained a remarkable ability to learn from every potentially devastating critique. Crutwell's demand for "honest" acting haunted Branagh's every speech; the teacher wanted his talented but still inexperienced pupil to find the poetry in the words he spoke, and to allow that poetry to guide his performance. "The first two terms at RADA let me see that I was gifted in particular ways—good at sight reading, good at accents, quick in most ways—but that this was not always a help," wrote Branagh. "Being betrayed into superficial performances by these accomplishments was a continual danger."

In 1981, desperate to find new ideas for his portrayal of Chebutykin in Russian playwright Anton Chekhov's *Three Sisters*, Branagh wrote to Sir Laurence Olivier. Olivier, one of the world's best-known actors, had directed stage and screen versions of the play, and had created the role with which Branagh was now struggling. Olivier wrote a short reply, concluding "If I were you, I should have a bash at it and hope for the best—which I certainly wish you." Although the letter offered little concrete advice, Branagh was heartened by the letter and threw himself into the role.

This small contact with one of the greats of the English theater was followed by another: John Gielgud, then RADA's president and another leading light in the acting world, saw Branagh rehearse a monologue from *Hamlet*. Though Branagh noted in his autobiography that his performance was terrible, he saw Gielgud brush away a tear. "He must have felt sorry for me," wrote Branagh of his struggle with one of the world's most daunting dramatic roles, one that Gielgud himself had performed definitively many years before. But perhaps Gielgud recognized the beginnings of greatness in the 21-year-old Branagh. In any case, the renowned actor provided a number of helpful suggestions to the awestruck student, who then performed the monologue in front of an audience that included several other famous actors as well as Queen Elizabeth and Prince Philip. Branagh had already chatted with the Queen follow-

ing the performance when Gielgud stopped to tell him how much he'd improved.

His first professional break came with a BBC production of a play slated to film in—of all places—Belfast. An ad in England's famed theater magazine *The Stage* sought an "actor, 16-24 with authentic working-class Belfast accent." Branagh got the part, and although he thought he'd have to back out because of conflicting dates with the performances of RADA's *Hamlet*, the production was able to work around him. He rehearsed the TV play, titled *Too Late to Talk to Billy*, during the day and performed as Hamlet at night. This manic schedule would eventually become the norm for Branagh, who seemed to overcommit himself continually, if only to prove he could accomplish it all.

Having completed the TV play and the RADA season, Branagh, just 21, was once again looking for work and had no prospects on the horizon. He went to see his idol Jacobi, who told him: "Actors are still just beggars, really." The next break came with a part in the play *Another Country*, along with an offer from the RSC. Branagh accepted the part in the play, passing on the RSC for the moment because he knew he'd start out playing small roles with the company. Encouragement came from another of Branagh's idols, British actor Albert Finney, who stopped by after a performance of *Another Country*, to which his company held the film rights, and spoke approvingly of Branagh's work. It was Finney who shortly thereafter delivered the news that Branagh had won RADA's prize for outstanding student of the year, the Bancroft Gold Medal. That same week *Too Late to Talk to Billy* appeared on television, filling his family with pride and for once easing his anxiety about being Irish. The teleplay was so successful that three sequels were made.

During this period Branagh also experienced the agony of waiting for a coveted part. He auditioned for the role of Mozart in Milos Foreman's film version of Peter Schaffer's popular play *Amadeus*. After making it through several callbacks, Branagh heard that he'd almost landed the part, that it was a veritable certainty, that just one more round of casting had been completed, and then that at the last moment the filmmakers had decided to cast American actors only. The frustration of this experience, however, was relieved somewhat by Branagh's being cast as the lead in the play *Francis*, the story of St. Francis of Assisi. The play was written by Julian Mitchell, author of *Another Country*, and though it never got the critical raves necessary to make it a hit, Branagh found the experience powerful and important. Branagh won the SWET award for "Best Newcomer" for his performance in *Another Country*, and offers began to come in steadily.

Branagh then decided on something really risky: a one-man show based on Alfred Lord Tennyson's poem *Maud*. He performed his version of this "monodrama," which he titled *The Madness*, and paid for its staging—knowing full well that the show could be a total loss. Despite an uncertain beginning, the show opened to strong reviews: the London *Times* called Branagh "the most exciting young actor in years." Following these notices Branagh played to sold-out houses. After these performances he would begin crafting his version of the role that would bring him international fame: Henry V.

He was 23 years old, playing Shakespeare's shrewd young king in what *Interview* called "the most auspicious Stratford debut since Richard Burton's." Branagh was typically fanatical in his preparation for this coveted role: he read piles of history books, studied different approaches to the play, and even asked Prince Charles, heir apparent to the throne of England, for some perspective on the private experience of the monarchy. To his surprise, he was granted an audience with the prince and had a candid discussion with him. Prince Charles—who confirmed the young actor's sense that figures of royalty experienced "an extraordinary melancholy"—would later become something of a patron to Branagh.

The production was very successful, though Branagh described in his autobiography moments of mortification (a pair of gloves that served as the focus of a crucial speech were missing during one performance, motivating Branagh to ad lib a speech in Elizabethan blankverse to get a fellow actor offstage to look for them) and provided several milestones for its star. Branagh's parents came to see the production—on the same night that Prince Charles and Princess Diana put in an appearance.

After appearing in the play *Golden Girls*, Branagh returned to the RSC as Laertes in *Hamlet*. But he began to feel, despite the satsifaction of the plays themselves, that the RSC had moved away from its original greatness. The directors, rather than the actors, were the focus, and the feeling of camaraderie and growth Branagh had read about in older actors' biographies was missing. Branagh wrote a play about his predicament titled *Tell Me Honestly*, which spoke to the concerns of fellow actors but which London *Times* reviewer Irving Wardle felt "only reinforce[d] the stereotyped view of actors as vain and neurotic . . . and directors as cold-blooded manipulators

solely interested in their careers." Branagh wanted to be part of an actors' theater, a company dedicated to presenting strong plays without the diffused energy and directorial stardom of the RSC. The disillusionment of this period led to the birth of an idea: he would start his own theater company. In September of 1985, having finished his run in *Hamlet*, he left the RSC to make the idea a reality. It would be called Renaissance.

Before the year was out Branagh appeared with two of his acting heroes, Judi Dench and Michael Gambon, in a television production of Henrik Ibsen's play *Ghosts*, and wrote a draft of a play about Northern Ireland called *Public Enemy*. He began to do more film and television work, saving money to finance his theater company. He appeared in the feature film *High Season*, a comedy filmed in Greece co-starring Jacqueline Bisset; he spent all his spare time on the set planning his production of *Romeo and Juliet*, phoning Renaissance co-conspirator and fellow actor David Parfitt and eagerly discussing plans.

On the set of the BBC series *Fortunes of War* he met the woman he would later marry, actress Emma Thompson. Though they were attracted to one another during the filming, they both recalled later, it was not until afterward that they began to take their romantic interest seriously. Thompson would prove a formidable presence in Branagh's professional life as well as his personal life. The pair managed to wed without too much publicity in August of 1989.

Despite the risks, and in the face of several predictions of dire failure, Branagh committed his earnings to the troupe that had become his obsession. Early in 1987 the Renaissance Theater Company made its debut with a production of *Public Enemy*, starring Branagh as Tommy Black, a Belfast youth who idolizes—and imitates—1930s film star Jimmy Cagney. London *Times* reviewer Harry Eyres wrote approvingly of the "vein of genuine innocence running through the fantasy" and of "Kenneth Branagh's charmingly whimsical, mercurial, physically magnetic performance." The company also presented John Sessions's one-man show about Napoleon, directed by Branagh, and arranged to have several major stars of the British stage appear in and/or direct Shakespeare plays. Derek Jacobi stunned Branagh by telling the young actor he'd like to direct him in *Hamlet*. This production was part of the 1988 Renaissance tour, which also included Judi Dench's production of *Much Ado About Nothing* and Geraldine McEwan's production of *As You Like It*, in which Branagh played the fool Touchstone.

1988 was most memorable for Branagh in that it saw him conquer a new prize: film. He had longed for some time to bring *Henry V* to the screen, despite its scale—the battle of Agincourt is the epic center of the play—and the fact that Branagh's great predecessor Olivier had made a celebrated film of it in the 1940s. If raising the money for Renaissance productions was difficult, funding the film would prove Herculean; but Branagh, as usual, knew what he wanted and set about getting it. During the course of financing the picture he was rehearsing Jacobi's *Hamlet* as well as appearing in *Much Ado* and *As You Like It*: "In that first week with moody Dane [Prince Hamlet]," he recalled in his book, "I was rehearsing from 10 am, breaking at 5:30 pm, playing one of the comedies, then having design meetings over a late supper for a movie that might or might not happen. Was I doing too much? Yes. Was it any good for Hamlet? God knows."

The production was of *Hamlet* successful—the company received a standing ovation after the first performances—and played several other venues, including the Opera House in Belfast. Branagh noted in his autobiography that this appearance helped him to reconcile himself with his lost "Irishness." In fact, he wrote, "I was being accepted for what I was and not what people thought I should be." Around this time Prince Charles invited the company to perform a Shakespearean "miscellany"—assorted scenes from different plays—for a private party in Windsor. It was another landmark for Branagh, who directed the scenes, and another chapter in an ongoing relationship between royal and actor.

Despite such highs, the uncertainty of funding for the film version of *Henry V*—David Puttnam, producer and movie dealmaker extraordinaire, was both hot and cold in his estimates of the film's chances of being made—took its toll on Branagh. Even the excitement of performing *Hamlet* in Elsinore Castle in Denmark, the play's setting, couldn't offset the anxiety of the film project. At last the funding was secured, however, and Branagh assembled many of the leading lights of Renaissance—Paul Scofield, Ian Holm, Jacobi, Dench, McEwan, Thompson, Alec McCowen, and many others—to form his cast. The close-knit and highly professional ensemble helped steady the fledgling director's nerves, though he noted in his autobiography that on his first day, when a shot was set up, he noticed nothing was happening. An assistant whispered that he had to say "action." These sorts of embarrassments, though, were minimally stressful compared to the challenge of acting and directing simultaneously. Eventually, an experienced cast and crew lent him the confidence

he needed, and Henry's leadership—its triumphs and crises—gained new resonance for the "king" of the film set.

The finished product rewarded Branagh's efforts. "Branagh is a marvel," wrote Peter Travers in *Rolling Stone*. "You just can't take your eyes off him." Travers praised the depth of characterization in the film, concluding that the "film is more than a promising first try: It's thrilling." Stanley Kauffmann, while more critical of some aspects of the film, largely praised its filmmaker-star in the *New Republic*: "The muck of reality, as against the pomp of circumstance, is very much the Branagh tone," the reviewer wrote, contrasting the new film against Olivier's patriotic and ceremonial version of 1944. "On the evidence here Branagh is not yet near Olivier as a classical actor," Kauffmann concluded, "but as director, as artistic entrepreneur, as sheer charge of filmworld energy, he has won his own Agincourt." *Time*'s Richard Corliss answered his own question about how well Branagh had succeeded Olivier: "Well, he's done it: created a *Henry* for a decade poised between belligerence and exhaustion." The New York Film Critics Circle named Branagh best new director; the film received Academy Award nominations for best actor and best director, and won the Oscar for best costumes. Branagh's conviction that Shakespeare could have mass appeal was vindicated: he was an instant international star, and even more respected at home.

In 1990 Branagh began work on his next film. It was a marked departure from Shakespeare: a supernatural thriller with elements of screwball comedy called *Dead Again*, which was released by Paramount in 1991. The script, by Scott Frank, interwove two narratives. In one—the portion Branagh directed in black-and-white—the tempestuous 1940s marriage between composer Roman (Branagh) and his glamorous pianist wife Margaret (Emma Thompson) ends in Margaret's murder. Roman goes to the electric chair for her death, though he carries a secret to his grave. In the other part of the story, a present-day tale in color, Los Angeles detective Mike Church (Branagh, again) attempts to cure an amnesiac woman (Thompson, again) and finds out—via a psychic, played by Derek Jacobi—that their previous lives were shared as the illustrious Roman and Margaret. Branagh's direction made reference to countless Hollywood classics, most notably Welles's *Citizen Kane*, and made splendid use of a diverse acting ensemble that included Andy Garcia, Hanna Schygulla, and—in an uncredited cameo—Robin Williams.

While reviews for *Dead Again* were mixed, the film was phenomenally popular, earning $20 million—it cost $15 million to make—in its first three weeks. David Ansen noted in his *Newsweek* review that fans of *Henry V* would expect a lot from the new film. "Well, do yourself a favor and lower those expectations. Branagh's second effort is highly entertaining claptrap." The *New Yorker*'s Terrence Rafferty agreed, calling the thriller an "entertaining exercise in high-style inconsequentiality." The film didn't gather the high praise and awards of *Henry V*, but it cemented Branagh's connections in Hollywood; though an old man of 30, he clearly had a trick or two left up his sleeve.

The same fanatical hard work that got Branagh into acting school also got his films made, and the awards and critical raves, while no doubt satisfying, are clearly not the main concern of acting's newest workaholic. An article about him in *Entertainment Weekly* drew to a close by joking that "before he plunges into his next project, Branagh plans another career breakthrough: a vacation." Perhaps there is no one who so enjoys returning to work.

Selected writings

Public Enemy (play).
Beginning (autobiography), St. Martin's, 1989.

Sources

American Film, September/October 1991.
Entertainment Weekly, September 20, 1991.
Interview, October 1989.
New Republic, December 4, 1989.
Newsweek, February 19, 1990; September 9, 1991.
New Yorker, September 9, 1991.
People, February 12, 1990.
Publishers Weekly, March 23, 1990.
Rolling Stone, November 30, 1989; February 8, 1990.
Time, November 13, 1989; February 5, 1990.
Times (London), August 17, 1985; February 18, 1987.
Times Literary Supplement, October 20, 1989.

—*Simon Glickman*

Francesco Clemente

Artist

Born in 1952 in Naples, Italy; son of Marchese Lorenzo Clemente di Luca (a judge); married Alba Primicieri; children: four. *Education:* Studied architecture in 1970.

Addresses: *Home*—Via del Riari 59, 00265 Rome, Italy. *Agent*—Sperone Westwater, 142 Greene St., New York, NY 10012.

Career

Painter and photographer. Individual exhibitions include those at Galleria Area, Florence, 1974; Galleria Gian Enzo Sperone, Rome and Turin, 1975; Galleria Paolo Betti, Milan, 1977; Centre d'Art Contemporain, Geneva, 1978; Art and Project, Amsterdam, 1978; Lisson Gallery, London, 1979; Galerie Paul Maenz, Cologne, 1979; Sperone Westwater Fischer Gallery, New York, 1980; Vereniging voor het Museum van Hedendaagse Kunst, Ghent, 1981; Anthony d'Offay Gallery, London, 1981; University of California, Berkeley, 1981; Galerie Daniel Templon, Paris, 1982; Galerie Bruno Bischofberger, Zurich, 1982; A Space, Toronto, 1983; Akira Ikeda Gallery, Tokyo and Nagoya, Japan, 1983; Kunsthalle, Basel, 1983; James Corcoran Gallery, Los Angeles, 1983; Fruitmarket Gallery, Edinburgh, 1983; Arts Council Gallery, Belfast, 1983; Nationalgalerie, then West Germany, 1984; Sperone Westwater/Leo Castelli Gallery, New York, 1985; Mary Boone/Michael Werner Gallery, New York, 1985; Metropolitan Museum of Art, New York, 1985; Museum of Modern Art, New York, 1986; Galerie Ascan Crone, Hamburg, 1986; Fundacion Caja de Pensiones, Madrid, 1986; Art Institute of Chicago, 1986; Winnipeg Art Gallery, 1988; Philadelphia Museum of Art, 1990; Sperone Westwater, New York, 1990; Kunst Museum, Basel, 1991. Group exhibitions include *India and the Contemporary Artist*, Museum of Modern Art, New York, 1985; *Avant-Garde in the Eighties*, Los Angeles County Museum of Art, 1987.

Sidelights

Francesco Clemente is as mysterious a person as his many self-portraits. His bristly head, wide mouth, and almond-shaped dark eyes stare out from many paintings, drawings, and collages, challenging the viewer to decipher the intentions and inspirations of the artist and his work. Clemente divides his time between New York City, Rome, and Madras, India; each city reveals a facet of his character and has a profound impact on his art. While his diverse work seems to some to form a coherent whole, many critics and viewers are bewildered by the enigmatic and very personal content of Clemente's photographs, paintings, drawings, collages, and miniatures. His most characteristic themes are about the body and its functions, ranging from the erotic to the disturbing, with orifices and polymorphous perversity galore. Critics are divided about Clemente's style; some say he is primitive, stylized, and representational, while others say he is just "hurried." The artist himself says he wants his work to be "effortless," to best relay the expressions of his subconscious to the canvas. Some paintings rival those of Pablo Picasso or Marc Chagall for their invention and emotion, but Clemente does not truly resemble any other painter, even himself, as he juggles and merges techniques. The artist is more likely to contextually contradict himself than to invent series of rules and guidelines for himself that would therefore make his art more accessible.

There are critics, however, who charge that Clemente is not genuinely complex, that he has little to share, and that he has been riding on a surge of undue popularity with less of a genuine artistic vision to share and more of an ego-driven profit motive. He and his wife partake somewhat of New York social life, and Clemente actually modeled clothes in a catalog for Comme des Garcons. Clemente has been prolific, and in 1985 (when he had three shows running simultaneously at different galleries), he was accused by *Time* art critic Robert Hughes as being too commercial. "He wittily exploits the affinity between artist and charlatan," Hughes remarked. Is Francesco Clemente pursuing a serious artistic path or is he playing with his rather extended fifteen minutes of fame? Is he exploring different art forms and religious influences or exploiting them? Clemente, of course, would much rather complicate these issues for his viewers than explicate them.

Clemente began to paint seriously on his own at age eight, by his own reckoning. When he was only 12, his parents published a book of his poems. (He has since kept his poetry private—Clemente found it impossible to write for years afterwards.) He studied architecture in 1970, and spent most of that decade following his mentor and early influence, Italian artist Alghiero Boetti, through India and Afghanistan. Clemente also traveled at that time with Alba Primicieri, who would become his wife, and with whom he has four children. Some critics speculate that a more feminine double of Clemente seen in many of his paintings is Alba.

Clemente's work was shown widely in the late 1970s in Italy and other European countries. He only became known to Americans, however, in 1980, alongside two other Italian artists, Sandro Chia and Enzo Cucchi, who have not retained their popularity into the 1990s. Clemente was labeled a neo-expressionist in 1980 although his work remains more typically postmodern in its combination of styles, media, and tangled message. Clemente, it

would seem, purposefully obstructs the viewer's understanding of his paintings with his statements of purpose. Many of these statements are equivocal and ambivalent. In 1988 Clemente told John Ashbery, a writer for *Interview*, that "My work is supposedly a continuous proliferation of images. These are static—like my beginnings. I like stuff that doesn't show my effort—whatever that means. I'm spending a lot of my energy not doing things at the moment." By inserting "supposedly" and "whatever that means," he seems to devalue his very assertion, daring the reader to take him or his critics seriously.

Clemente's messages are even further blurred by self-contradiction. He reported to *Interview* in 1988 that "for the last couple of years, I've been going through an 'I'm dying' phase and now I'm in an 'I'm dead' phase. Very relaxing." And yet two years later he complained in the *Los Angeles Times:* "People say there's a lot of death in my paintings, and I have no interest in death. I've never subscribed to the West-

> *"As to whether I see the flesh as a means of achieving transcendence or an obstacle in that pursuit, it can go either way."*

ern understanding of it, which is that it's an ending." These contentious remarks notwithstanding, Clemente's work clearly reveals several ongoing concerns: religion, the self, and sex. Revealing his knowledge and contemplation of these elements, he told the *Los Angeles Times*, "The West perceives a big split between spirit and flesh, whereas in India they're seen as intertwined. As to whether I see the flesh as a means of achieving transcendence or an obstacle in that pursuit, it can go either way."

The sensuous quality of many of his paintings reflect Clemente's ideas about the relationship of art to the body. The artist told Henry Geldzahler in a 1991 *Interview* piece: "I've been thinking of the body as a line that divides what you see inside and what you see outside of you, so the body for me is a border, a line that continues into the line of the painting." A possible interpretation is that Clemente thinks of the canvas as the physical place to express ideas about the body; as an extension of the line of division between self and the world, the canvas is the place for explanation and exploration. For instance, 1981's

Two Men shows a man reclining in bed sucking another person's toe. The view of the figures is from directly above the bed, and we see the man's face and torso, but only the forked legs (one bent back) of the other figure. The pattern on the sheets and pillow is that of a snake biting its tail. The man's nipple and belly button repeat the snake motif. Clemente may be comparing the self-consumption or the snake to the activity between what the title informs us is two men. The style is flat and representational; the man's nose seems a purposefully awkward perspective study, such as any beginning art student might produce. At first glance the painting seems crudely sexual, but the snake and the style hint that Clemente had more in mind.

Another work, a pastel from the *Three Worlds* exhibit of 1990 called *Everything I Know*, shows four figures. One, a mummified torso, appears at the bottom; on its head is a reclining figure full of eyes. *New York* writer Kay Larson called this figure an "analogue of Buddhist mindfulness." On the right side of the work are two figures, one the recognizable self-portrait with bright red, sensuous lips, and the other probably Alba, standing behind Clemente. One of these figures is clothed and the other apparently not—they are obscured by the right edge of the drawing, as if about to run out of the frame completely. The background is a yellow glow that disappears on the left side of the picture. Aside from the religious reference, this drawing is full of personal imagery that is not explained to the viewer, but Clemente again hints of his own wisdom. This work and *Two Men* taken together show that Clemente may be teasing the viewer by revealing little clues to the meaning of these works, then changing his mind. Not everyone cares to know so much; *Time* art critic Robert Hughes said, "Even in today's morass of worthless 'personal' imagery, it would be hard to find a sillier painting [than the one by Clemente showing a] green whirlpool ... with a man and his separated genitals disappearing into it." While perhaps irritated with the work, Hughes nevertheless remarked that "Clemente's work lives a tremulous, only part decipherable life at the juncture of Eros and cultural memory."

As Hughes suggests, not all of Clemente's symbols are purely personal. To draw from cultural memory, Clemente uses talismanic symbols drawn from Christianity, alchemy, astrology, mythology, and the Tarot. The religions of India have apparently affected him most profoundly; references appear often, in ways that seem central to the meaning of the works. Clemente commented about his religious background to the *Los Angeles Times:* "I was raised Catholic but

for several years I've been studying the religious traditions of India and the East. I've had no formal religious training and I don't meditate, although I certainly pray—for me, prayer goes on constantly in one form or another. I've had a few pivotal experiences in the course of my spiritual studies and have met some extraordinary people."

Clemente seems to have cultivated a strange hybrid urbanity born of the different cities where he makes his homes: As he told the *Los Angeles Times*, "The faces in my paintings all look alike because I want the figures to have the quality of just faces in the crowd—because that's what we all are." In *Interview* Clemente revealed a curious mixture of naivete and savvy when he said, "In New York, most of the time, I see people I can't stand. The ones you really like you want to leave alone, for their sake." He told the interviewer, "I feel the way you do about journalism and interviews, but someone from the magazine called and they said they had done too many rock stars and wanted to put an artist on the cover, 'and besides,' they said, you're *cute.*' So I said sure." While he can play the media and enjoy it (in a way that to some recalls Andy Warhol), Roberta Smith of the *New York Times* protested that Clemente seems "untarnished by such [extra-art] activities."

Clemente titled his 1990 show *Three Worlds* to reflect the three countries in which he lives and their influence on his art, influences that complicate and diversify his "cultural memory." Kay Larson of *New York* described the overall impressions of the cities from his works this way: "Italy is weighed down by an air of the antique, by the dragging feet of history. America is about light and openness, freedom and potential. India unites both sets of qualities—an immense, ancient past, freedom from 'rules'—under the spiritual dome of Hinduism and Buddhism .... He may live in New York, but Madras, you sense, is where he's from." Roberta Smith agreed that "the works most strongly influenced by [India's] culture are the best."

Clemente's time in that country as represented in *Three Worlds* was taken up with the painting of miniatures, created in collaboration with young Indian apprentices. The style is flat and colorful, more representational than realistic. The theme for these 24 works is again the human body. Larson astutely compared Clemente's "amputated limbs that dance like [Henri] Matisse's bathers." Yet at least one other critic put forth the belief that Clemente's heart is in his native country, and that his most serious impulses are inspired by Italian style. *New Yorker* critic Adam Gopnik told the *Los Angeles Times* that

"Clemente seems to be trying to recapture a historical dimension that's been absent for several decades as painting has become increasingly abstract and ironic . . . he has a very self-conscious relationship to his painting and for me, everything in his work seems to be held in quotation marks . . . . And I wonder if it's possible to restore a kind of classical, Mediterranean high seriousness to painting—and that seems to be one of Clemente's intentions."

Clemente's *Three Worlds* exhibit was a target for those who fault him with a *lack* of seriousness. Roberta Smith criticized the artist in the *New York Times* for not pulling off the "balance between self-obsession and self-effacement . . . . [the works] are empty of psychological content; they could have been produced by any number of artists from the 1970's and 80's. They reflect a conviction that art and life are one, but . . . the sense of an individual life, a particular motor powering a particular engine, is missing." Perhaps there is an element of truth in Smith's criticism, because while an artist may invent a different and secret language for self-expression, he or she cannot be surprised or disappointed if the garbled meanings of private symbols do not always enthrall the audience. The different cities, the different styles and media, the different religions—all serve to give Clemente a fresh insight into himself. Self-examination seems to be the real impetus for Clemente, and his worldliness, his multiple understandings and experience serve ultimately as a mirror.

While self-regard is traditionally scorned in the west, it has provided Clemente with provocative subject matter and work. The proliferation of his work, self-centered as many critics have judged it to be, offends some who believe that an true exploration cannot be conducted with many works, only with a grand opus that represents years of patient labor and implied torture. Despite Clemente's desire for "effortlessness," there are decided phases to his works and a growing effectiveness in his favored media. Clemente said, "I view the work as an ongoing ebb and flow," the *Los Angeles Times* reported. "There are ideas and themes that interested me 10 years ago that no longer seem too compelling, so yes, you do bring things to a conclusion. But in a larger sense the paintings don't change at all. The mysteries that exist in life are eternal, so although the way one approaches those mysteries might change from year to year, the mystery remains the same." *Los Angeles Times* reporter Kristine McKenna assessed Clemente's character by saying that he refuses to "draw rigid conclusions about life." Perhaps he wishes his critics and viewers to do the same with him and with their own lives.

Sources

Books

Auping, Michael, *Francesco Clemente*, Abrams, 1985.

Periodicals

Interview, March 1988; November 1991.
Los Angeles Times, August 19, 1990.
New York, November 19, 1990.
New York Times, December 2, 1990.
People, March 7, 1988.
Time, April 22, 1985.

—*Christine Ferran*

Mario Cuomo

AP/Wide World Photos

Governor of New York

Full name, Mario Matthew Cuomo; born June 15, 1932, in New York, NY; son of Andrea (a grocery store owner) and Immaculata (Giordano) Cuomo; married Matilda N. Raffa, June, 1954; children: Margaret, Andrew, Maria, Madeline, Christopher. *Education:* St. John's University, B.A. (summa cum laude), 1953, LL.B., 1956. *Politics:* Democrat. *Religion:* Roman Catholic.

Career

New York State Court of Appeals, judicial assistant, 1956-58; Corner, Weisbrod, Froeb & Charles (law firm), Brooklyn, NY, member, 1958-63, partner, 1963-74; secretary of state, New York, 1974-78; lieutenant governor, state of New York, 1979-82; governor of New York, 1983—. Has won re-election twice.

Addresses: *Office*—State Capitol, Albany, NY 12224.

Sidelights

Mario Cuomo is a political enigma—a front-running, though unofficial, candidate for national office who has twice formally declined to enter the presidential race. The charismatic Cuomo has been governor of New York State since 1983 and has been an articulate and outspoken opponent of the administrations of former President Ronald Reagan and President George Bush.

The lifelong Democrat has not sought his party's nomination to Washington, D.C., although on several occasions he seemed ready to do so. This ambivalence towards a run for the White House has led reporters to dub Cuomo the "Hamlet on the Hudson," a term that hardly does justice to the governor's decades of political service.

"Mario Cuomo is blessed—or cursed—with the ability to see both sides of any argument," wrote Richard Stengel in *Time.* "As a lawyer, he was trained to plead pro and con and was always deft at making his case. As a man, he is inclined to argue inwardly, to question his motivations, his ambitions." Likewise, *Esquire* contributor Andrew Kopkind noted of Cuomo: "He seems to understand better than anyone what dangers lurk, what it takes to put things right, how great are the stakes, and how small are the chances of success by the standards he sets for himself. With ambivalence like that, it's not hard to talk yourself out of a job."

On December 20, 1991, Cuomo announced that he would not run for president in 1992. The three-time New York governor had been virtually on the brink of filing for candidacy in the New Hampshire primary, but his state's budget problems stayed his hand. "It seems to me I cannot turn my attention to

New Hampshire while this threat hangs over the head of the New Yorkers that I've sworn to put first," Cuomo told the *New York Times*. "It is my responsibility as Governor to deal with the extraordinarily severe [budget] problem," he continued. "Were it not, I would travel to New Hampshire today and file my name as a candidate in its Presidential primary." Cuomo and the state legislature in New York face an $875 million gap between income and expenditures in the 1992 budget, a situation that has led to heated negotiations between Cuomo and Republicans in the New York State Senate. "For months I have focused my energies on dealing with the state's budget problem," Cuomo told the *New York Times*. "I had hoped by now to have some resolution. But the Republicans have responded to every reasonable offer of compromise by the Assembly and Governor with new and predictably unacceptable demands."

Cuomo put forth a similar argument in 1987—simply that his pledge to the citizens of New York must come before any presidential aspirations. This has not kept him from being considered a future president, however. Much of the mail he receives in Albany, New York's capitol, consists of pleas for him to run. The *Philadelphia Inquirer* quoted one such letter, from a man in Jackson, Mississippi, who wrote: "Please, please, please, take the reins at the helm and lead your people, Americans, out of bondage." *Readers Digest* contributors Rowland Evans and Robert Novak have claimed that such wholehearted faith in Cuomo only proves that he is "the brightest, toughest, and most interesting Democrat around."

Mario Matthew Cuomo is a first-generation American, the son of immigrant parents from Salerno, Italy. He was born on June 15, 1932, in the borough of Queens in New York City. The governor told *American Heritage* magazine that the immigrant experience is part of the foundation of his life. "When my mother and father came [to America], they could not speak the language," he said. "They had no skills. They had one thing: a willingness to give labor. But it had to be at the lowest level. My father was literally a ditch digger in New Jersey, *literally*." Cuomo himself could not speak English when he entered public school in Queens. "I first learned about the country the way most first-generation children do," he said. "Not from my parents, because my parents didn't know anything about the country; they barely knew anything about their own country—they hadn't been educated there or here. And my neighborhood wasn't educated. I learned about the country not from my parents, not from the priests, but from the schools."

Eventually Cuomo's father was able to open a neighborhood grocery store on a corner in South Jamaica, Queens. The family moved into an apartment nearby, and as a youngster Cuomo was rarely allowed to go out of sight of either home or the store. The curfew was severe, but Cuomo turned it to his advantage by spending time reading and listening to the radio serials. He told *Gentleman's Quarterly* that the grocery store itself was "a terrific place." He added: "The miracle of my mother and father's grocery store is they both spoke Italian to people who spoke Polish, German, Irish—I don't know how they did it. The only thing they had in common were the numbers. The black crayon on the bag, and in the book that was the credit book."

Cuomo's father prospered in time, and the family moved to a home in Queens. Cuomo was also able to attend St. John's preparatory high school in his own neighborhood. He was a good student and an

> *"Republicans believe that the wagon train will not make it to the frontier unless some of the old, some of the young and some of the weak are left behind."*

excellent athlete, playing baseball so well that he earned a contract with the Pittsburgh Pirates right out of high school. In *Reader's Digest*, Evans and Novak quote the baseball scouting report on the young Mario Cuomo: "Potentially the best prospect. Could go all the way. Aggressive and intelligent. Very well-liked by those who succeed in penetrating the exterior shell. Will run over you if you get in his way."

Cuomo was serving as the center fielder for the Brunswick, Georgia, Pirates when a wild pitch hospitalized him for a month with a severe head injury. That experience convinced him that he would never make the major leagues. He went home to Queens and enrolled at St. John's University. He received a scholarship that he was able to supplement by playing semiprofessional basketball. He earned a bachelor's degree with top honors in 1953 and went on to St. John's law school, where he finished at the top of his class in 1956.

Kopkind wrote: "The young Cuomo was turned down by all the tony Manhattan law firms he applied to for a job. Although he looked like a liberal and acted like a liberal, he did not make the same noises that Manhattan liberals made." Stung but undaunted by the rejection, Cuomo joined a Brooklyn firm and was made partner in 1963. It was through his early work as an attorney that Cuomo began to receive notice on the political front. In 1964 and 1965 he represented the people of Willett's Point, Queens, when a developer wanted to clear away the area's scrap-processing plants and junkyards to make the World's Fair site more attractive. Later in the decade he helped 69 families save homes that were slated to be razed for construction of a high school and massive athletic facilities.

In May of 1972, New York City mayor John Lindsay commissioned Cuomo to assess a proposed low-rent public housing project scheduled to be built in the middle-class borough of Forest Hills, whose residents opposed such a project. Cuomo found a sane compromise by agreeing that the proposed project would be too large and would overwhelm the neighborhood's facilities. He further argued that such a large low-rent project would simply segregate its residents within their designated area. His proposal for a down-sized project was acceptable to the residents of Forest Hills and the poor who would be joining that community.

With an eye toward political office, Cuomo ran for lieutenant governor in 1974, but his ticket lost in the Democratic primary. The man who did win the governorship, Hugh Carey of Brooklyn, was a friend from St. John's. Carey appointed Cuomo secretary of state and made him an important troubleshooter and adviser. Cuomo took a largely honorific title and made it a full-time job. He investigated abuses in state-run nursing homes, mediated a Mohawk Indian lands claim dispute, and helped to settle a rent strike at the Co-op City apartment complex. Cuomo expanded the duties of secretary of state, but he was still able to reduce the costs of the office by 40 percent.

In 1977 Cuomo became a candidate for mayor of New York. He was narrowly defeated by Edward I. Koch in both the primary and the general elections. Cuomo returned to Albany and his duties as secretary of state, and the following year he was asked to join Carey's ticket as lieutenant governor. The Carey-Cuomo ticket handily defeated all Democratic rivals and won the general election. In addition to his responsibilities as lieutenant governor, Cuomo ran former President Jimmy Carter's 1980 re-election campaign in New York. He also served as a delegate to the 1980 Democratic National Convention.

In January of 1982 Carey announced that he would not seek reelection as governor of New York. Cuomo announced his candidacy for the job in March, some weeks after the popular Edward Koch had already begun a spirited campaign for the office. Cuomo proved himself Koch's equal, even in New York City neighborhoods that were strongly in favor of the mayor. For the Democratic primary, Evans and Novak reported, "Cuomo had fashioned a coalition of blacks, Hispanics and union members, combined with anti-Koch upstaters, to win the nomination with 52 percent of the vote." With one-fourth the campaign funds of his Republican opponent, Cuomo won a narrow victory in 1982 and was sworn in as governor of New York in January of 1983. He has been in office ever since, having won re-election twice.

Cuomo became a national figure during the Democratic National Convention in San Francisco in 1984. He was invited to give the keynote address to begin the convention—possibly the most difficult role in the entire affair. By that time Cuomo had experienced the effect of Reagan-era budget cuts on federal programs in his state. Like most Democrats, he was shocked by the direction he saw the nation taking. On the other hand, he did not consider himself an orator; he was very nervous and was convinced that some of the ideas in his speech were simplistic. On the contrary, he was about to enter national politics with a bang.

"From the first few words of the speech, it was clear to me that these people [at the convention] were desperate for something worthwhile," Cuomo told *American Heritage*. "They all got quiet. They didn't know who I was; there was nothing riveting about the guy or the first few sentences, but when they came to attention the way they did, what they were saying was: 'Hey, look, we're dying for something to cheer. We *need* something. We're going to give you every chance we can. *Give* us something.'" What Cuomo gave his fellow Democrats was a rousing indictment of the Reagan administration, its values, and goals. "Republicans believe that the wagon train will not make it to the frontier unless some of the old, some of the young and some of the weak are left behind," he told the crowd. "Democrats believe that we can make it all the way with the whole family intact."

Kopkind remarked: "Cuomo's keynote speech to the national convention in San Francisco . . . was not only a piece of stirring oratory, but it foreshadowed the configuration of post-Reagan politics: the revolt against greed, the re-emergence of social concern, the quest for community, and the search for new coalitions that Cuomo calls 'family' and 'the politics of inclusion' and [Jesse] Jackson terms common ground.' All the Democrats and many of the Republicans starting out...have adapted, if not adopted, the essence of what Cuomophiles now call, simply, 'the speech.'"

By 1988 Democratic party regulars were giving Cuomo the presidential nod, but the governor was besieged then, as he is now, with budget deficits and plunging popularity in his home state. In 1988, and again more recently, Cuomo declined to run for president after appearing to be on the very brink of announcing his candidacy. Almost inevitably, racist rumors about Cuomo began to make the rounds—his Italian ancestry led some to assert that he had won the governorship with "mob money," that his family had been involved with the Mafia, and that he must have "skeletons in his closet." In a *New York* magazine expose, Nicholas Pileggi stated that "the most prevalent rumors about the 'mob' skeletons in Cuomo's family closet turn out to be misleading or false." Pileggi quoted Edward McDonald, head of the Organized Crime Strike Force of the U.S. Attorney's office in Brooklyn, New York, who said: "I have never heard of Cuomo connected with any wiseguys in any way whatever. It shouldn't be worth denying, but still, the calls keep coming in."

Republican strategists believe Cuomo is vulnerable in more concrete ways. Cuomo is a liberal who believes government has a duty to serve its neediest citizens and that higher taxes should be levied on those who can most afford to pay them. Michael Barone and Kenneth T. Walsh claimed in *U.S. News & World Report* that the Bush camp planned in the event of Cuomo's candidacy to characterize Cuomo as "an out-of-touch leftwinger similar to previous opponent Michael Dukakis." One Bush political adviser told the magazine that Cuomo would be "the easiest type of Democrat to run against."

Such glib remarks underestimate Cuomo's ability to muster support with reasonable arguments, forcefully presented. In the wake of Cuomo's announcement that he would not run in 1992, *Philadelphia Inquirer* correspondent Robert L. Turner wrote: "Cuomo has been the most forceful and persistent critic of the Reagan-Bush retreat from support of state and local government. His hammering of Bush can be counted

on to help the other Democrats....[In a Cuomo campaign] there would have been no lack of substance. Cuomo has articulated detailed proposals on many issues, including a finely targeted approach to stimulating a national economic recovery."

"The problem for Cuomo is not his arguments with everybody from God to Bush, but his endless arguments with himself," wrote Sidney Blumenthal in the *New Republic.* "The only institution in American politics more raucous and divided than the Democratic Party is Mario Cuomo's mind; this is why the roots of his indecision cannot ultimately be located in any poll or scenario.... He remains enigmatic, even to himself." Kopkind similarly stated of Cuomo: "His famous charisma is compounded of a killing contradiction: the projection of leadership and the reality of retreat. It is immensely attractive, the allure of a public figure who seems so gifted and at the same time so modest in describing his gifts."

Indeed, Cuomo gives his opinion on himself quite frankly. He *is* concerned about more than New York's state budget. "Is it theoretically possible that you could conclude that you should run for president?" he asked in *Gentleman's Quarterly.* "Yes, it's theoretically possible, but to do that I would have to conclude that I was the best one available. Very hard for me to imagine...that there is nobody in the Democratic Party better than me. I know what I can do and I know what I can't do. I'm a good governor. But to say that I should lead the free world and that you don't have anybody better than me, that's a very tough obstacle."

Selected writings

Forest Hills Diary: The Crisis of Low Income Housing, Random House, 1974.
(Editor with Harold Holzer) *Lincoln on Democracy,* Harper, 1990.

Sources

American Heritage, December 1990.
Esquire, June 1988.
Gentleman's Quarterly, November 1990.
National Review, February 28, 1986.
New Republic, September 17-24, 1984; May 6, 1991.
Newsweek, July 23, 1990.
New York, November 2, 1987; September 16, 1991.
New York Times, December 21, 1991.
New York Times Magazine, January 29, 1984.

Philadelphia Inquirer, December 11, 1991; December 24, 1991.

Reader's Digest, July 1986.

Time, March 2, 1987.

U.S. News & World Report, July 23, 1984; March 5, 1990; November 12, 1990.

—Anne Janette Johnson

W. Edwards Deming

UPI/Bettmann

International business consultant

Born William Edwards Deming in 1900 in Sioux City, Iowa; son of a lawyer; married and widowed twice; children: three daughters. *Education:* University of Wyoming, B.S., 1921; University of Colorado, M.S., 1924; Yale University, Ph.D., 1928.

Addresses: *Home*—4924 Butterworth Pl., Washington, DC 20016.

Career

Western Electric, Cicero, IL, statistician, 1924-27; U.S. Department of Agriculture, Washington, DC, statistician, 1927-39; U.S. Bureau of Census, Washington, DC, adviser in sampling, 1939-45; consultant to numerous industries and government bureaus in the United States, Japan, and elsewhere, 1945—. Professor of statistics at New York University and Columbia University.

Member: International Statistics Institute, American Society of Quality Control, National Academy of Engineering, American Statistical Association (fellow), Royal Statistical Society (fellow), Institute of Mathematical Statistics, Market Research Council, Biometrics Society (honorary life member), Union of Japanese Scientists and Engineers (honorary life member), Japanese Statistical Association (honorary life member).

Awards: Honored by establishment of annual Deming Prizes in Japan, 1952; member of Engineering and Scientific Hall of Fame, 1986—; decorated with Second Order Medal of the Sacred Treasure by the Emperor of Japan; numerous honorary degrees from American universities.

Sidelights

American business leaders facing a crisis in productivity and quality control are turning to the advice of W. Edwards Deming, a ninety-plus-year-old management specialist and statistician. For years Deming and his revolutionary ideas were virtually ignored in this country, but they found an enthusiastic audience in Japan. There, Deming's philosophy of quality control and plant management has become a formidable economic weapon, enabling Japan to rise from the ashes of World War II and become an industrial giant among nations.

"W. Edwards Deming has seen the future and it works—at least for Japan," wrote a *U.S. News & World Report* correspondent. "Deming is the father of Japan's quality revolution. He is a turning point of business history made flesh, an American guru who sports in his lapel the Second Order Medal of the Sacred Treasure, awarded to him by the late Emperor Hirohito." Concern for his own country's dwindling reputation as a producer of quality products, Deming has brought his theories to American audiences through numerous articles, books, and seminars. His age—and a pacemaker in his heart—have not stopped him from spreading his philosophy and his practical methods for "total quality management." *Philadelphia Inquirer* contributor Mary Walton noted: "Like Japanese companies, Deming's American followers regard improvement as a never-ending process, not a quick fix aimed to make the financial quarter look good."

It is ironic that an American is responsible for the institution of practices that have made Japanese products the favorites of the world's consumers. "The world has come to rely so heavily on the value and durability of goods 'Made in Japan' that it's easy to forget that only 30 years ago the phrase was a joke, a synonym for shoddiness," claims Clare Crawford-Mason in *People*. "W. Edwards Deming . . . may deserve as much credit as anyone for the new image and performance of Japanese industry."

The Japanese themselves readily admit their admiration for the truculent American statistician. As

---

"We have been in an economic decline for three decades."

Washington Post correspondent Hobart Rowen reported, "What is a novelty here is almost a religion there. In Japan, Deming is a household name." That country's industrial leaders have honored Deming by creating an annual award in his name that is bestowed upon the industry that shows the most growth, quality, and creativity.

Deming's philosophy flies in the face of current American business practices, so it is sometimes a bitter pill to swallow among the management corridors in the United States. *Chicago Tribune* reporter Ronald E. Yates contended that many American chief executive officers "still look a bit askance at the man who is considered a living legend in Japan but remains a prophet without honor in his native America." Some top managers have become converts, however. Robert Baggs, Jr., director of training and development for Rudolph/Libbe, Inc., told the *Chicago Tribune:* "Deming's whole message is that if a company is not doing well, it is management's fault, not the workers' fault. The message is cooperation and looking at everything: workers, production, finance, management as part of a system. The

message is to optimize the system and then manage *it*, not people."

Deming's life began in extreme hardship. He was born in 1900 in Sioux City, Iowa, the son of a lawyer. While he was still a youngster, his family moved to Powell, Wyoming, a small town near Cody. The Demings lived in a tar-paper shack, where they literally struggled to survive the harsh Wyoming winters. Even while in grade school, Edwards had to work at odd jobs to help support them.

The family's economic circumstances improved over time, and Deming was able to stay in school and complete his public education. He enrolled at the University of Wyoming as an electrical engineering major in 1918 and earned his bachelor's degree in 1921. From there he went to the University of Colorado, earning a master's degree in 1924, and on to Yale University for a doctorate in mathematical physics in 1928.

During his years as a graduate student, Deming spent the summers working as a statistician at Western Electric's Hawthorne Works plant in Cicero, Illinois. The plant employed some 46,000 people—one quarter of whom were inspectors—and quality control was a major objective. There Deming met and worked with Walter Shewhart, a physicist from Bell Laboratories who suggested that uniformity of product should be achieved *during* the manufacturing process. Massive inspections of finished items could then be scaled back, and the plant would be less wasteful.

Deming and Shewhart also felt that the production quota system was a detriment to the manufacturing process. Deming discovered that the quota system encouraged workers to disregard quality. It also put a ceiling on production. While at Hawthorne, Deming began to formulate the fourteen-point message that has become the bedrock of his business philosophy.

In 1931, Shewhart published *The Economic Control of Quality of Manufactured Product*. The work proposed a new system of statistical process control that would reach throughout a manufacturing system. As *Fortune* magazine contributor Jeremy Main wrote: "Even other statisticians found Shewhart hard to understand. It devolved on people like Deming to spread the message."

During the 1930s Deming worked with the Department of Agriculture in Washington, D.C. In 1939 he joined the U.S. Census Bureau and helped to devise the sampling techniques first used in the 1940 census. His work as a consultant to industries began during the Second World War, when he went to work for the Defense Department. Applying the statistical quality controls that he and Shewhart had advocated, he was able to insure that certain munitions, airplane parts, and other engine components were produced without dangerous variations.

At the time Deming was already painfully aware of the pitfalls in the American manufacturing process. He told the *Chicago Tribune:* "In the year 1910 the U.S. made half the manufactured products of the world.... Our quality was just good enough to create an appetite for more. A further advantage came to North America for a decade after World War II. North America was the only part of the world that could produce at full capacity. The rest of the industrial world lay in ruins. The rest of the world were our customers, willing buyers for whatever North America could produce.... What happened? Everyone expected the good times to continue. It is easy to manage a business in an expanding market, and easy to suppose that economic conditions can only grow better and better. We were simply lucky— not smart. In contrast with expectations, we find, on looking back, that we have been in an economic decline for three decades."

Deming first went to Japan in 1947 as part of General Douglas MacArthur's occupation force. The island nation was trying to struggle back from the battering it had taken during the war, and Deming offered suggestions to the Japanese on how they might structure their industries. His initial lectures in 1947 intrigued the Japanese industrialists enough that in 1950 Deming was invited back again—this time by the Union of Japanese Scientists and Engineers.

The message that Deming brought to Japan was revolutionary. At a time when American industry was the world model, he told the Japanese *not* to emulate American business practices. He urged the Japanese to seek constant improvement in every manufacturing process, never to rest on their laurels. He encouraged them to abolish fear in the workplace by dumping quota systems and worker evaluations. He stressed the importance of satisfying the consumer through well-made products and innovation. Foremost, he said, the improvement of quality must envelop the entire production process, from the incoming raw materials to the very top seats of management. Defects could be removed by steadily reducing statistical variances along the production line.

Deming offered this and other advice to the Japanese at 8 a.m. to 6 p.m. seminars in nearly every large Japanese city. He was able to address approximately 80% of all of Japan's top business and industry leaders, a feat "unprecedented in Japanese history," to quote Yates. Yates added that the Japanese might not have been convinced by Deming's arguments had the American not backed them with mathematical formulas and statistical proofs. Today, copies of Deming's statistical analyses can be found framed in numerous Japanese businesses.

Deming told *Fortune:* "In 1950 I was the only person in Japan who believed the Japanese could produce quality that would invade markets the world over in five years." Indeed, the effects of Deming's advice began to be felt in Japan by the end of the 1950s, and he became a cult hero in that nation. It has only been in the last fifteen years that American industries have "discovered" him and invited him to apply his expertise to their endeavors.

One of the first major American companies to seek Deming's help was the Nashua Corporation in Nashua, New Hampshire, an office supply and equipment company. Deming first visited the company in 1979 at the request of chairman William E. Conway. At that time the plant was having trouble with the consistency of its carbonless paper and was considering the purchase of a new $700,000 coating head for the production line. Using his statistical methods, Deming was able to prove that the expensive equipment was not necessary. Existing processes were adjusted, the testing method was changed, and a supplier was urged to provide a more consistent raw material. Conway told *Fortune* that Deming's suggestions saved Nashua $800,000 the first year alone. "It was like a miracle," the chairman said.

In 1980, NBC-TV ran a documentary called *If Japan Can, Why Can't We?* The show featured Deming and his contribution to Japan's success. Almost immediately some of America's biggest industries called upon Deming for aid—Ford Motor Company hired him for monthly consultations and within several years improved its reputation for safe, reliable automobiles. General Motors followed suit, and AT&T, Xerox, and Western Electric have utilized Deming's expertise as well. He is not always a welcome visitor, apt as he is to blame top-level management for shoddy workmanship and waste. As Pontiac Division general manager William E. Hoglund put it in 1984, "They have to scrape me off the wall sometimes after he has been here."

Deming is best known in the business community for his four-day seminars, which he conducts several times a year in various large cities. Top executives pay thousands of dollars to attend these sessions, hoping to apply Deming's methods to troubled American industries. Main wrote that in a typical seminar, Deming "singlehandedly holds his audience with drama, scorn, humor, anger, sadness. His sonorous voice booms out rhythmically . . . when he rails against management. Occasionally the volume drops to a whisper as he speaks of the misguided manager 'just doing his best . . . making things worse.'"

Now in his nineties, Deming keeps a pace that might floor a man half his age. He travels extensively, continues to teach at universities, and offers as many as six seminars a year. His home is the same Washington, D.C. townhouse that he bought sixty years ago—his office is in the basement. Twice widowed, he has three grown daughters.

Deming expresses little confidence about future economic growth in the United States. As Yates put it, "Deming insists that most of American management still hasn't seen the light and that the nation's business schools are still content to perpetuate destructive ideas of 'management by objective' or 'results-oriented management.'" Yates noted that the Japanese, on the other hand, "practiced what Deming preached. And the rest, as they say, is history. Japanese corporations today are the envy of the world-profitable, well-managed, competitive, and growing."

Asked in the *Chicago Tribune* how he would like to be remembered in his native land, Deming replied: "I probably won't even *be* remembered." After a pause, he added: "Well, maybe . . . as someone who spent his life trying to keep America from committing suicide."

Selected writings

The Economic Control of Quality of Manufactured Product, 1931.
Quality, Productivity, and Competitive Position, 1982.
Out of the Crisis, 1986.

Contributor of numerous articles to professional publications.

Sources

Books

Aguayo, Rafael, *Dr. Deming: The American Who Taught the Japanese About Quality,* Carol Publishing, 1990.
Gabor, Andrea, *The Man Who Discovered Quality: How W. Edwards Deming Brought the Quality Revolution to America—The Stories of Ford, Xerox, and GM,* Random House, 1990.
Walton, Mary, *The Deming Management Method,* Dodd, Mead, 1986.
Walton, Mary, *Deming Management at Work,* Putnam, 1990.

Periodicals

Chicago Tribune, December 29, 1991; February 16, 1992.
Fortune, June 25, 1984; August 18, 1986.
People, September 8, 1980.
Philadelphia Inquirer, June 9, 1991; February 16, 1992.
San Francisco Chronicle, January 6, 1991.
U.S. News & World Report, April 22, 1991.
Washington Post, July 25, 1991.

—Mark Kram

Matt Dillon

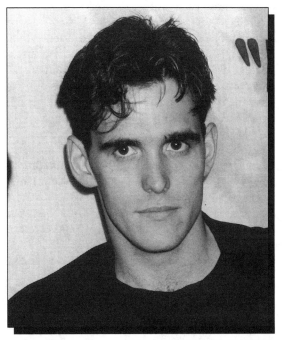

Tom Gates/Archive Photos

Actor

Born February 18, 1964, in New Rochelle, NY; son of Paul (an investment manager) and Mary Ellen Dillon. *Education:* Attended Mamaroneck High School.

Addresses: *Home*—New York, NY. *Office*—c/o Vic Ramos, 49 West 9th St., New York, NY 10011.

Career

Actor in motion pictures, 1978—. Films include *Over the Edge*, 1979; *Little Darlings*, 1980; *My Bodyguard*, 1980; *Liar's Moon*, 1982; *The Great American Fourth of July and Other Disasters*, 1982; *Tex*, 1982; *The Outsiders*, 1983; *Rumble Fish*, 1983; *The Flamingo Kid*, 1984; *Target*, 1985; *The Big Town*, 1987; *Drugstore Cowboy*, 1989; and *A Kiss Before Dying*, 1991. Also appeared in films *Rebel*, *Kansas*, *Native Son*, and *Bloodhounds of Broadway*.

Sidelights

When 14-year-old Matt Dillon played a brooding, directionless adolescent in his first feature film, he didn't need much acting technique to create a convincing portrayal. At that time he was in fact bored, alienated, and on his way to becoming a genuine juvenile delinquent. His success in the role marked the beginning of a busy dramatic career, and although he continued to play many inarticulate, violent individuals, acting transformed the real-life Dillon into a disciplined and highly motivated youth, considered to be among the most talented actors of his generation.

Talent scouts for casting agent Vic Ramos discovered Dillon in 1978. They had come to Hommocks Junior High School in Larchmont, New York, looking for non-actors to star in a small independent film entitled *Over the Edge*. Dillon caught their attention as he loitered around his locker while cutting class. When they approached him about auditioning, he agreed, but he certainly didn't take the offer too seriously. "I really didn't give a crap," he informed *People* contributor Richard K. Rein. "I went down [to Ramos's Manhattan office] with a couple of buddies to wise off at all these movie people. I used to make fun of the kids in school who acted or went to dance class." Dillon's intense gaze and cocky attitude struck just the right note with Ramos, according to *Over the Edge*'s director, Jonathan Kaplan. He stated in *Gentleman's Quarterly* that after Dillon left the office, Ramos declared: "That's him. That's the kid. I don't care if we look at 6,000 more, he's the one." Soon Dillon learned that he had been selected to play Richie, the second lead in *Over the Edge*.

The screenplay was based on real events that had transpired several years earlier in a San Francisco-area development called Foster City. In the movie, the condominium development—named New Granada and set in an unspecified Western state—is populated by middle-class refugees from big cities. The newcomer families see their new home as a place where they can enjoy a safer, more wholesome lifestyle. Their children, however, have a different perception of New Granada. To them, the half-finished, isolated community, with its winding, dead-end roads, is a soulless prison. Dillon's character transforms his peers' ennui into a spree of escalating vandalism. When a policeman overreacts and shoots him dead, his friends riot and destroy New Granada's high school.

According to *American Film* contributor Bret Easton Ellis, *Over the Edge* "tuned into adolescent frustration more keenly than any movie of its era. There was real poetry in its hard-edged B-movie suburban lyricism and, even though it now looks like a period

> *"[In Drugstore Cowboy] we didn't want to batter people over the head with sermons.... We tried to be true to the characters and figured that if we succeeded, the morals would fall in place."*

piece set in the late 1970s of Cheap Trick and Aerosmith, it doesn't feel dated. Dillon was only in *Over the Edge* for less than half its running time, but his presence dominated the picture. He gave a classic tough-guy adolescent performance." Dillon, whose only previous acting experience was playing Benjamin Franklin in an elementary school pageant, told *Mademoiselle:* "I was *so* intense when I started out that people assumed I was heavily into method acting. But I wasn't. What I *was* was fourteen. In *Over the Edge,* they didn't have to tell me to put my hand through a pane of glass. I had the raw energy. I did what I felt." The film was released in 1979 just as another gang epic, *The Warriors,* was linked with violent outbreaks at theaters across the country. Fearful that *Over the Edge* would generate a similar response, its distributors barely promoted the film at all, and it disappeared from theaters in less than a month. Since then, it has become something of a cult classic.

Vic Ramos had become Dillon's agent, and the next role he won for his client was that of Randy, a silent, surly youth who gives Kristy McNichol her sexual initiation in *Little Darlings.* The movie was a hit in the summer of 1980 and gave Dillon his first significant exposure. Quite suddenly he was the object of desire for teenaged girls across the country. Ramos capitalized on that phenomenon by saturating teen fan magazines with pinups of Dillon and founding a Matt Dillon Fan Club. Infatuated girls lay in wait for their idol outside of his house and school. Their devotion only intensified that fall when he appeared as the school bully in *My Bodyguard.* "Having young girls flip out . . . was appealing at first," Dillon admitted in *Gentleman's Quarterly,* "but it was never what I was in [the business] for, ever." The novelty of being a teen heartthrob quickly wore thin, but it was something he would have to put up with for years to come.

Dillon seemed close to being typecast as a hood until he worked in the 1982 melodrama *Liar's Moon.* In it, he portrayed a sweet, innocent farm boy who falls in love with a rich girl in post-World War II Texas. He broadened his range still further that year in *The Great American Fourth of July and Other Disasters,* a PBS adaptation of one of playwright Jean Shepherd's humorous recollections of growing up in the Midwest. Neither of these productions reached a large audience, but they were important to Dillon because they proved that he could play something other than an icon of teen angst. Although he turned 18 that year, he did not graduate from high school, and obtaining an equivalency degree is still on his list of future projects.

Dillon fever flared up with renewed intensity among adolescent girls in late 1982 with the release of *Tex,* an adaptation of the S. E. Hinton novel of the same name. Scenarist Tim Hunter had been looking for a story to serve as his directoral debut, and Dillon suggested the novel, which focuses on a boy's complex relationship with his older brother/surrogate father. Hunter worked in collaboration with Hinton and Charlie Haas to create the screenplay, then cast Dillon in the title role. The finished film was a tremendous box-office success, and although many reviewers felt that it was overburdened with subplots about class conflict, drugs, and old family secrets, most concurred that Dillon's performance was reason enough to see *Tex.* The *New Yorker's* Pauline Kael felt that Hunter's greatest achievement was "that he allows Dillon's mysteriously effortless charm to shine." *Time's* Richard Schickel wrote: "No one has more accurately captured the mercurial quality of adolescence than he has, with anger, rebelliousness, gallantry, goofiness all tumbled together to create a confused, wholly believable vulnerability." During the making of the film, Dillon became close friends with author Hinton, and it was through her that he secured his next role, in Francis Ford Coppola's adaptation of her book *The Outsiders*.

Dillon was in stellar company in *The Outsiders*. His fellow cast members in this tale of lower-class toughs tormented by upper-class rivals included Tom Cruise, Rob Lowe, Patrick Swayze, Ralph Macchio, and Emilio Estevez. The film did fairly well at the box office, but Coppola was widely faulted for turning Hinton's wry, somewhat humorous story into a pretentious, leaden film. In the role of gang leader Winston Dallas, Dillon was singled out by many commentators as the best thing about *The Outsiders*. Bret Easton Ellis wrote in *American Film* that "he embodied the greaser soul of Winston with a natural, restless authority, and he easily outshone a sizable cast . . . . He helped guide this grandiose teen psychodrama to its hyperbolic hilt and went out of the picture in full operatic splendor." For *New York* critic David Denby, Dillon's acting provided "the only moments of pleasure" in the film.

Despite the less-than-favorable evaluations of *The Outsiders*, Coppola followed it up with an adaptation of another Hinton book, *Rumble Fish*. In this effort, the director indulged in bizarre photographic techniques and surrealistic imagery, which some reviewers found brilliantly creative and others denounced as tedious and affected. The plot concerned an alcoholic father (Dennis Hopper) and his two sons, the burned-out, deranged "Motorcycle Kid" (played by Mickey Rourke) and Rusty-James (Dillon), who hero-worships his older sibling. In the climactic scene, Rusty-James carries out his brother's crazed dream to liberate the animals in the local pet shop— even the colorful fighting fish of the title, who have been isolated from each other for their own protection. Dillon rates *Rumble Fish* as his favorite among all the films in which he has worked.

After completing the trio of Hinton adaptations, Dillon opted for a change of pace in director Garry Marshall's *The Flamingo Kid*, the story of a working-class boy awed by the wealth that surrounds him in his summer job at a beach club. This light comedy became his most successful picture to date. From there he began moving into more adult roles, starring with Gene Hackman in the 1985 spy thriller *Target*, portraying a soldier in the World War II drama *Rebel*, and playing a revolutionary in *Native Son*. The late 1980s saw him playing adult versions of the danger-

ous characters that had made him famous: he was a psycho drifter in *Kansas*, a gambler in *The Big Town*, and a thug in *Bloodhounds of Broadway*. None of the six films made after *The Flamingo Kid* were moneymakers or critics' favorites, however, and for a time Dillon worried that he was becoming an "unbankable" actor.

Those doubts were dispelled in 1989, when he appeared in the highly acclaimed *Drugstore Cowboy*. Like his first film, it was based on a true crime story. He played Bob Hughes, the film's narrator and the leader of a band of junkies who supported their habits by robbing pharmacies in the Pacific Northwest. To research his character, Dillon spent days in the shooting galleries of New York City and even shot himself up with a real needle during filming— using a vitamin solution. He also spent time with William S. Burroughs, a guru of the Beat Generation and author of classic drug-oriented literature such as the novels *Junky* and *Naked Lunch*. (Burroughs also appeared in the film.)

While *Drugstore Cowboy* exposed the grimness and paranoia of the addict's world, it was also truthful about the euphoria that can be found in a needle. Such authenticity inevitably led to charges that the film glamorized drug use, but Dillon disagreed. "So many times in films, the drug addict is portrayed as a guy who is miserable getting high," he was quoted as saying in *Rolling Stone*. "Those films get it wrong. When Bob is high, that's when he thinks everything is great. I felt obligated to be honest about that . . . . We didn't want to batter people over the head with sermons . . . . We tried to be true to the characters and figured that if we succeeded, the morals would fall in place." Indeed, it was the absolute truthfulness of *Drugstore Cowboy* that impressed critics most.

Dillon was quoted in *Mademoiselle* as saying that he'd like to play "some regular guys," but in his follow-up to *Drugstore Cowboy*, he had his first role as a bona fide murderer. *A Kiss Before Dying*, the remake of a 1956 thriller starring Robert Wagner, saw him cast as a seductive, upwardly mobile killer who plans to do away with wealthy twin sisters in order to further his own ambitions. "He's a real Eighties guy," the actor commented of his character to *Gentleman's Quarterly* writer Lucy Kaylin. "I think if you were to ask him if he enjoys killing people, his answer would be an honest no. But he has a goal." Of his own personal goals, Dillon told *Mademoiselle*: "What counts is paying consistent attention to work. When I was fourteen I thought I knew it all, but over time you see the bigger picture. So you make a few great movies—and a few that are not-so-great. I'm an actor . . . not a teen star. I'm not in it for the fan club. I'm in for the long haul."

Sources

American Film, February 1991.
Gentleman's Quarterly, April 1991.
McCall's, January 1983.
Mademoiselle, July 1989.
Newsday, March 14, 1982.
People, September 29, 1980.
Rolling Stone, November 25, 1982; November 30, 1989.
Seventeen, July 1980.
Vanity Fair, April 1991.

—Joan Goldsworthy

Perry Farrell

©1990 Chris Cuffaro/Visages

Singer, artist, and filmmaker

Born Perry Bernstein in 1960 in Queens, NY; son of a jewelry business owner and an artist; married Casey Niccoli (a filmmaker) in 1991.

Career

Lead singer and songwriter for Los Angeles-based rock and roll band Psi-Com, 1981-85; lead singer and songwriter for Jane's Addiction, 1986-91; director, with wife Niccoli, of the film *Gift*, Warner Bros., 1991.

Awards: Jane's Addiction voted best underground band and best hard rock/metal band by *L.A. Weekly*, 1987; *Nothing's Shocking* was nominated for a Grammy Award for Best Heavy Metal Album; gold record for *Ritual de lo Habitual*, 1990; Perry Farrell named artist of the year by *Spin*, 1991.

Sidelights

Perry Farrell is an unlikely voice of a generation. In the early 1980s, as a struggling artist/musician, he was living with his girlfriend out of his car in the streets of Los Angeles. By the end of 1991, Farrell had become one of the most recognized social and political spokespersons for the legions of post-baby boom teenagers and twentysomethings who had taken to calling themselves Generation X. After fronting an obscure L.A. art/rock band called Psi-Com, Farrell formed Jane's Addiction in 1986 with guitarist Dave Navarro, bassist Eric Avery and drummer Steve Perkins. The band released one

independent live album in 1987 and two successful albums for Warner Bros. in 1988 and 1990. The two major-label records, *Nothing's Shocking* and *Ritual de lo Habitual*, brought the band as much notoriety for the controversial covers as for the ferocious yet melodic swirl of guitars and vocals contained therein.

Riding a huge wave of popularity in 1991 after *Ritual de lo Habitual* went gold, Jane's Addiction headlined Farrell's brainchild, the "Lollapalooza Festival," an eclectic mix of seven musical acts and numerous booths displaying art and trumpeting the latest political causes. In a year that most promoters characterized as a very slow one for the concert business, Lollapalooza was the most successful show of the season, playing to nearly half a million people in 21 cities. Farrell envisions Lollapalooza to be an annual alternative lifestyle event, complete with art, politics and, of course, music. But it appears that Lollapalooza will no longer feature Jane's Addiction. Fearing the trappings of success and commercialism, the band broke up in 1991, following a short series of post-Lollapalooza concerts. The controversial Perry Farrell performed his last show with Jane's Addiction while nude onstage in Hawaii.

Farrell was born Percy Bernstein in 1960 in Queens, New York, the son of a 47th Street jeweler in the city's diamond district. Sometimes the young Farrell would accompany his father on large transactions to "charm the customers," wrote *Rolling Stone*. "[The customers] would buy jewelry off me," Farrell recalled in *Rolling Stone*. "They couldn't say no because I was so damn adorable in my Beatle haircut and Beatle suit." When Farrell was four, his mother, an artist, committed suicide. He alludes to this briefly in the song "Then She Did . . ." from 1990's *Ritual de lo Habitual*, in which he sings in a pained voice to an ex-lover who overdosed, "Will you say hello to my ma?/She was an artist, just as you were/She was unhappy just as you were." After his mother's death, which Farrell refuses to discuss with the media, the family moved to Woodmere, Long Island, and later to Miami, Florida, where Farrell attended high school.

Farrell moved west to attend college in Oceanside, California. He supported himself by working in a vitamin factory, according to *Rolling Stone*, but quit

---

"When your fans start to look like you, it's time to move on. I don't want to be king of the ring-nose dreads."

---

after chemicals made his eyelashes and eyebrows fall out. Dropping out of college during his freshman year after suffering a nervous breakdown, Farrell later worked a series of odd jobs, including one delivering liquor; the job led him to a private club in Newport Beach where he was asked to model and dance. "They were also pushing prostitution," Farrell remarked in *Rolling Stone*. "I had to wear a pair of Speedos. It was pretty sleazy stuff." Dancing at the club, and lip-syncing some tunes, gave Farrell a taste of the spotlight and he enjoyed it.

"I wanted to try singing," he said. "There's not many things I'm better suited for. I don't know—I just *look* like a singer." Farrell eventually quit the dance club, bought a public address system, and changed his name to Perry Farrell, taking his brother Farrell's first name as his surname and at the same time creating a pun on the word peripheral. Having no musical training, Farrell began experimenting with tape recorders and headphones, creating songs from scratch.

In 1981 Farrell formed a band called Psi-Com and hit the insular Los Angeles underground music scene. "The self-described 'art' scene—depressed, black-clad musicians playing music almost as performance art, usually as an ironic comment on the state of pop culture—produced a lot of bands and venues but not many fans," commented Jonathan Gold in *California*. Psi-Com stayed together for four years, long enough to record an independent album that received some college airplay. When half the members left the band to join a religious cult, Psi-Com called it quits, but not before bassist Eric Avery auditioned for the band. Avery played the same bass riff for 45 minutes while Farrell improvised vocals. When 18-year-olds Steve Perkins and Dave Navarro later joined on drums and guitar, respectively, the Jane's Addiction line-up was born. Farrell took the band's name from a prostitute friend who helped support him and the band and who was also the inspiration for one of the band's most popular tunes, the haunting acoustic "Jane Says."

Jane's Addiction was based on Farrell's vision of a band that "wouldn't fit," observed Dave Handelman in *Rolling Stone*. It was to be a band to challenge contemporary thought and moral values, confronting head-on the issues of censorship, drugs and sexuality. The band formed in the mid-1980s, an era that was ripe for a group like Jane's Addiction to enter the scene and shake things up. "By the end of 1986," wrote Gold, "the thrashings of Hollywood postpunk had all but withered away; what rose up in its place was plain old heavy metal again." Straightforward L.A. metal groups like Poison and Motley Crue rode MTV to stardom. At the same time, a different, slightly more melodic type of metal was blooming in L.A.'s underground, personified by such groups Guns N' Roses and Jane's Addiction. Both bands became popular with the metal club circuit, playing regularly to boisterous crowds at the club Scream, and the Roxy. Farrell, usually clad in a nose-ring and dreadlocks with dark mascara, led his band through high-energy, high-voltage shows that observers say were never alike. "The standard comparison in those days," surmised Gold, "put Jane's Addiction as Led Zeppelin to Guns N' Roses' Aerosmith, because Farrell's voice was shrill, the song structures powerful and abstract."

When *L.A. Weekly* named Jane's Addiction best underground band and best hard rock/metal band of 1987, it became clear that the group would soon be signed to a major label. After releasing a live album on the independent Triple X label, Jane's Addiction began negotiations with several different major labels. Maintaining creative control was important to

Farrell. "Why give somebody else the reins when we've worked to get this sound?" Farrell said, as quoted in *Rolling Stone.* "It's like if you had a baby and somebody said, 'I want to raise your kid for you. I'll give him back when I'm done.'" The band signed with Warner Bros. for a $300,000 recording fund and two guaranteed albums, the first to be made with engineer Dave Jerden coproducing with Farrell.

The band's first LP was 1988's *Nothing's Shocking;* its title was underscored by the jacket cover, a Farrell-created nude sculpture of his girlfriend, Casey Niccoli, as Siamese twins with their heads ablaze. The songs included one about Ted Bundy as well as numerous references to heroin, a problem drug for all band members but drummer Perkins. Nevertheless, *Nothing's Shocking* was recognized by the usually conservative Academy of Recording Arts and Sciences, which nominated it for a Best Heavy Metal Album Grammy. "Naming the album *Nothing's Shocking* was Farrell's way of pointing out how blase and numb people have become in the eighties," explained Michael Goldberg in *Rolling Stone.* "The point, of course, is that there is plenty we should be shocked about."

Critically, the band's debut album was hailed as "superbly produced hard rock" by *Guitar Player's* Joe Gore and given four stars by *Rolling Stone's* Steve Pond. The inevitable comparisons to Led Zeppelin abounded, but were largely a result of the band's multi-layered guitars and Farrell's multi-tracked falsetto whine. Musically, the group's sound went beyond Led Zeppelin. "Guitarist Dave Navarro's densely layered overdubs recall those of Jimmy Page, without ever actually *sounding* like them," declared Joe Gore. "Furthermore, Jane's Addiction knows which Zepisms to avoid: the inept blues covers, the macho posturing and the lame lyrics." In addition, Pond found that "Jane's Addiction's version of Led Zeppelin is stripped of [lead singer] Robert Plant's fairy-tale whimsy."

Farrell and Jane's Addiction continued to address weighty material on the follow-up to *Nothing's Shocking,* 1990's *Ritual de lo Habitual.* The band's second album caused a furor before the plastic was even unsealed. Many stores refused to carry the album because of the cover, another Farrell creation depicting two naked women and a naked man along with icons of the Mexican spiritual movement, Santeria. The LP was reissued to many stores in a plain white jacket with the band's name, album title, and a reprinting of the First Amendment. Inside, Farrell penned a scathing diatribe that begins, "To the Mosquitoes: We have more influence over your

children than you do, but we love your children. Most of you love them too, very much. You want what's best for them. Consider them when planning the future . . . . Do you take the time to explain things to them, or do you blame the rest of the world for their mistakes? . . . I used to wish sometimes that I was a woman. A woman is the most attractive creature nature has to offer a man. Why then is it such a shame to see her unclothed? I feel more shame as a man watching a quick-mart being built." Farrell goes on to attack man's abuses of nature and the government's restrictions of freedoms, and chronicles how he was seemingly awakened by the sting of censorship: "Sometimes to realize you were well someone must come along and hurt you. I have aligned with all those who have been stung by suppression. As heirs to this planet, we must maintain, honor and enjoy the gift of freedom. A cause to validate everyone's life? Indeed."

The music on *Ritual de lo Habitual* generated nearly as much excitement as the cover controversy. In *Guitar Player,* Joe Gore said the album "reeks of the funky danger that's been missing from most mainstream rock for 20 years." In *Stereo Review,* Parke Peterbaugh found that "in Perry Farrell's world, there is no right and wrong and no sin except the subversion of self-expression." Such amoralistic thinking is plainly present in songs like "Ain't No Right," in which Farrell moans, "Ain't no wrong now, ain't no right/Only pleasure and pain." The oppression of interracial relationships is addressed on "No One's Leaving": "My sister and her boyfriend slept in the park/She had to leave home 'cause he was dark/Now they parade around in New York with a baby boy/He's gorgeous!"

Their hedonistic themes and raucous live shows made Jane's Addiction one of the hottest tickets on the U.S. concert circuit. Farrell's shaman-like stage antics earned him a warm rapport with his audience. "When I talk to an audience," Farrell told Gold, "I like to get the feeling that I'm at a party and I'm the guy who knows all the songs they like. I'll sing them, but it's my party. I like having something to say when everybody stares at me." While the band would swing in a tribal groove, Farrell would deliver his sociopolitical views to the masses. One night in Indiana in 1991, Gold related, Farrell talked about leaders. "I've been thinking about creative leaders," he told the crowd. "I've been thinking about our president. He found a way to kill off a country by dropping bombs, but can he make love? And if he could make love, would he need to drop bombs?" And, at a Halloween concert in Hollywood, Farrell offered each person present five dollars to come up on stage and touch his or her crotch.

The live energy and politically charged atmosphere of a Jane's Addiction tour reached its zenith with the Lollapalooza Festival in the summer of 1991. The 21-city, seven-act tour featured such varied performances as the hardcore rap of Ice-T, the angst-ridden punk of the Henry Rollins Band, the guitar grunge of the Butthole Surfers, the industrial disco of Nine Inch Nails, the sociopolitical rock of Living Color, the ethereal pop of Siouxsie and the Banshees, and the headliners, Jane's Addiction. The hugely successful tour was also a free market of ideas. As Farrell told *Spin*, "I don't like the idea of the world being controlled by the news media. We need to exchange ideas somewhere else, another forum. The cafes aren't being used anymore, so let's try it at a festival." Tents and booths were set up for magic acts, artwork displays, and activist organizations ranging from Greenpeace to the National Abortion Rights Action League. Also on hand were voter registration booths and forums for discussing censorship, handgun control, and environmental causes. Farrell continued in *Spin* that he plans to make Lollapalooza an annual event, have it headlined in 1992 by the Red Hot Chili Peppers, and to eventually take it around the globe.

On October 16, 1991, Farrell's drug use got him into legal trouble. A maid cleaning his Holiday Inn hotel room found assorted drug paraphernalia and an unidentified white powder. When Farrell returned, he was arrested by two police officers. "He was extremely intoxicated," one was quoted as saying in *Rolling Stone*. "His balance was poor; he was not completely coherent; his speech was thick and slurred, like a real bad drunk."

On the heels of the breakthrough success of Lollapalooza, Jane's Addiction self-destructed. The band members were not especially close to begin with; Farrell and Avery had barely spoken in two years, according to *Rolling Stone*. But friction was apparently not the major impetus for the break-up, success was. "I've taken it as far as I can without losing the element of fun," Farrell commented to Gold in *California*. "The size of the crowds has increased, the level of musicianship has increased . . . . As an actor, you leave a part behind when you leave the role, but as a musician you carry a role with you always. Men age, and I want to do something that doesn't involve guitar solos . . . . When your fans start to look like you, it's time to move on. I don't want to be king of the ring-nose dreads."

Selected discography

With Jane's Addiction

Jane's Addiction, Triple X, 1987.
Nothing's Shocking, Warner Bros., 1988.
Ritual de lo Habitual, Warner Bros., 1990.

Also recorded the single "Ripple" for *Deadicated: A Tribute to the Grateful Dead*, Arista, 1991.

Sources

California, August 1991.
Guitar Player, December 1988; January 1991; March 1991.
Rolling Stone, October 22, 1987; October 20, 1988; February 9, 1989; February 7, 1991; September 19, 1991; November 28, 1991.
Spin, December 1991.
Stereo Review, December 1990.

Other sources include album liner notes to *Ritual de lo Habitual*, Warner Bros., 1990.

—*John P. Cortez*

Matthew Fox

Roman Catholic priest

Mari Kane/Carlson-Kane Studios, S.F., courtesy of Matthew Fox

Born Timothy James Fox, December 21, 1940, in Madison, WI; son of George Thomas and Beatrice (Sill) Fox. *Education:* Aquinas Institute of Philosophy, Dominican College of St. Rose of Lima, River Forest, IL (now Aquinas Institute, St. Louis, MO), M.A., 1964; Aquinas Institute of Philosophy and Theology, Dubuque, IA (now Aquinas Institute, St. Louis, MO), M.A., 1967; Institut Catholique de Paris, S.T.D. (summa cum laude), 1970; postdoctoral study at University of Muenster, 1970. *Politics:* Independent. *Religion:* Roman Catholic.

Addresses: *Office*—Institute in Culture and Creation Spirituality, Holy Names College, Oakland, CA 94619.

Career

Entered Ordo Praedicatorum (Order of Preachers; Dominicans; O.P.), 1960, ordained Roman Catholic priest, 1967; Aquinas Institute of Philosophy and Theology, Dubuque, IA (now Aquinas Institute, St. Louis, MO), assistant professor of theology, 1970-71; Emmanuel College, Boston, MA, assistant professor of theology, 1971-72; Loyola University of Chicago, IL, assistant professor of theology, 1972-73; Barat College, Lake Forest, IL, professor of religious studies and chairman of department, 1973—; lecturer for Thomas More Association, 1973—; founder and director, Institute in Culture and Creation Spirituality, first at Mundelein College, Chicago, IL, then at Holy Names College, Oakland, CA, 1976—.

Member: Secretariat of Lorscheid International Movement of Dominicans, 1969; Catholic Theological Association.

Sidelights

Labelled by some a New Age guru in priest's clothing, by others a prophet calling Christians to deeper faith, Dominican priest Matthew Fox has stirred great controversy among Christians, particularly within the Roman Catholic church. As director of the California-based Institute in Culture and Creation Spirituality, author of more than a dozen books, and editor in chief of *Creation Spirituality* magazine, Fox has enjoyed a widening forum for his interpretation of biblical teaching, which focuses on what he calls "original blessing" rather than on the doctrine of original sin. Fox has garnered an enthusiastic following for his brand of creation spirituality among both Catholics and mainstream Protestants.

Born Timothy James Fox, Matthew Fox was the fourth of seven children born to Beatrice and George Fox, an assistant football coach at the University of Wisconsin in Madison. Fox's parents greatly influenced their son. Having escaped the slums of Chicago and an abusive family situation through the influence of the Augustinian priests who schooled him through Villanova University, George Fox was strictly pious throughout his life. The elder Fox's dominant personality and iron-fisted rule of the household was not softened by that of his powerful, independent wife, Beatrice, who, raised a liberal Episcopalian, eventually converted to Catholicism.

At age 12 Timmy Fox was struck down by polio, which was then sweeping the country in epidemic proportions. He survived the initial onslaught of the disease but found his legs paralyzed, a difficult blow in a family where athletic ability was valued. Fox spent the better part of a year isolated in the hospital; even his family had to speak to him through special windows. During this time a Catholic brother from the Dominican order came to visit the boy. This gentle man was both a person the elder Fox would admire and his opposite in temperament. Six months after his illness began, the young Fox regained use of his legs, and when he left the hospital it was evident

> *"I don't deny original sin, but I insist that we start with original blessing."*

that he was a changed person—solitary, impatient, with his sights set on an unspoken goal.

Timothy Fox formally joined the Dominicans at age 19 and spent his first year at the Dominican novitiate in Winona, Minnesota, overlooking the Mississippi River. As is the custom, in a special ceremony he left his old self behind and was renamed Matthew. The routine was rigorous: Dominicans rose at five and filled their days with chanting, chores, prayer, and meditation. "They were not conscious about what they were doing," Fox told Lawrence Wright of *Rolling Stone.* "We were celibate because Dominicans have always been celibate, we don't eat meat at this time of year and we fast at this time of year; they didn't have any reasons for any of this. I think that's why I eventually decided to get my doctorate in spirituality: I wanted to understand what's the rationale for all this."

After that first year Fox was sent to the Aquinas Institute in River Forest, Illinois, where he proved to be a brilliant student. He later earned a doctorate in theology with highest honors from the Institut

Catholique in Paris. Fox did not want to be a priest who routinely performed Mass, weddings, funerals, or the numerous other pastoral tasks typical of a Catholic community. Instead, he focused on and taught theology at various universities and conducted his own theological investigations.

In 1972 Fox published *On Becoming a Musical, Mystical Bear,* a book on prayer. He explained how many Christians feel boxed in by a religion that is geared financially, institutionally, and intellectually toward children and is not ready to serve adults. Fox attempts to replace childish notions of prayer with a mature definition of spirituality—a response to life based on mysticism—experienced as enjoyment of life—and prophecy—experienced as the fight to share life and criticize its enemies. Fox was then offered the head position in the religion department at Barat College in Lake Forest, Illinois. When he was asked to study the teaching of spirituality in America, he wrote a critique of the entire theological education system and provided his own model.

When in 1976 authorities at Mundelein College in Chicago asked him to implement his plan, the Institute in Culture and Creation Spirituality (ICCS) was formed. The faculty included experts in a variety of disciplines, including theology, philosophy, psychology, dance, music, and art. It offered a master of arts degree and advertised: "Artists, scientists, Jungian analysts, and theologians lead participants to develop a mystical prophetic vocation while studying the creation-centered tradition. Intellectual courses go hand in hand with extrovert meditation courses of dance, photography, acupressure/massage, art, music, and clay and culminate in a compassion practicum for social transformation."

After seven years in the Chicago area, Fox felt the need for a change of scene. With the permission of his superiors, Fox moved ICCS to Holy Names College, a liberal arts college in Oakland, California. With the 1983 move its faculty became ever more diverse and included instructors in Native American ritual, feminist studies, new shamanism—a belief that good and evil spirits may be influenced by religious leaders—dreams, and pre-Christian rituals. Its advertising literature reads: "A nine-month graduate program dedicated to in-depth transformation of the individual and society. Innovative curriculum develops both inner awareness and commitment to social change. Native American, feminist, Celtic, Rhineland mystic and Biblical sources shape our educational philosophy, as does the emerging scientific paradigm. Creativity is activated through 'art as meditation' courses, weekly rituals and individual and group process. Passionate and compassionate response to injustice and oppression is the goal of the ICCS experience."

Original Blessing: A Primer in Creation Spirituality is Fox's manifesto for a more mystical and ecologically based theology, with far less emphasis on such traditional themes as sin and redemption and more on blessing and creativity. "I don't deny original sin, but I insist that we start with original blessing," Fox told Sam Keen of *Psychology Today*. "We inherited an earth that is hospitable toward us.... There were 19 billion years or so of history and God's creative activity before human beings appeared on the scene and invented sin.... In creation spirituality, we begin with the idea that each of us is born a unique expression of divinity, an image of God." Fox sees God as panentheistic (that is, as naturally present in all things), but believes that God transcends the created order. He draws on the work of medieval mystics Hildegard of Bingen, Francis of Assisi, Mechtild of Magdeburg, Meister Eckhart, and Julian of Norwich, as well as other theologians, artists, and scientists.

Fox outlines creation spirituality by describing four paths of renewal: Delight, Letting Go, Creativity, Compassion. In the first path a joyful attitude toward the Mother Earth is shown through affirming the senses: eating, drinking, dancing, singing, and love-making. The second path focuses on the world's mysteries and darkness, including evil, suffering, and death. The path of Creativity is the act of creation, attributed to the right side of the brain. The final way, Compassion, includes concern for Mother Earth, justice, and peacemaking.

"We should begin with a positive accent, the spirit of wonder, awe or radical amazement we have when we first attend to the original blessing, to the beauty that is around and within us," Fox explained to Keen. "Only then do we enter into the darkness... the awareness of evil, suffering and death. We must confront our wounds, but not without the empowerment that comes from the awe and wonder of the universe.... Once you experience the awe and face the darkness, creativity is unleashed. It's not something you have to manufacture. Creativity is utterly natural in us. It's our divine power.... Creativity gives us the impulse and power to transform ourselves and society."

Fox's emphasis on creativity rather than original sin, his tolerance of homosexuality, his portrayal of God as both father and mother, and the presence of a self-styled "witch" named Starhawk on the faculty of ICCS set him on a collision course with church officials. In 1984 the Vatican's Sacred Congregation for the Doctrine of the Faith demanded that the Dominicans investigate Fox's theological work. A three-man committee was assigned the task and focused on three of Fox's tomes, *Original Blessing, Whee! We, Wee All the Way Home,* and *On Becoming a Musical, Mystical Bear.* Early the following year the committee reported that though there were some "defects" in his works, Fox should be commended for his hard work and creativity.

The commission suggested that Fox's future work be reviewed by his Dominican superiors, an idea to which Fox was receptive. In late 1985, Cardinal Joseph Ratzinger, head of the Congregation for the Doctrine of the Faith, told the Dominicans that the recommendation was inadequate. According to *National Catholic Reporter* writer Bill Kenkelen, Ratzinger called *Original Blessing* "deviant and dangerous," an "altogether personal, gratuitous and subjective interpretation of Christian spirituality.... One notes especially his practically total neglect of the magisterium [divinely inspired true doctrine] and his manner of citing what he likes in the Bible and interpreting it his own way." Ratzinger further suggested that Fox be removed as director of ICCS and that Starhawk be fired.

In *The Coming of the Cosmic Christ: The Healing of Mother Earth and the Birth of a Global Renaissance,* Fox promotes what he believes is a long-suppressed tradition of joyful, sensuous, egalitarian, ecumenical, and ecologically sensitive Christian mysticism. Fox believes that humankind needs a new cosmology—a story of the universe and our place within it—because the old cosmology of the Enlightenment—which understood the universe as a machine and tried to understand that machine in order to control it—no longer works, as the eighteenth-century philosophy has led to the brink of ecological and social disaster. According to Fox, science, mysticism, and art must work together to birth a "living" cosmology that will transform culture and its institutions, including education and religion. Science tells the story of the universe's origins; mysticism is the human response of amazement to the universe; and art is the response to the mysticism that allows for creative change in all areas of life.

Writing in *Earth Island Journal*, Fox stated, "Meister Eckhart taught that 'God is a great underground river,' and that the world's great religions are all wells tapping into that power. We must unleash the wisdom of all religions—Western and Eastern, as well as Native American and Goddess traditions—to reveal the Cosmic Christ [the image of God present in all things]." Fox believes that a shift to a living cosmology could launch an era of "deep ecumenism," that is, the unleashing of the wisdom of all world religions. "This unleashing of wisdom holds the last hope for the survival of the planet we call home," he wrote in *The Coming of the Cosmic Christ*, "for there is no such thing as a Lutheran sun and a Taoist moon and [a] Jewish ocean and a Roman Catholic forest. When humanity learns this we will have learned a way out of our anthropocentric dilemma that is boring our young, killing our souls, trivializing our worship, and exterminating the planet."

Fox believes that the symbol of the Cosmic Christ appropriate to the turn of the twenty-first century is that of Jesus as Mother Earth, an earth that is being crucified, yet resurrected daily. According to Fox, Mother Earth is a unique expression of divine wisdom, caring, creativity, and fruitfulness; yet because humans have set out to control nature—instead of realizing their interdependence with nature—they have brought about disasters of all kinds: ecological, social, religious. Only with a living cosmology does he see hope for the survival of Mother Earth and all her inhabitants.

Fox's work has been the focus of controversy for many reasons, among them his challenge to the institutional church to revitalize itself—to not neglect its mystical traditions, to make its rituals more meaningful, to allow the fuller participation of women and the marriage of priests, and to challenge church members to creativity and compassion in all areas of their lives. Some critiques, while noting that Fox's creation spirituality should not be dismissed, maintain that he oversimplifies complex issues and his scholarship is flawed, adding that he distorts the work of the medieval mystics with unreliable translations and questionable emphases to fit his own agenda. To others he is seen as un-Christian because his concept of the Cosmic Christ smacks of the Hindu doctrine monism and his deep ecumenism of the empowerment jargon that is so much a part of the New Age movement.

Rather than shielding Fox from this new criticism as they had previously, Fox's Dominican superiors ordered him to refrain from preaching, teaching, and lecturing for one year beginning December 15, 1988. Fox created a stir when the California-based "Friends of Creation Spirituality" paid for a full-page advertisement in the *New York Times* with copies sent to the national news media. In it, Fox accused the Church of "fundamentalist zeal," listed his academic credentials, provided a summary of Vatican charges

brought against him, and passionately defended his creation-centered spirituality. Sales of his books rose dramatically and letters of support flooded into the institute, which numbers 25,000 adherents. "That is something of an irony that the Vatican—in over-reacting to creation spirituality—has spread the seeds more broadly," Fox told *Detroit Free Press* reporter David Crumm. "There's no question that the interest is more broadly disseminated than it was before."

During his forced sabbatical, Fox traveled extensively, visiting Holland, Italy, Latin America, Australia, and New Zealand. When he resumed his vigorous schedule of writing, speaking, and teaching, Fox began his first public appearance by saying, "As I was saying before I was so rudely interrupted fourteen months ago . . . ." He in effect picked up where he had left off.

By mid-1990 Fox had become something of an embarrassment to his Dominican supervisors. The Central province chapter of the order assigned him to St. Pius Priory in Chicago and asked him to be there within a few weeks. Fox insisted that he could not leave ICCS on such short notice, a statement that was accepted. By 1991 it was plain that Fox had no intention of obeying the order to leave California. His *Creation Spirituality: Liberating Gifts for the Peoples of the Earth*, a brief outline of his theology, sold 25,000 copies in its first month of publication, and his work at ICCS went on as usual. If Fox refuses to return to Chicago a third time, he may be forced to leave the Dominican order, but he hopes for support from some influential members of his order. In the meantime, Fox remains at ICCS and at his home in Oakland, which he shares with his dog, Tristan. "I am against abortion," Fox told Peter Hebblethwaite of the *National Catholic Reporter*, "and I'm not going to abort my work here in California."

Selected writings

Religion USA: An Inquiry Into Religion and Culture by Way of Time Magazine, Listening Press, 1971.
On Becoming a Musical, Mystical Bear: Spirituality American Style, Paulist Press, 1972.
Whee! We, Wee All the Way Home: Toward a Sensual, Prophetic Spirituality, Consortium, 1976.
A Spirituality Named Compassion and the Healing of the Global Village, Humpty Dumpty, and Us, Winston Press, 1979.
(Editor) *Western Spirituality: Historical Roots, Ecumenical Routes*, Fides/Claretian, 1979.
(Author of introduction and commentary) Meister Eckhart, *Breakthrough: Meister Eckhart's Creation Spirituality in New Transition*, Doubleday, 1981.

(With Brian Swimme) *Manifesto for a Global Civilization*, Bear and Company, 1982.

(Author of introduction) *Meditations with Meister Eckhart*, Bear and Company, 1982.

Original Blessing: A Primer in Creation Spirituality, Bear and Company, 1983.

Illuminations of Hildegard of Bingen, Bear and Company, 1985.

(Editor) *The Hildegard Reader: Operatione Dei and Letters by Hildegard of Bingen*, Bear and Company, 1986.

The Coming of the Cosmic Christ: The Healing of Mother Earth and the Birth of a Global Renaissance, Harper, 1988.

Creation Spirituality: Liberating Gifts for the Peoples of the Earth, Harper, 1991.

Sheer Joy: Conversations With Thomas Aquinas on Creation Spirituality, Harper, 1992.

Sources

America, July 12, 1980; September 15, 1984.

The Catholic World, July/August 1990.

Christianity Today, June 16, 1989.

Commonweal, December 4, 1981; April 23, 1982; June 16, 1989.

Creation Spirituality, November/December 1991.

Detroit Free Press, March 15, 1990.

Earth Island Journal, Winter 1988-89.

National Catholic Reporter, October 21, 1988; October 28, 1988; November 4, 1988; December 23, 1988; February 10, 1989; April 28, 1989; May 12, 1989; February 16, 1990; January 24, 1992.

New York Times Book Review, January 15, 1989.

Psychology Today, June 1989.

Rolling Stone, November 14, 1991.

—*Jeanne M. Lesinski*

Robert M. Gates

CIA Director

Full name, Robert Michael Gates; born September 25, 1943, Wichita, KS; son of an auto parts salesman; married, 1966; wife's name, Becky; children; two. *Education:* William and Mary College, B.A., 1965; Indiana University, M.A. in Russian history, 1966; Georgetown University, doctorate in Soviet and Russian history, 1974.

Addresses: *Office*—Central Intelligence Agency, Washington, DC 20505.

Career

Joined the CIA career training program, 1966, served as a current intelligence analyst, later specialized in Soviet affairs; U.S. Air Force, 1966-68; National Security Council staff, 1974-1980; national intelligence officer on Soviet Union, 1980-82; deputy director of intelligence, 1982-86; deputy director of CIA, 1986-88, briefly serving as acting director in 1987; served as assistant to the president and as deputy for national security affairs, 1988-91; director of Central Intelligence Agency, 1991—.

Awards: Distinguished Intelligence Medal; Intelligence Medal of Merit; Arthur S. Fleming Award (presented annually to the ten most outstanding young men and women in federal service).

Sidelights

Robert M. Gates has geared his entire career toward becoming director of the Central Intelligence Agency. From the time he joined the agency in 1966, he took challenging assignments and drew praise for his performance and clear-thinking analysis. He chose the right mentors—notably George Bush and Robert Casey—and was always loyal to his bosses. In 1987, Gates got his chance. Following Casey's death, Gates was nominated to succeed him as director of the CIA. At the time, however, the Iran-Contra affair was raging and Gates was a peripheral figure in the scandal. After several days of stormy Senate hearings, he withdrew his name from nomination.

Four years later, Gates got something that few in Washington ever get: a second chance. President Bush again nominated him for the CIA's top post and, despite ongoing reservations from some members of the Senate, he was approved. The agency Gates now heads seeks to adapt to a changing world in which there is one Germany and no Soviet Union. He is regarded as one of America's leading authorities on Russia, possessing knowledge that will be important in helping the United States draft its policy in upcoming years.

Robert Michael Gates was born during the middle of World War II in a quiet, suburban neighborhood of Wichita, Kansas. He was an avid Boy Scout who became an Eagle Scout and a straight-A student in high school. After graduating, he traveled east to William and Mary College in Virginia, where he earned high honors in history, an award for service, and a reputation as a workaholic. From there, Gates moved to the University of Indiana's Institute on Soviet and East European Studies, where he earned a master's degree and met his wife, Becky. In the fall of 1966 the couple moved to Washington, where Gates—then 23 years old—began working as a Soviet affairs analyst for the CIA. Several years later he became one of two assistant national intelligence advisers to the strategic arms limitations talks.

From the beginning, Gates believed that the CIA's analytical studies of the USSR were inadequate and ill-conceived. "He was aware of the shortcomings," Gates's former CIA colleague, David Aaron, told the *Washington Post.* "He and I used to sit around and fantasize about why couldn't we get half the people from *Time* or *Newsweek* and have them put out the *National Intelligence Daily,* and have no intelligence people involved at all." In 1974, Gates earned his doctorate from Georgetown University. His 290-page doctoral dissertation, which focused on 15 years of Soviet-Sino relationships, quickly became regarded as the authoritative statement on the issue. Gates's status at the CIA began to soar and he drew the attention of then-CIA director George Bush.

He also drew the attention of President Gerald Ford's White House. Late in 1974 Gates was assigned to the administration's National Security Council staff under director Brent Scowcroft. He stayed with the NSC even after the election of President Jimmy Carter, working under Zbigniew Brzezinski. He earned a reputation as a loyal and diligent worker, albeit, one source told the *Washington Post* in 1987, "not a warm guy, not the kind of guy you'd like to spend a weekend with."

Working for the White House first exposed Gates to the policy-making side of government. David Aaron recounted for the *Washington Post* that in 1977 NSC officials were concerned about rising Islamic fundamentalism in Turkey. Aaron asked Gates for a CIA paper on the subject. Gates inquired of the agency several times, getting nothing back. Finally, he learned no one had studied the issue. "He thought it was appalling," Aaron recalled, "and he was more appalled because he wasn't sure that they would even go out and find out about it."

In January 1980, Gates returned to the CIA to work for director Stansfield Turner as national intelligence officer on the Soviet Union. Two years later, under director William J. Casey, he was promoted to deputy director for intelligence gathering, the agency's top

analytical job. He distinguished himself in this job, allotting extra funds for travel, study and language training for the analysts. He also sought to improve contacts with the academic community and encourage more competitive analysis. In 1983, Gates became Casey's deputy director. Critics and supporters acknowledged that Gates had established himself as a top Soviet scholar with unsurpassed intelligence credentials.

Through the 1980s, Gates's views about the Soviets served as a consistent counterpoint to the political mind-set of President Ronald Reagan's White House. The *Los Angeles Times*'s David Lauter wrote in 1991, "During the early days of the Reagan Administration, many White House officials viewed Gates as too soft. He was not an 'evil empire' believer. In 1983, for example, Gates ordered a study of Soviet military spending, which concluded that Moscow's military budget had stagnated since 1976 at a level far lower

> *"CIA and U.S. intelligence must change—and be seen to change—or confront irrelevance and growing sentiment for their dismantlement."*

than the Pentagon had been saying. Subsequently, however, as Reagan became more and more enamored of his relationship with Mikhail S. Gorbachev, Gates began sounding warnings. In the first ten months of the Bush Administration, he was widely seen as a hard liner."

The flash point came in October 1989, when Gates wrote a speech that was highly pessimistic about Soviet President Gorbachev's chances of achieving genuine reform in his country. "There are very real limits to the democratization intended by Gorbachev," Gates wrote. "No opposition party will be tolerated . . . . Elections were rigged . . . . Every element of political reform seems to have been designed to increase Gorbachev's personal power." Secretary of State James Baker read the speech—and killed it—before Gates could deliver it.

Though Gates began his career as a Soviet specialist, many in the CIA regarded him as a better bureaucrat than analyst. In an opinion piece in the *Washington Post* in 1991, Tom Polgar, a former CIA "super-grade" who opposed Gates's nomination as CIA chief, wrote, "Through more than 20 years' service, Gates earned a reputation as an able staff officer, outstanding briefer (no small task), reliable subordinate and a non-competing deputy. These are qualities much sought after in Washington, particularly during periods when management is valued more highly than leadership." Sources said that by 1985, Casey was talking privately about Gates as a future CIA director. Gates had another key supporter in then-Vice President Bush who, after swearing in Gates as the CIA's deputy director in 1986, told the small crowd of family, friends and co-workers present that Gates was like a son to him.

In December 1986 Casey was incapacitated with a brain tumor. When Casey resigned two months later, President Reagan nominated Gates as his successor. Initially, Congressional leaders praised his selection, but Gates soon came under fire for his apparent role in the Iran-Contra scandal, in which profits from the sales of arms to Iran were illegally diverted to Contra rebels in Nicaragua. An independent report on the affair commissioned by President Reagan said that Gates had misled Congress in 1986 when he testified that Casey knew only "bits and pieces" about the possible diversion of arms sales funds. The report concluded that Casey knew much more than that.

In addition, Congressional leaders raised questions about Gates's actions, or lack of them, during the Iran-Contra affair. Gates said he had been aware of the covert scheme since December 1985, and voiced his protests over it to Casey. But his relative silence on the issue bothered some congressmen. Senator William Cohen, R-Maine, told the *Philadelphia Inquirer* that Gates was a man who was "not prepared to lay his career on the line over a matter he did not create."

Gates was also questioned on allegations that he may have advocated a U.S. invasion of Libya in 1985. Gates vehemently denied the charges, characterizing them for the *Los Angeles Times* as "outrageous" and "false." Still, after two days of hearings it became clear to the Reagan Administration that Gates's name would have to be withdrawn in order to avoid a drawn-out fight that could have lasted as long as the congressional investigation of the Iran-Contra affair. Gates took the initiative to make the move, telling the *Los Angeles Times* that "a prolonged period of uncertainty (over his nomination) would be harmful to the CIA."

Gates stayed on as acting director until May, 1987, when then-FBI Director William Webster was confirmed for the position. He returned to the post of

deputy director until December 1980, when President-elect Bush brought him back into the White House as deputy national security adviser, again serving under Scowcroft. Bush took minor heat at the time for promoting someone with a minor involvement in the Iran-Contra affair, but Gates's solid credentials seemed to overshadow that criticism. Retired Adm. Bobby Inman, who preceded Gates as deputy director of the CIA, told the *Los Angeles Times* that Gates "is an extraordinarily bright, capable public servant and one of the country's premier students of the Soviet Union."

As deputy national security adviser, Gates headed the Deputies Committee, a panel of representatives from leading agencies that serves as a sort of executive committee for the Administration's foreign policy. In that post, he participated in such major events as the Gulf War, but also was the White House manager for many lower-level crises that did not require direct presidential involvement and received little public attention. Gates viewed the post as important, but made no secret of his desire to eventually head the CIA. "You know the great thing about the DCI (director of Central Intelligence) job," he told the *Los Angeles Times* in 1991, "is that it's the only job in government where you're free to promote anyone you want."

In 1991 he got that chance again. Despite Gates's confirmation problems four years earlier, President Bush again nominated him to head the CIA. A few members of Congress said at the time that they still had serious doubts about Gates's willingness to be fully candid with them. But White House officials felt they had enough support to go ahead. Before the confirmation hearings, Senate investigators conducted a four-month examination, including a painstaking review of Gates's answers to a comprehensive set of 80 interrogatories.

The hearings, in September 1991, were not easy for Gates. Senators questioned Gates's insistence that he knew little of the Iran-Contra diversion until long after the fact. If so, some suggested, didn't that suggest that he was out of touch with agency activities? Gates was also questioned on other unauthorized covert deals with Iraq, political tailoring of intelligence on the Soviet Union and Iran and a stifling bureaucratization of the CIA intelligence directorate he once ran.

Gates's supporters vouched for his objectivity. John N. McMahon, deputy director under Casey from 1982 to 1986 while Gates was running the CIA's analytical branch, told the *Washington Post* that he could not recall any instance in which Gates had slanted intelligence to please policy-makers. There would be 2,000 analysts in the agency, McMahon said, "who would be headed by Bob Gates, walking out the front door if they thought that the CIA was going to become a policy tool of any administration."

On November 5, 1991, the Senate confirmed Gates by a 64-31 margin. At age 40, he became the youngest man ever to head the CIA, as well as the first career analyst to run the agency. "Most of the past directors were American government people, and they learned foreign affairs after being appointed," Kenneth de Graffenreid, the National Security Council's intelligence expert during the Reagan era, told the *Los Angeles Times*. "Gates, by contrast, is actually a person who likes foreign policy."

Gates told senators that his first task as CIA director would be to recommend that President Bush launch a sweeping reassessment of intelligence needs for the post-Soviet era. "CIA and U.S. intelligence must change—and be seen to change—or confront irrelevance and growing sentiment for their dismantlement," he told *Congressional Quarterly*. He endorsed the idea that more attention be focused on "human intelligence" gathered by individuals, rather than on intelligence-gathering through the expensive, high-tech equipment that has been used to monitor the Soviet threat in recent decades.

Gates also vowed to chance the super-secret image of the CIA, telling the *Lexington Herald-Leader* that he planned to take "symbolic steps that would suggest that the mentality of the Cold War has changed." However, the first proposal he made—to publish the overall figure the United States spends on intelligence—was killed by President Bush. He also approved new procedures aimed at encouraging CIA employees to be on the lookout for criminal activities outside the agency as well as within it.

The plan, approved in January 1992, included the addition of legal issues to the training courses for new CIA officers, guidelines outlining some of the improper or potentially illegal activities that should be reported, and the designation of three offices at the agency to review the reports and coordinate follow-up inquiries. And he pledged as well to make intelligence more useful in response to complaints that reports had become inapplicable. "We publish too much intelligence of questionable relevance to policy makers," he told *Congressional Quarterly*. "Less and better should be the rule."

Sources

Boston Globe, November 5, 1991; November 13, 1991; December 11, 1991.
Chicago Tribune, February 3, 1987; March 3, 1987; December 29, 1988.
Congressional Quarterly, October 1991; November 1991.
Lexington Herald-Leader, January 14, 1992.
Los Angeles Times, December 29, 1988; May 15, 1991.
USA Today, September 16, 1991.
Washington Post, February 3, 1987; November 29, 1987; December 29, 1988; May 28, 1989; June 23, 1991; September 15, 1991; September 16, 1991; September 22, 1991; October 18, 1991; January 26, 1992.

—*Glen Macnow*

Kathie Lee Gifford

Talk-show host and entertainer

Born Kathie Lee Epstein, August 16, 1953, in Paris, France; raised in Maryland; daughter of Aaron (a U.S. naval officer) and Joan Epstein; married Paul Johnson (a gospel composer), 1977 (divorced); married Frank Gifford (a football Hall-of-Famer and sportscaster), 1986; children: Cody Newton. *Education:* Attended Oral Roberts University.

Addresses: *Home*—Greenwich, Connecticut.

Career

Performed as a folksinger at age 14; named Maryland's Junior Miss at age 17, began singing and acting in commercials, TV pilots, and on the soap opera *Days of Our Lives* at age 20; featured singer on the game show *Name That Tune*, 1977; costarred on the sitcom *Hee Haw Honeys*; continued to work in television and nightclubs until 1982; then became reporter and substitute anchor on *Good Morning America*; cohost, with Regis Philbin, of syndicated talk show *Live With Regis and Kathie Lee*, 1985—. Spokesperson for Carnival Cruise Lines, Ultra Slim Fast, the Home Furnishings Council; entertains for Children's Charity, Multiple Sclerosis, and Special Olympics.

Sidelights

The secret to Kathie Lee Gifford's success is that she simply has no secrets. As the outspoken cohost of the widely syndicated *Live With Regis and Kathie Lee*, she shares her loves, hates, worries, embarrassing moments, triumphs, and trials with a national audience, five days a week. Never mind that she's rich and famous, talented, and undeniably gorgeous. She has endeared herself to millions of fans with her sassy one-liners and genuine emotions.

Live With Regis and Kathie Lee, a New York talk show that went national in 1988, is a challenging exercise in spontaneity. Live, unrehearsed, and unscripted, without even the usual seven-second tape delay for emergencies, the show is a throwback to the early days of live television. The intrepid cohosts rely on personality and nerve to pull them through an unpredictable hour-long show. The fact that they are surviving and more—in spite of the sometime disdain of the critics—is either a tribute to their professional talent, or a sign of audience backlash against the competition. *Live* is a standout in a crowded field of gabfests featuring daily topics of taboo. Viewers turned off by the parade of talk show trash are finding, according to the ratings, solace in the normalcy of Regis and Kathie Lee.

The format is simple. The pair opens with a 15-minute "host chat" focusing on small-talk topics of everyday life. Fans find out what their spouses are *really* like, how Regis and wife, Joy, sat around and watched TV the night before, and Kathie Lee and her husband, former pro football player and sportscaster Frank Gifford, "finally" got out to see a movie, leaving baby Cody with their trusty nanny, Christine. There's no doubt Regis and sidekick are living life in the fast lane, but somehow they make it seem like no big deal. And when they tell about attending the odd premiere, or lunching at the White House, or spending the weekend with Marla Maples and Donald Trump, they're a little awestruck themselves—like, "Can you believe this is really happening to me?" And their fans seem to be happy things are going so well for them.

Personality plays a big part in their routine. Regis is something of a grouch, whining and complaining about the inconveniences of life, while Kathie Lee is a perfect foil, sunny, irreverent, and delivering him an occasional—verbal—kick in the pants. They follow up their "host chat" with the usual mix of celebrity guests, actors, authors, acrobats, entertainers, and everyday people experiencing their 15 minutes of fame. Somehow, it all works. *Live* is the fastest-growing syndicated talk show in the nation, and is overtaking *Donahue*, *Geraldo*, and *Sally Jessy Raphael* in many markets.

When *TV Guide* sponsored a phone-in survey to name the Most Beautiful Woman on TV in 1990, *Live*'s loyal and large audience came through. Kathie Lee won in a landslide. The magazine logged nearly 18,000 calls for Gifford; the number-two vote-getter, Jaclyn Smith, received less than 4,000. Of course, no other contender used her own show to muster support. According to *TV Guide*, "With an ambition and resolve few Miss Americas would flaunt, this determined beauty-queen wannabe turned her syndicated daily variety show...into a gigantic vote-for-me campaign." She admitted to being "totally, totally shameless" in her quest for the title. "There is no accounting for my behavior," she confessed. "It's hysterical. Of course I'm not the most beautiful woman on TV—but for one week, it would be great to think so." And the publicity certainly didn't hurt.

As Regis Philbin told *Good Housekeeping*, "She's got a lot of *chutzpah*, she's unafraid, and she's got a lot of feeling and emotion inside her. And sometimes, maybe, there's a war going on between the *chutzpah* and the warmhearted feelings, so it's fascinating." "I'm human," Kathie Lee told *TV Guide*, "and I'm not afraid to show it on the air."

Kathie Lee Gifford may be a new household word to many, but she's no "instant" success. Her father, Aaron Epstein, a naval officer stationed in Paris when Kathie Lee was born, and mother Joan mailed birth announcements prophetically headlined A

STAR IS BORN. When she was five, the family, including older brother David, now a minister, and younger sister Michele, a singer, moved to Maryland. Aaron played jazz saxophone with a group called the Five Moods, and Joan sang on the radio. Following their lead, Kathie Lee and her siblings staged numerous backyard productions for their neighbors. With four years of piano lessons, Kathie Lee embarked on her professional career at age 14. She and her sister formed a folk group called Pennsylvania Next Right, for which they arranged the music, made the costumes, and booked gigs in coffeehouses.

> *Once, while introducing a* Good Morning, America *segment on Princess Diana's positive influence on British fashion, she quipped, "Maybe she can help the Queen!"*

The daughter of a Jewish father and Christian mother, Kathie Lee attended Methodist Sunday school and was a born-again Christian by junior high. The folksingers switched to gospel music. In 1971 Kathie Lee won Maryland's Junior Miss title, a $1,000 scholarship, and the friendship of pageant cohost Anita Bryant, who hired her as a girl Friday/baby-sitter, and steered her toward Oral Roberts University. After several appearances on Roberts's television show, she left the school one semester shy of graduation and headed for Hollywood at age 20.

A well-timed visit to a friend on the set of the daytime soap *Days of Our Lives* resulted in a year-long stint as Nurse Callahan, a minor character on the show. The exposure led to more television work in commercials and network pilots. In 1976 she married gospel music composer Paul Johnson, whom she met while taping an Oral Roberts show. In 1977 she became a featured singer on the game show *Name That Tune*, and her nightclub career expanded into an opening act for headliners Bill Cosby, Rich Little, and Bob Hope. Next, she worked as costar on a musical situation comedy, *Hee Haw Honeys*, and subbed as host on *A.M. Los Angeles*, Philbin's old show.

In 1982, with her marriage to Johnson dissolving, Kathie Lee accepted an offer in New York from *Good Morning, America* to substitute-anchor for Joan Lunden and cover human interest stories. She raised eyebrows there with her off-the-cuff ad libs. Once, while introducing a *GMA* segment on Princess Diana's positive influence on British fashion, she quipped, "Maybe she can help the Queen!" In 1985, she added the *Live* job to an already challenging schedule. A year of racing between two studios each morning took its toll, and she left *Good Morning, America* for a permanent spot on *Live.* Here outrageous comments about wrinkled thighs and dowdy queens were a hit.

One happy by-product of her time on the *Good Morning, America* set was meeting and working with Frank Gifford, who would become her second husband. She and the former football star/ABC sportscaster became fast friends. Gradually, the friendship turned to romance, and in 1986 Kathie Lee accepted a five-carat, emerald-cut diamond ring, and they married. Since Frank is 23 years older than Kathie Lee, and already has three grown children by his first wife, babies were not originally part of the plan. But with characteristic candor, Kathie Lee explained that when she miscalculated her fertile

phase while vacationing off the coast of Italy (courtesy of Carnival Cruise Lines, for which she is spokeswoman) little Cody Newton Gifford was conceived. Not so much a surprise, his mom protests, as a blessing. Never was a pregnancy more publicized. Viewers heard all about her morning sickness and stretch marks. After the March 22, 1990 birth, fans learned about breast-feeding and weight loss (made easier by Ultra Slim Fast products, which she endorses). Cody made his television debut at a tender six weeks, and Kathie Lee remodelled her dressing room to accommodate his crib. As would be expected, the new mother didn't keep her philosophy on childrearing a secret.

"I didn't have [Cody] so I could leave him at home," she told *Good Housekeeping.* "You have a very short time to be a child, and we're in such a rush to raise our children to be adults that they miss out on childhood. I had one of those glorious, radiant childhoods that I wouldn't trade for anything in this world. And I want my son to have that as much as possible. I wasn't taught to read when I was one and given math tests when I was two. There's enough

Kathie Lee Gifford and television show cohost Regis Philbin pose with the Miss America Crown at a press conference announcing they would host the 71st Miss America Pageant in September, 1991. AP/Wide World Photos.

time in life for all that pressure. I know it's a competitive world, but a child who has love and a wonderful childhood will have a competitive edge over anybody who's been stuck in a room with a book. I want Cody to be a wonderful human being. The rest is just going to happen."

Kathie Lee isn't standing still while this happens. Besides the *Live* show, she continues to perform sell-out nightclub engagements, endorse a variety of products, is researching her family tree for an autobiography, and works for several charities. In September of 1991, she and Philbin cohosted the nationally televised Miss America Pageant. "I wish I were a little less ambitious, frankly," she admitted to *Good Housekeeping.* "My problem is that now I don't have the time to pursue things the way I did when I didn't have someone at home whom I adore. My challenge is to balance it all in a healthy way. And I'm not always successful at that."

Before a solo singing engagement in 1991 at New York's Rainbow and Stars showroom, Kathie Lee fretted to a *New York Times* reporter, "I'm nervous about the show. I really want it to be good. I did Freddy's five years ago and got lousy reviews, but I sold out and got standing ovations. Why? I don't waste time thinking about it. The people paid and had a good time and that makes it a success."

In fact, she set a new house record during the two-week Rainbows and Stars engagement. "People will love it, the critics will hate it," she correctly predicted in the same interview. "That's the story of my life. But that's O.K. I may not be everyone's cup of tea, but I might be someone's glass of Champagne."

Sources

Chicago Tribune, November 16, 1990.
Good Housekeeping, August 1991.
New York Times, March 7, 1991.
People, September 5, 1988; May 21, 1990; September 30, 1991.
TV Guide, August 25, 1990; September 7, 1991.

—*Sharon Rose*

Alan Greenspan

UPI/Bettmann

Chairman of the Federal Reserve Board

Born March 6, 1926, in New York, NY; son of Herman Herbert and Rose (Goldsmith) Greenspan; married Joan Mitchell (an artist), 1952 (marriage annulled, 1953). *Education:* New York University, B.S. in economics (summa cum laude), 1948, M.A., 1950, Ph.D., 1977; advanced graduate work at Columbia University.

Addresses: *Office*—Federal Reserve System, 20th and Constitution Ave., NW, Washington DC, 20551.

Career

Served as chairman and president of Townsend-Greenspan & Co., Inc., 1954-74, and 1977-87; chairman of the President's Council of Economic Advisors, 1974-77; chairman of the National Commission on Social Security Reform, 1981-83; other appointments include President's Foreign Intelligence Advisory Board, Commission on Financial Structure and Regulation, Commission on an All-Volunteer Armed Force, Task Force on Economic Growth, and Economic Policy Advisory Board; chairman, Board of Governors of the Federal Reserve System, 1987–. Has served on the board of trustees of the Rand Corporation, as director of the Institute for International Economics, and on the board of overseers at the Hoover Institution at Stanford University.

Member: Economic Club of New York (vice-chairman and trustee), Conference of Business Economists (chairman), National Association of Business Econo-

mists (president and fellow), National Economists Club (director).

Awards: John P. Madden Medal, 1975; joint recipient of Thomas Jefferson Award for greatest public service performed by an elected or appointed official, 1976; joint recipient of William Butler Memorial Award, 1977; fellow, American Statistical Association, 1989; honorary degrees from Pace, Hofstra, Colgate, and Wake Forest universities.

Sidelights

Alan Greenspan does not hold elected office, but he serves a constituency larger than that of any politician. As chairman of the Federal Reserve Board, this bespectacled, owlish, 66-year-old commandeers U.S. monetary policy, and in so doing, exercises a power that stretches well beyond any political or geographic border. When he speaks, either before a private group or a congressional committee, the world turns an ear: If his message, like his countenance, is morose, stock markets tumble and the value of the dollar overseas sinks; if he is upbeat, markets rally to record highs, consumers feel a sense of confidence in buying new products, and a sense of economic well-being descends to pacify investors, mortgage payers, and Wall Street brokers. As James Risen wrote in the *Los Angeles Times* in 1991, "Greenspan has become the premiere force in American economic policy today, with influence that in many ways extends beyond that of George Bush."

President Ronald Reagan appointed Greenspan as the U.S. top banker in 1987, replacing Paul Volcker, whose imposing physical presence—he is 6'7''—and anti-inflation zeal were legendary. Admitting to *Time* magazine in 1987 that it would be a "major challenge to fill Volcker's shoes," the smaller, quieter Greenspan took the helm of the "Fed" amid concerns that the new Mr. Dollar would not be as hawkish on inflation as his predecessor had been.

In reappointing Greenspan to a second term in 1991, President George Bush concurred with the *Washington Post,* which said the first term of the conservative chairman had been "marked by outstanding performance." Greenspan's tenure has been largely free of criticism, even in the midst of a recession, primarily because economists admit that many factors affecting the long-term economy, most notably fiscal policy, are well beyond the control of the Fed. He has also eluded most of the naysayers' barbs because while he knows how to play the political game, he is generally not viewed as a policy maker who succumbs to political pressure or presidential bullying. His intellectual integrity is said to prevail over partisan scraps.

Erudite economic theory was not the first love of Greenspan, who was born to divorced parents in New York City in 1926. He studied music at the prestigious Juilliard School, and afterward played tenor saxophone in the well-known Henry Jerome swing band. But his fascination with numbers was insuperable, and as New York's jazz golden age whirled about him, he managed the band's payroll and took time out to read college textbooks on banking. At 19, Greenspan put his musical instruments in their cases for good and began his study of economics at New York University. He did advanced graduate work at Columbia University under scholar and then-future Fed chairman Arthur F. Burns.

The free-market economic theories Greenspan would bring to government work years later were forged in the early 1950s, when he became a disciple of writer and social critic Ayn Rand. Greenspan found an intellectual ally in the conservative Rand, whose famous philosophical novels, *The Fountainhead* and *Atlas Shrugged,* denounced government regulation and intervention, while stressing the importance of individualism. As a contributor to Rand's publication, the *Objectivist,* Greenspan wrote: "The welfare state is nothing more than a mechanism by which governments confiscate the wealth of the productive members of society."

In 1967, while running the successful economic consulting firm he had co-founded, Townsend-Greenspan & Co., Greenspan took his first step along the political trail, becoming presidential candidate Richard Nixon's director of domestic-policy research. Greenspan was named chairman of the President's Council of Economic Advisors in 1974, a month before Nixon resigned in disgrace following the Watergate scandal, and continued in that position in President Gerald Ford's administration. But while the economist was climbing the government ladder, the pragmatism and savvy that would later emerge as his defining features were still a few rungs beneath him. "Everyone was hurt by inflation," he said at a 1974 hearing. "If you want to examine percentagewise

> *"Having pushed Mr. Greenspan out to sea to steer the U.S. economy with only a single oar—monetary policy—the kibitzers in Congress and the White House are now telling him how to row."*
> —Paul A. Gigot

who was hurt most . . . it was Wall Street Brokers." He later retracted the statement, having learned the political hazards of a free-spirited tongue. "Obviously, the poor are suffering more," he said.

Greenspan continued his career with free-lance political work after leaving the Ford administration. He advised such disparate politicians as Senator Edward Kennedy, George Bush, and Ronald Reagan on their presidential aspirations for the 1980 election. As chairman of the National Commission on Social Security Reform from 1981 to 1983, he was praised for fashioning a compromise plan to rescue the social security system from insolvency.

When President Reagan tapped Greenspan to become Fed chairman in 1987, several economists worried about his lack of international financing experience. They also feared that Greenspan would not be as aggressive in keeping down inflation—the prices of products—as his nearly mythic predecessor had been, even though Greenspan stated that he had a hard-line zero-inflation goal. It was not surprising that in response to Reagan's announcement that he had nominated Greenspan, the Dow Jones average of 30 industrial stocks on the New York Stock Exchange lost 22 points, and the dollar tumbled against foreign currencies. But the market and the dollar rebounded the following day, as economists and newspaper editorial writers, still slightly shocked at Volcker's imminent departure, came to grips with the succession.

Greenspan is head of an institution that was created by Congress in 1913 to manage the nation's money supply, centralize and strengthen the regulation of banks, and provide a flexible currency for a country that was trying to wean itself from the gold standard. The United States was one of the last industrialized countries to establish a central bank; other central banks include the Bank of England, the Banque de France, and the Bank of Canada. In subsequent years, the power of the Fed was expanded to cover such financial issues as margin requirements—the minimum amount of cash that must be put down when a security is bought.

Greenspan is the powerful chairman of a presidentially appointed Board of Governors that sets policy for Federal Reserve district banks and helps determine the lending practices of all deposit-taking institutions throughout the country. There are three basic tools the Fed uses to drive the economy, the most important of which is what is called open-market operations. If Greenspan believes the country is facing a credit crunch, he can lobby the Board to buy government securities from banks, thereby infusing the banks with cash which they can in turn lend to citizens who want to buy homes, cars, and other commodities. On the other hand, if Greenspan senses a credit glut—that is, if banks are lending too much, which can drive up inflation—he can advise *selling* securities to banks, which would take money from the institutions and reduce lending. The Fed can also change the discount interest rate of its district branches, which lend money to banks. Lowering the rate encourages a bank to borrow from its district branch and allows that bank to pass the savings on to its customers in the form of lower-interest-rate loans. By raising the discount rate, the Fed discourages the bank from borrowing and lending. The Fed's third tool concerns reserve requirements, the amount of cash banks must keep on hand but cannot lend. If the Fed lowers the requirement, cash is freed up and banks can increase lending. If the requirement is raised, the banks must

lock away more cash, thereby reducing the amount of money they have to lend.

Although the board, including the chairman, is appointed by the country's reigning politician, it is an independent agency that does not answer to any elected official. The Fed finances itself, so economic pressure cannot be placed on it, and the president, or any member of Congress, cannot compel the Board to act in a certain way.

Such independence plays to Greenspan's strengths. Norman Jonas wrote in *Business Week* in 1987, "What drives him as an economist is his conviction that policy-makers must look beyond palliative actions that may please the public in the short run but hurt it in the long term." Because he is largely free from political pressure, Greenspan is better able to exercise his Rand-inspired *laissez-faire* philosophy, which favors letting economic conditions improve on their own without much government tinkering with monetary policy.

As an arch-conservative, Greenspan also sees a danger in relying on monetary policy adjustments to cure the country's economic woes. If he pushes interest rates too low, credit floods into the economy and inflation can skyrocket. By raising interest rates to cut down on inflation, he faces the prospect of greater unemployment because business owners do not pursue the loans that enable them to keep existing workers or hire new workers. Of his approach to monetary policy, Greenspan said in 1975, "I'm not a Keynesian. I'm not a monetarist. I'm a free-enterpriser."

Some economists argue that Greenspan has taken that hands-off principle too far, that he has not acted strongly enough when the economy has been ailing. But the Fed chairman has been praised for recognizing that many of the factors driving the U.S. economy have less to do with monetary policy and more to do with fiscal policy, which is largely the domain of the president and Congress. Greenspan has said that changes in tax policy and decisions regarding the U.S. deficit will contribute to the long-term health of the economy far more than any monetary policy ever could.

Prior to Greenspan's 1991 reappointment, several political observers criticized President Bush for relying on Greenspan to jump-start the recessionary economy solely with monetary action. "Chairman Greenspan is actually President Bush's biggest economic asset," Paul A. Gigot remarked in the *Wall Street Journal* in 1991. "Yet having pushed Mr. Greenspan out to sea to steer the U.S. economy with only a single oar—monetary policy—the kibitzers in Congress and the White House are now telling him how to row."

Despite his ability to withstand the political pressure of presidents, Alan Greenspan is known in Washington as one of the most politically savvy government officials. His ability to look beyond partisan infighting and galvanize compromise has endeared him to both Democrats and Republicans, including four presidents. Robert S. Strauss (see *Newsmaekrs 91*), former chairman of the Democratic National Committee and the U.S. ambassador to Moscow, was quoted as saying in the *New York Times* in 1990, "Alan Greenspan is a great listener, and he exposes himself to people who know what's going on in this town, who are moving around the town, and he knows how to digest that information. His political antenna is always up. He's very sensitive to what's taking place politically on [Capitol] Hill, in the executive branch, in the media, and that's a tremendous strength for a person in his position."

He is credited with achieving consensus not only among rival political parties but also among governors on his board, many of whom embrace sharply conflicting economic theories. In 1990, speaking in scholarly rather than partisan terms, Greenspan was able to convince the Federal Reserve Board to lower bank reserve requirements, making $12 billion available for new loans to hurting Americans and helping the flagging financial industry by increasing yearly bank profits by $1 billion. The vote was unanimous. He also enjoys the reputation of being flexible enough to look at anecdotal evidence as well as hard data in formulating an economic outlook for the future.

Occasionally, though, Greenspan is accused of entering the partisan fray. Economist David M. Jones, quoted in *Business Week*, suggested that Greenspan had fueled the impression that he is influenced by political pressure when the Board cut the discount rate after the embarrassing Republican loss in Pennsylvania's 1991 special Senate election. The normally soft-spoken Greenspan has also testified in Congress that he supports a reduction in the capital gains tax and an increase in consumption taxes—politically contentious issues in which, some say, the Fed chairman should not be meddling, because they go well beyond his role at the central bank.

Still, Greenspan has proven to many that a low-key individual can lead a high-profile life, and that a politically-minded economist can become one of the most influential non-politicians in the world.

Sources

Business Week, June 15, 1987; November 25, 1991.
Los Angeles Times, May 30, 1991.
New York Times, January 22, 1990; July 26, 1990.
Time, June 15, 1987.
U.S. News & World Report, December 17, 1990.
Wall Street Journal, March 4, 1988; May 17, 1991.
Washington Post, July 12, 1991.

—*Isaac Rosen*

Derek Humphry

Photo by Frank Capri, NYC, courtesy of the National Hemlock Society

Suicide rights advocate

Born c. 1931 in Bath, England; married first wife, Jean, c. 1953 (died, 1975, in a suicide assisted by her husband); married second wife, Ann Wickett, 1976 (divorced; Wickett's death, a probable suicide, reported October 8, 1991); has married for a third time; children: (first marriage) three.

Addresses: *Office*—c/o Hemlock Society, Eugene, OR.

Career

Former writer for the London *Sunday Times* and the *Los Angeles Times;* cofounder and national director of Hemlock Society, a suicide advocacy group, 1980; author.

Sidelights

The most controversial book of 1991 may also be the most bizarre "how-to" ever to reach the best-seller lists. *Final Exit: The Practicalities of Self-Deliverance and Assisted Suicide for the Dying* is the end product of advocate/author Derek Humphry's efforts to bring euthanasia into the public eye.

For the British-born Humphry, whose parents separated while he was still a child and who educated himself by listening to BBC news broadcasts, dealing with death has been a sad constant in his life. The former journalist witnessed his first wife, Jean, fade under the ravages of cancer; in 1975, after 22 years of marriage, the couple participated in an assisted suicide when Humphry laced a cup of coffee with

secobarbital and codeine, gave it to Jean, and stayed at her side as she passed from consciousness and died some 50 minutes later. "One thing about that sort of death," he told Erica E. Goode in a *U.S. News & World Report* interview, "is you accept it. You say goodbye to each other, and everything is clear." As *Time* added, Humphry also assisted two other family members in their suicides: a brother who was subsisting on life-support, and a father-in-law who chose sleeping pills as his form of "exit."

Humphry was able to detail his role in Jean's life and death in the 1978 book *Jean's Way.* One point that especially bothered him, as he related to Goode, was the possibility of botching the job: "Why did I have to risk having to smother her [should the drugs not take effect]?" he asked. "How much better if a doctor had administered the drugs. I would have done my part."

The publication of *Jean's Way* brought Humphry a number of letters from readers who confessed that "they, too, had helped a terminally ill family member die but kept it secret, or had contemplated such actions but held back out of fear," as Goode reported. Humphry and his second wife, Ann Wickett, responded by cofounding the Hemlock Society, a suicide advocacy group named after the poisonous plant that ancient philosopher Socrates used to end his life.

The Hemlock Society, whose motto is "Death with Dignity," kept a relatively low profile for years, while publishing books and pamphlets for its 38,000 members. One such member, according to Daniel S. Levy in a *Time* article, was Steven Schragis of the Carol Publishing Group. Around the early 1990s, Schragis persuaded Humphry "to move beyond philosophical arguments to practical guidance," as Levy described; Schragis offered to distribute a book on the subject.

Final Exit, for which Humphry took sole authorship, was published under the Hemlock Society banner in April of 1991. The 192-page book, though, "at first languished unnoticed," noted Levy. "Then, after a *Wall Street Journal* feature and stories on ABC's *Good Morning America* and CNN, sales skyrocketed."

The book's speedy public acceptance generated an unusual circumstance: "Given how controversial the topic is, *Final Exit* has generated surprisingly little heat," Levy noted. "No prosecutor has attempted to suppress it. The National Right to Life Committee criticizes it in interviews but is not actively campaigning against it. A few booksellers decline to carry it, generally on moral and religious grounds."

One reason for *Final Exit*'s popularity may be in the changing role of patients in American society. "Doctors have always been in control, but now it's not just doctors and patients," as Ruth Macklin, professor of bioethics at Albert Einstein College of Medicine, was quoted as saying in a *Newsweek* cover story. "There are hospital administrators, in-house attorneys and risk managers.... These are the people who are *really* in control." This increasing lack of control among the sick and dying, the *Newsweek* piece suggested, accounts for the sudden rise of *Final Exit*, which instructs readers on a variety of different "exit" techniques.

Levy listed some of the book's "recipes" for suicide. The volume, he said, "includes charts of lethal dosages for 18 prescription drugs, primarily pain killers and sleeping tablets; it debates and debunks the merits of cyanide; it offers abundant practical advice about asphyxiation by plastic bag or auto exhaust. Seemingly every detail is addressed: mixing pills with yogurt or pudding so that the patient does not vomit or pass out before ingesting a lethal amount; *not* turning off the telephone or message machine, because 'any changes will only alert callers to something unusual happening'; having family members avoid any direct physical assistance, so

they cannot be prosecuted; and, if concealment of the cause of death is sought, telling heirs to object to an autopsy."

The author's attention to detail extends to bystanders, according to the *Newsweek* review of *Final Exit*. He "urges anyone compelled to use a hotel room to leave a note 'apologizing for the shock and inconvenience'—along with a big tip."

As it happened, *Final Exit* came at a time when the "right to die" debate was raging in other quarters. In a related issue, Jack Kervorkian (see *Newsmakers 91*), a Michigan physician, had invented a so-called "suicide machine," with which a patient could self-administer lethal doses of drugs. Public sentiment over euthanasia was turning, as the *Newsweek* article reported: "Only 41 percent of the respondents in a 1975 Gallup poll said they believed that someone in great pain, with 'no hope of improvement,' had the

> *"My book pleads with the depressed to go to a psychiatrist. But it's addressed to the 6,000 people who die every day, not the handful who commit suicide."*

moral right to commit suicide. By 1990, that figure had risen to 66 percent."

But, as Goode observed, "There are those who do not see Humphry as purely the selfless champion of a graceful exit. Rita Marker, director of the International Anti-Euthanasia Task Force and a vocal enemy of the Hemlock leaders, sees in [Humphry's] avowals of compassion the maneuvers of a 'charlatan,' who in a 'cold and calculating' manner hastened his [first] wife's demise. Henry Brod, who resigned as director of operations for the Hemlock Society after a disagreement with Humphry, describes him as a difficult man whose 'strong ego' is both his strength and his weakness."

As the book's subtitle implies, *Final Exit* contains advice meant for the dying, to plan and facilitate their deaths. The relatively simple instructions—"prescription drugs with a plastic bag over the head is Humphry's preferred method," a *Newsweek* reviewer noted—led some to believe that the physically sound but emotionally ill may take the volume in hand to commit suicide. Humphry decrys any such implication. "My book pleads with the depressed to go to a psychiatrist," he told Levy. "But it's addressed to the 6,000 people who die every day, not the handful who commit suicide."

Eventually, though, one such case of depression-induced suicide did arise, and the victim's relatives made their views known in a *Time* interview. Ethel Adelmen, whose son Adrian took his life, blames *Final Exit* for his suicide. "He was 29," Adrian's brother, Alan, told the magazine's Bonnie Angelo. "He had been suffering from major depression for seven months. As far as we know, he became a member of the Hemlock Society . . . by sending them a check for $25. They don't screen members." Added Ethel: "Some people want to kill themselves, but they can't find an easy way. Humphry outlines it step by step, even to fooling your doctors to get [the drug] Seconal. This is why we're angry."

Elaborating, Alan Adelman pointed out that Adrian "had followed the format in the book exactly. On page 81, the book says that if the survivors want to cover up the suicide, they can refuse an autopsy on religious grounds. Unless, of course, the state has a compelling reason to perform the autopsy, the wishes of the family will be respected." Asked if she had let Humphry know how she felt about his book, Ethel Adelman replied no: "I honestly don't think he cares. He is indifferent to who might read it." The debate continued in *Time*'s Letters section, where one reader wrote to say that *Final Exit* "prevented my 69-year-old friend from committing suicide. After he placed the book on his hospital bedside table, he immediatly received more effective treatment."

Outside of *Final Exit*, Humphry created a more personal controversy when it was disclosed that early in 1990 he allegedly walked out on his second wife, Ann, when she was diagnosed with cancer—ironically, the same disease that afflicted the author's first wife. A *New York Times* article by Robert Reinhold stated that "the couple offer differing versions of what happened." In Ann Humphry's view, Derek "panicked" at the news of her condition, was "unable to cope with the fact that his wife of 13 years was struck with a life-threatening illness," and "simply walked out."

Humphry countered with the statement that the split was "the culmination of years of marital troubles," as Reinhold put it, quoting the author as saying it "was a very shaky marriage." Reinhold added that the Humphrys "had lost mutual trust four to five years ago and had frequently asked each other for divorce." The news of Ann's cancer "was a terrible blow to both of us but I did not on the spot consider leaving her," Humphry told Reinhold. In a statement titled "Why My Marriage to Ann Wickett Failed," Humphry, as a *People* article revealed, claimed that his wife "kept insisting she was terminally ill even after the oncologists assured both of us that she was not so . . . . [Wickett] literally demanded that I cry for her in the same way as the book *Jean's Way* reports that I did for my first wife." Ann Wickett's body was found in an Oregon wilderness area on October 8, 1991; her death has been determined a probable suicide, as reported by the Associated Press.

Though the marital dispute caused a rift among the Hemlock Society members, the news didn't stem the sales of *Final Exit*. Some 15 years have passed since Karen Anne Quinlan, who lived for years in a vegetative state on life-support following irreversible brain damage sustained in a car accident, triggered the "right to die" debate in America. Before that, *Final Exit* "would have been unimaginable," said Katrine Ames in *Newsweek*. Ames and other critics have noticed that as much as technique, "etiquette" enters into the suicide instructions in the book. Though the volume is straightforward, Ames wrote, it does not lack emotion. "I wanted it to say, 'Be considerate of others, go careful with your life and other people's feelings,'" Humphry was quoted as saying in the *Newsweek* article.

That he has become something of a spokesman for death is a fact that Humphry apparently accepts—to a point. "He shrugs off the namecallers who brand him a second Hitler, the evangelists who say he does the Devil's work," Goode remarked. "But prod him, and there are places where the skin is thinner: 'It's not much fun when you walk down the street and people say 'Derek Humphry is a murderer,' he has said. He recalled the time an anti-euthanasia demonstrator dressed up as his dead wife, Jean, at a Hemlock meeting and paraded down the center aisle of the auditorium shouting, 'Derek, I've come back to you!' while he stood, speechless, at the podium."

Humphry, as Levy noted, "argues that he will not make suicide easier—just more reliable, less painful, less messy and above all less solitary. He urges those who choose suicide to gather family and friends around them for solace as they slip away. That gesture might require the biggest social and cultural change of all. Many people who could accept the idea of ending a loved one's pain would find it impossible to watch, and be complicit in, the actual suicide. For the one who dies, there may be a final exit. But those who live on might have to dwell with ceaseless doubt, guilt or scorn."

If Humphry ever writes his autobiography, Goode quoted the author as saying, "it will be called 'Seesaw,' because his life has had 'deep valleys, but also moments of incredible joy.'" Listening to the author speak on the subject he knows most about, added Goode, "one hears the echoes of his own lifelong search for closure. It's a search he keeps returning to, campaigning publicly for people's right to say farewell fully and thoughtfully to loved ones." "The roots of human life are in the dying process," said Humphry to Goode. "It can be very beautiful."

Selected writings

Jean's Way, 1978.

Final Exit: The Practicalities of Self-Deliverance and Assisted Suicide for the Dying, Hemlock Society, 1991.

Sources

Detroit News, October 9, 1991.
Newsweek, August 19, 1991; August 26, 1991.
New York Times, February 8, 1990.
People, March 13, 1990.
Time, August 19, 1991; November 18, 1991; December 9, 1991.
U.S. News & World Report, September 30, 1991.

—*Susan Salter*

Patricia Ireland

AP/Wide World Photos

President of National Organization for Women (NOW)

Born c. 1946; raised outside Valparaiso, IN; daughter of James (an engineer) and Joan (Filipek) Ireland; married second husband, James Humble (an artist), 1968. *Education:* University of Tennessee, graduated with a degree in German, 1966; law degree from University of Miami Law School, 1975.

Career

Worked as a flight attendant for Pan Am, 1966-75; lawyer, beginning 1975; elected executive vice-president of National Organization for Women (NOW), 1987; appointed president of NOW, 1991.

Sidelights

In its 25-year history, the National Organization for Women has seen unity and infighting, triumph and disappointment, and more than its share of controversy. As the 1990s began, a spate of events precipitated turmoil among feminists—including the Clarence Thomas (also in *Newsmakers 92*)/Anita Hill debate and the possible repeal of *Roe vs. Wade*, the landmark abortion-rights bill. Into this fray stepped a soft-spoken Miami lawyer, Patricia Ireland, as acting NOW president following the sudden resignation of president Molly Yard (see *Newsmakers 91*) due to illness. No sooner had Ireland, former executive vice-president of NOW, taken office than a personal revelation resulted in headlines and notoriety.

Some five months after taking office, Ireland's picture appeared on the cover of the *Advocate*, the nation's leading gay- and lesbian-issues newsmagazine, with the headline "America's Most Powerful Woman Comes Out." In the ensuing interview, Ireland confirmed that while she has been married for more than 20 years to artist James Humble, she had been conducting a longtime relationship with an unnamed woman in Washington, D.C. The news "rocked the feminist community, which hoped Ireland—a more measured and mediagenic activist than her predecessors—might rescue NOW from its fringe image," commented Eleanor Clift in a *Newsweek* article. "Instead, her confession will give conservatives more ammunition to argue that liberal interest groups are out of touch."

Critics of Ireland and her organization saw opportunity in the revelation. As Clift added, a Republican consultant, Alex Castellanos, "savors the 'cultural gulf' that Ireland symbolizes." Castellanos was quoted as saying, "This is way deep in left field for the average taxpayer." Florida State Senator Dick Anderson, according to Karen S. Schneider in a *People* article, denounced NOW in a speech, calling its members "horrible, unfeminine shrews," adding, "except for that lovely Patricia Ireland. I can't believe *she's* mixed up with them."

In fact, feminist ideals had long been a part of Ireland's life, even before she joined NOW. Raised in a rural area of Indiana, Ireland "raised honeybees, attended Presbyterian church and studied at a two-room school," as Mary Voboril noted in a wire-service article appearing in the *Detroit Free Press.* This "average, typical teenager," as Ireland described herself to Voboril, had a maternal grandmother who "was one of the first women to tool around Chicago in a Model T," Voboril wrote. Ireland's mother, Joan, "was the first director of her Indiana town's Planned Parenthood clinic."

Tragedy struck the Ireland family when Patricia was five years old: her older sister, Kathy, was killed in an accident. But even this terrible moment provided fodder for Ireland's future instincts; in the years following, she "resolved to turn things around for her anguished parents, to somehow make things right," as Voboril explained. "That may have evolved into a determination to make things right for women." As Ireland recalled in the article, "I was well into my 40s before I started thinking what impact my sister's death had on me. My strongest defense is always denial."

Ireland entered DePauw University at age 16—her academic career was interrupted, however, by the news that she was pregnant. "Abortion [at that time] was illegal, so she had the procedure in Japan," Voboril reported. Rebounding, Ireland transferred to the University of Tennessee, where she met her second husband, artist James Humble (Ireland's first marriage took place during her tenure at DePauw).

Her degree in German qualified her to teach, but instead Ireland took a job as a Pan Am flight attendant. It was here that she first came into contact with NOW. "Ireland discovered the airline's health policy wouldn't pay for her husband's dental surgery because it covered only the spouses of male employees," as Clift recounted in the *Newsweek* article. "With the help of a Florida chapter of NOW, Ireland challenged the policy and won. The experience made her a loyal NOW member."

While Ireland was still with Pan Am, she enrolled in law school, taking weekend shifts to pay for her education. "It was the best of all worlds," she told *Advocate* interviewer Donna Minkowitz. "During the week, I would do this really intense intellectual work, and then during the weekends, I would fly off to Mexico City." But at the same time, Ireland became "acutely aware of what stereotypes do, because I was in a traditional woman's job, as a flight attendant. I would go up to someone at a party, and I'd say, 'I'm Patricia Ireland. I work for Pan Am.' And they'd say,

'Great. Can I get you a drink?' When I'd go up to somebody else and say, 'Hi, I'm Patricia Ireland. I'm a law student at the University of Miami,' they'd say, 'Oh, I wanted to talk to somebody about that case that just came down.'"

The moral she learned, Ireland continued, is that "my brain was the same, my ideas were just as worthy or unworthy, but there was a tremendous difference in the way that people perceived me and treated me. The way I was getting credibility was by moving into a man's job, which is a source of great irritation to me. I think traditional women's work is undervalued—teaching, health care, social work. That was part of the experience that made me want to be an activist."

Ireland plunged into feminist causes, making her name in Miami by fighting Dade County's anti-gay

> *Americans, Ireland believes, "are up to here and beyond with [politicians'] hypocrisy and their greed and their scandal. It would be very refreshing if people would talk honestly about their lives."*

referendum in 1977, according to Voboril. She also "chaired Florida NOW's lesbian rights task force and, on a ticket with Yard, ran for national executive vice president in 1987," Voboril noted. In addition, Minkowitz identified Ireland as "the architect" of NOW's Stand Up for Women committee on abortion rights. This group placed Ireland and cohorts in the path of anti-abortion activist Randall Terry (see *Newsmakers 91*) of Operation Rescue. "What Operation Rescue does is not stop abortion," she told the *Advocate* reporter. "What they're trying to do is create a media image. They're trying to portray themselves as the civil rights movement of the '80s and '90s. Our presence at the clinics not only keeps the clinics open in many cases but also shows a very strong image in pictures that we are mobilized, we're a majority, and we're not going to be pushed backward. We're not going to let a bully keep us from having health care."

While Ireland's trademark style had traditionally been an understated one—"she calls for 'shadow lobbying,' where lawmakers' wives and daughters work over their husbands and fathers at dinner," as Howard Fineman observed in *Newsweek*—on this most controversial issue she's willing to risk personal freedom. If *Roe vs. Wade* is overturned—'as many believe likely," offered Schneider, "Ireland has vowed to call for NOW's first-ever act of civil disobedience." As Ireland told Schneider, "We will break the law to make sure women have the right to safe, legal abortions." Countered antifeminist activist Phyllis Schlafly in the same article, "Patricia Ireland represents no change—NOW still has nothing to say to the average American woman."

"Almost from the beginning, sexual politics has been an issue at NOW," as Voboril commented in her article. In the *Advocate* interview, Ireland saw a chance for her organization to connect with other left-wing fronts. She noted that at a recent national board meeting, NOW passed a resolution in support of the actions of the radical gay-rights group Queer Nation, which at that time was waging civil disobedience against the Cracker Barrel restaurant chain. (The Cracker Barrel management had raised public ire by announcing that they would dismiss not only any employee who was openly homosexual, "but anybody who they thought might appear to the customers to be lesbian or gay," as Ireland described it.)

Politics aside, Ireland's personal revelation in Minkowitz's *Advocate* article has become the focus of much attention. After telling Minkowitz that she sees her husband "regularly"—the couple has no children—Ireland, after some prodding by the interviewer, conceded that she had a woman companion "and she's very important in my life. And that's the extent of what I would choose to reveal about how we live our lives." She did not reveal the woman's name, nor her occupation in Washington.

Still, Ireland hesitates to label herself bisexual. "I have not used labels most of my life," she told Minkowitz. "I don't mean to say that I don't have great respect for the people who are out lesbians or out gays. I think it's an important strategy. We've had a very strong policy in NOW of respecting people's privacy, and in my own particular life, the privacy of my family and friends is really important to me."

While admitting that the acknowledgment of a woman companion has caused controversy, and that such detractors as Randall Terry, right-wing senator Jesse Helms, "and anybody who wants to oppose us" might use the news to their advantage, Ireland thinks that in the long run attitudes could change. In particular, she believes that "there's a high, high level—post [Clarence Thomas] hearings—of cynicism about politicians." Americans, she related to Minkowitz, "are up to here and beyond with their hypocrisy and their greed and their scandal. It would be very refreshing if people would talk honestly about their lives. I think the upside of it far outweighs the downside of trying to hide and trying to pretend like I live my life in a way I don't."

To Ireland, some of the controversy can be summed up by an image problem that persists for lesbians, feminists, and women in general. She explains in the *Advocate* piece: "Until the charge of 'lesbian' carries no sting, it is a very powerful weapon to keep any woman from standing up and being independent: 'Oh, you don't want to define yourself through some man? You want to be economically independent? You want to stand on your own two feet? Then you must not be a real woman. You must be one of those others.' And as long as being called a lesbian means you can lose your home, your job, your custody of your children, your credit, and the love of your family and friends in some instances, we're going to be held back. All women are held back by that."

Though in the *People* article Ireland objected to the *Advocate*'s headline about her "coming out"—"it implies I've been hiding something, and I haven't"—she contends in the *Advocate* interview that the more people know about their homosexual neighbors, friends, and relatives, the better it is for gay rights. "The polling indicates that people who know they know a lesbian or a gay person are much more likely to support lesbian and gay civil rights. And that to me is a very strong recommendation for the strategy of being out. I have always been a very private person. And I think that my sense of privacy and family has only increased as I've become more of a public figure, because I have so little of it." She adds that she still would like to keep a sort of fence around her private life—"There seems to me to be some area that I ought to be able to have as my own and say, 'Nobody comes any closer than this.'"

It isn't only the general public that has opinions about her relationships, Ireland noted in the *Advocate*. "I think a lot of women in the lesbian community have drawn their own assumptions, and a lot of people, like in my law firm or my hometown, drew a certain set of assumptions. I'm always amused and amazed at the things people think they know."

Looking into the future, Ireland has her eye set on creating a third party for the American political system, one that would "have dramatic impact," as she noted to Minkowitz. "When we held hearings to convene it, testimony came from all communities, including the gay and lesbian community. It's clearly a community that is excluded from the current politics. There are more lesbian and gay elected officials than there ever used to be, but the number is still minuscule."

She thinks that strong support from gays and lesbians could also help her in her fight for legal abortions. "The overlap [between gay rights and abortion rights] is clear in terms of individual rights being respected," as she declared in the *Advocate*. "There is a connection between the fact that rape against women has increased dramatically and the fact that hate crimes against lesbians and gays have increased. There has been an increase in neo-Nazi and skinhead racist attacks as well."

Working at the helm of NOW, Ireland has seen the membership growing—numbers went up following the Clarence Thomas hearings. "That activism may be a tribute to NOW's influence, even if the group—and its leader—seem so far out of the mainstream," said Clift. To Ireland, the storm over her personal relations will pass and life will go on. "I will not let the world tell me who to love," she told Schneider. "I want the focus to be on the work that I do, not on the fact that I choose to love two people."

Sources

Advocate, December 17, 1991.
Detroit Free Press, December 15, 1991.
Newsweek, July 22, 1991; December 16, 1991.
People, January 13, 1992.

—Susan Salter

John Justin, Jr.

Boot manufacturer

Born in 1917 in Texas; married. *Education:* Attended Oklahoma A & M University and Texas Christian University. *Military service:* Served in U.S. Merchant Marine.

Addresses: *Office*—Justin Industries Inc., 2821 West 7th St., Forth Worth, TX 76107.

Career

Vice president of Justin Industries (formerly known as H. J. Justin & Sons), beginning in 1950; president, beginning in 1952; chairman of the board and CEO, 1974—.

Sidelights

The name of Justin has been associated with the boot business since 1879, when patriarch H. J. Justin first began making boots for the cowboys working the ranges of Spanish Fort, Texas. More than a century later, H. J.'s grandson John Justin, Jr. would not only help build the company into a major manufacturing concern (Justin Industries netted $315 million in 1990), but would figure in a modern-day corporate showdown.

Justin Industries, which has incorporated such well-known names as Tony Lama, Roper, and Norcona, is known for producing footwear that is hardy and stylish, often made of exotic leathers. But "alligators, eels and pythons aren't the only creatures whose hides [CEO John Justin] can display," noted Katherine Weisman in a *Forbes* article. In 1990 "he skinned

a couple of upstart corporate raiders named Barry Rosenstein and Perry Sutherland."

It all started in March of 1990 when Sutherland and Rosenstein, both in their early 30s, had acquired more than 14 percent of Justin stock. They entered an acquisition bid of $18.50 a share, or about $158 million. According to a *New York Times* report, Justin said he would consider the offer. Weeks turned into months with no agreement from the 74-year-old chairman. By September, Justin served notice that he had rejected the offer.

Although the two investors had publicly insisted that they meant to keep Justin Industries in business with its current management, John Justin tells a different tale. "They said they were going to break the company up," Justin maintained to Weisman. "They were going to sell land, break this up and that up." He added, "I didn't feel they had any feeling for what the company consisted of, and what it meant."

Still, Sutherland and Rosenstein already owned a considerable share of the company and were out to court fellow stockholders with an offer to "sell high." "How, then, did John Justin fend off a $28-a-share tender?" asked Weisman. "By expanding the company some more. In a conveniently timed acquisition, he paid $18 million cash and assumed $35 million in debt for $79 million (1989 revenues) Tony Lama, the prestigious but moneylosing bootmaker."

Suddenly, the two investors found themselves with a much more valuable company to bid for. The Lama deal "threw a monkey wrench into their financing plans," Weisman explained. "Their bankers, worried about the increased debt load, would now lend them money for only 71 [percent] of the shares." Sutherland and Rosenstein now needed an additional $50 million, and finding backing became troublesome.

"Then Justin got on the phone," said Weisman. "With his soft Texas drawl, he promised scores of local shareholders that the company's profits would rebound with the Texas economy, and begged them not to tender." The strategy worked—enough shareholders agreed not to sell, and Rosenstein and Sutherland "subsequently sold their 1 million shares to a group of private investors. They say they broke even on the deal," Weisman reported.

Though the sale of Justin Boot could have made its CEO a very rich man, he implies that tradition, not money, is what motivated him to almost single-handedly take on Wall Street. As for Sutherland and Rosenstein, "We didn't understand these people," Justin told Weisman. "They're not the type of people we deal with day to day."

Sources

Forbes, June 24, 1991.
New York Times, March 9, 1990; September 20, 1990; December 26, 1990.

—*Susan Salter*

Estee Lauder

Cosmetics company founder

Born Josephine Esther Mentzer; name changed to Estee Lauder in the 1930s; born c. 1908 in Corona, Queens, NY; married Joseph Lauter in 1930 (divorced in 1939; remarried in 1942); children: Leonard Allen and Ronald.

Addresses: *Office*—767 Fifth Ave., New York, NY 10153.

Career

Estee Lauder Inc., chief executive officer, 1946-82, chairman of the board, 1982—.

Awards: Neiman Marcus Fashion Award, 1962; named one of 100 women of achievement, 1967, and one of top ten outstanding women in business, 1970, by *Harper's Bazaar*; spirit of achievement award, 1968, from Albert Einstein College of Medicine; Kaufmann's Fashion Fortnight award, 1969; Bamberger's designer's award, 1969; Gimbel's Fashion Forum award, 1969; international achievement award, 1971, from Frost Bros.; Pogue's annual fashion award, 1975; Golda Meir 90th anniversary tribute award, 1978; decorated chevalier, Legion of Honor, France, 1978; medaille de Vermeil de la ville de Paris, 1979; fourth annual award for humanitarian service, 1979, by the Girls' Club, NY; 25th anniversary award, 1979, from the Greater New York Council of Boy Scouts of America; L. S. Ayres Award, 1981; achievement award, 1983, from the Girl Scouts USA, 1983; outstanding mother award, 1984; Athena Award, 1985; named laureate of National Business Hall of Fame, 1988.

AP/Wide World Photos

Sidelights

A legend in the cosmetics industry, Estee Lauder has built an empire of four distinct product lines that generate sales of nearly $2 billion a year. Lauder's exclusive fragrances and cosmetics have cornered the department store market. Her success can be traced to a genius for marketing, a microscopic attention to detail, and an unflagging belief in her ability to bring beauty to an elite clientele.

But Lauder did not always move in such fashionable circles. She was born in less-than-glamorous Corona in Queens, New York, around 1908. Her parents named her Josephine Esther Mentzer. Eventually, Lauder embarked on a sales career by persuading beauty salons to carry skin creams concocted by her chemist uncle. She persisted until department stores also agreed to sell the products. Lauder had hit the jackpot: Saks Fifth Avenue was her first big customer, in 1948. She had cleverly offered to treat the troubled complexion of the buyer's daughter prior to the sale, and the treatment worked. Such instinctive sales strategies were to become Lauder's hallmark.

In 1930 Lauder married Joseph Lauter. Their first son, Leonard Allan, was born in 1933. Josephine Esther Mentzer Lauter became Estee Lauder at some point before 1939, when she and Joseph were divorced. After the divorce, Lauder became romantically involved with the late Arnold Lewis van Ameringen. He was 16 years older than Lauder, married, and was also involved in the beauty business. The relationship reportedly ended when it became clear van Ameringen would not leave his wife.

Then, in 1942, Lauder remarried Joseph and they had a second son, Ronald. Later, van Ameringen assisted her in creating her first fragrance. Accounts differ concerning how he helped: either by extending her credit while she developed the scent, or by actually providing the formula for it. In 1953 Youth Dew bath oil appeared in department stores and was a smash hit. Sales at Estee Lauder Inc. began at $300 to $400 a week, then climbed to an unprecedented weekly $5,000. Lauder sold exclusively to department stores, because it was too costly to employ personnel to handle the drugstore market. This only added to the mystique of the products.

The company then expanded to include four completely different lines of cosmetics and scents: Estee Lauder, Clinique, Prescriptives, and Avis. Estee Lauder came first, catering to women in the 50s-to-70s age range, who tend to be loyal customers. Model Paulina Porizkova can be seen in print ads for this line of hypoallergenic products. And one campaign advertising the fragrance Beautiful includes vocals by rock singer Joe Cocker. The Estee Lauder label also encompasses Lauder for Men and is the largest moneymaker, bringing in an estimated $600 million per year as of 1989. Actor Bruce Boxleitner was hired to highlight these products. The sleekly packaged Prescriptives line is geared toward women in their 30s and 40s. It is the newest line, with annual sales of $42 million. Created with the sophisticated career woman in mind, Prescriptives started turning a profit in 1987. Clinique is targeted for young women in their teens and early twenties. Especially attractive to new customers, it is responsible for $475 million in annual sales. Another men's line, Aramis, brings in $75 million a year.

By 1987 Lauder had cornered 38 percent of the market. The closest rival was Cosmair, owner of L'Oreal and Lancome, which represented 14 percent of cosmetics sales. Part of Lauder's success can be credited to the image she projects—she *is* the company, in the eyes of the consumer. She is also a gifted strategist. It is Lauder who is credited with the idea of giving away free samples of scents, for example, at a time when an advertising budget was out of the question. Most people enjoy presents, she

reasoned. This approach eventually became widespread in the industry.

Throughout her career, Lauder also cleverly cultivated friends and clients in high places. According to one account, she orchestrated a "chance" meeting with the Duchess of Windsor. She made sure the press just happened to be there to record the event. The encounter went well, and the two became friends. Nowadays, however, she no longer needs to stage meetings with world-renowned personalities. Diana, Princess of Wales, asked that Lauder be included at a White House dinner held in the princess's honor in 1985. And former Russian first lady Raisa Gorbachev sought out Lauder during a visit to New York in 1989.

Lauder's success can also be attributed to a penchant for detail. She not only pays attention to the packaging of her products, but also insists that her

> *Lauder once even lectured a Salvation Army employee working on the street on the art of being well dressed. "God is in the details," is one of her sayings.*

cosmetics counter salespeople dress stylishly. And she trains personnel to touch customers, in order to promote a sense of intimacy and therefore more sales. Reportedly, Lauder once even lectured a Salvation Army employee working on the street on the art of being well dressed. "God is in the details," is one of her sayings, according to Lisa Belkin in the *New York Times Magazine*.

Since about 1989 the competition for the number-one spot in cosmetics has started closing in on Estee Lauder Inc., although it still enjoys the largest share of the market. Some of the top French cosmetics firms have expanded to the United States, including Clarins, Chanel, and Christian Dior. L'Oreal's Lancome brand has done well in the United States. And the English and Dutch company Unilever joined the competition when it took over Elizabeth Arden and Faberge. The Revlon Group is also in the running.

When Lauder became chairman of Estee Lauder Inc. in 1982, her eldest son Leonard took over as chief executive officer. In order to combat the encroaching competition, and with his mother's support, Leonard adopted some new strategies. The company has moved into more international markets, including highly desirable France and Japan. It will no doubt maintain its prime positioning in the more elite department stores, such as Bloomingdale's, where it enjoys the best positioning and accounts for the largest sales at the cosmetics counters. Aramis is the only label that has dropped in status. Its skin care products for men are geared toward counteracting this trend.

And the firm can now dole out $62 million in advertising per year for all of its lines. New product development is another strategy, although the company is careful not to steal sales from any of its already successful brands. And prices have risen in the Estee Lauder line by between 30 and 50 percent. Customers apparently were not intimidated by the increase. When Lauder's Perfect Lipstick hit the stores at $15.00 per tube, for example, it still sold out in record time.

From humble beginnings in Queens, New York, Estee Lauder has elevated herself to the level of the world's most elegant and sophisticated people. Her summers are spent in the Hamptons of New York; her winters in Palm Beach, Florida. Lauder reached the pinnacle of her field by parlaying homemade face cream into four distinct product lines worth nearly two billion dollars. She explained the approach that brought her to the top in *Fortune* magazine: "I never dreamed about success. I worked for it." Since 1982, it has been up to Lauder's son Leonard to keep the family firm going. With his formidable forecasting abilities and excellent track record, it is likely Estee Lauder Inc. will endure.

Sources

Business Week, September 4, 1989.
Fortune, October 12, 1987; March 14, 1988.
Insight, August 28, 1989.
New York Times Magazine, November 29, 1987.
Vogue, January 1990; May 1990.

—Victoria France Charabati

Simon LeVay

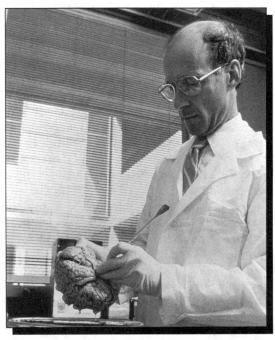

Neurobiologist

Born August 28, 1943, in Oxford, England; son of David LeVay and Marjorie Hare. *Education:* University of Cambridge, M.A., 1966; University of Gottingen, Germany, Ph.D., 1971.

Addresses: *Office*—Salk Institute for Biological Studies, San Diego, CA.

Career

Harvard Medical School, Cambridge, MA, 1971-84, began as instructor, became associate professor of neurobiology; Salk Institute for Biological Studies, San Diego, CA, associate professor, 1984-92; West Hollywood Institute for Gay and Lesbian Education, West Hollywood, CA, co-director, beginning 1992. Adjunct professor of biology, University of California, San Diego.

Sidelights

When a paper from the technical journal *Science* is featured on the front pages, the network news and the morning talk shows," noted Sharon Begley in a *Newsweek* article, "you can be sure the subject is not the behavior of a pulsar." The study that caused all the commotion in fact came from Simon LeVay, a neurobiologist at San Diego's Salk Institute, and the topic was an explosive one— whether, as LeVay theorized, homosexuality could be biologically determined.

LeVay's interpretation is "a logical extension of two decades of work on the differences between male

and female brains," wrote Denise Grady in *Discover* magazine, which also named LeVay's findings one of the 50 top science stories of 1991. The researcher based his theory on some of his studies of a group of brains. As J. Madeleine Nash reported in *Time*, LeVay "found that one tiny region in the brain of homosexual men was more like that in women than that in heterosexual men." As Nash elaborated, LeVay studied the hypothalamus, located in the brain's center, "in an area of the brain that is known to help regulate male sexual behavior. Within this site, LeVay looked at four different groupings of cells, technically referred to as the interstitial nuclei of the anterior hypothalamus, or INAH for short. Other researchers had already reported the INAH 2 and 3 were larger in men than in women. LeVay hypothesized that one or both of them might vary with sexual orientation as well."

Of the 41 brains LeVay examined, 19 had come from homosexual men who had died of AIDS. "So had six of the 16 presumed heterosexual men and one of the six women," noted Nash. "After careful examination of the brain samples, he found that the INAH-3 areas of most of the women and homosexual men were about the same size. In straight men this region was on average twice as large—or about the size of a grain of sand."

LeVay's paper "touched off a frenzy," as Begley wrote. "Some gay activists raised the specter of a homophobic state requiring gay men to have brain surgery to set them straight, while others said the findings overthrew once and for all the notion that homosexuality is an aberrant lifestyle or a mental illness, whose practitioners should be shunned or put on an analyst's couch."

Certainly the nature-versus-nurture aspect of homosexuality has traditionally added heat to an emotional issue, but for LeVay, who is openly gay, the genetic findings may help turn around a longstanding stereotype about the "causes" of homosexuality. In a *Newsweek* cover story on the subject, LeVay recalled that as a child he saw qualities in himself that perpetuate the gay image: "not liking sports, preferring reading, being very close to my mother" among them. A distant relationship with his father is "the classic clincher," as *Newsweek* put it. But LeVay offered this opinion supporting genetics: "My point would be that gays are extremely different when they're young and as a *result* they can develop hostile relationships with their fathers. It's just a big mistake to think it's the other way around and the relationships are causal."

As much as LeVay's research has brought him recognition, "he and others in the field acknowledge that the paper needs replication, since such studies are difficult and somewhat subjective," as *Science* writer Marcia Barinaga reported. Possible repudia-tions of the scientist's findings include the idea that it was AIDS itself that caused the discrepancy in size of the INAH-3 nuclei in the brains LeVay studied.

Still, some of LeVay's colleagues are stepping forward to support his views. "Simon is very good; he's extremely well-equipped to make those observations," one neurobiologist told Barinaga, adding, "but we ought to put off big speculation until it is confirmed." In the same article, another scientist, Laura Allen of UCLA, said LeVay "is probably correct" in his theory, since the heterosexual men's brains contained larger INAH-3 nuclei whether or not they had died of AIDS.

"Over the years much research on homosexuality has been motivated by a desire to eradicate the behavior rather than understand, let alone celebrate, diversity," concluded Nash. "LeVay and others hope their work will enable humans to view homosexuality the way other species seem to see it: as a normal variation of sexual behavior."

Sources

Discover, January 1992.
Newsweek, September 9, 1991; February 24, 1992.
Science, August 1991.
Time, September 9, 1991.

—*Susan Salter*

Steve Martin

Comedian and actor

Born in 1945 in Waco, TX; son of Glenn and Mary (Lee) Martin; married Victoria Tennant (an actress), 1986. *Education:* Attended Long Beach State College (now California State University, Long Beach) and the University of California, Los Angeles.

Career

Comedian, actor, writer, and producer. Stand-up comedian and writer for television comedy shows, c. 1966-70. Began making appearances on television shows in the 1970s, including *Andy Williams Presents Ray Stevens,* 1970; *The Sonny and Cher Comedy Hour,* 1972-73; *The Smothers Brothers Comedy Hour,* 1975; *The Johnny Cash Show,* 1976; and *The Tonight Show* (often as guest host). Occasional host of *Saturday Night Live,* beginning c. 1976. Star of television specials *Steve Martin: A Wild and Crazy Guy,* 1978; *Comedy Is Not Pretty,* 1980; and *Steve Martin's Best Show Ever,* 1981.

Actor in feature films, 1979—, including *The Jerk,* 1979; *Pennies from Heaven,* 1981; *Dead Men Don't Wear Plaid,* 1982; *The Man with Two Brains,* 1983; *The Lonely Guy,* 1984; *All of Me,* 1984; *Little Shop of Horrors,* 1986; *Three Amigos,* 1986; *Roxanne,* 1987; *Planes, Trains, and Automobiles,* 1987; *Parenthood,* 1989; *Dirty Rotten Scoundrels,* 1989; *My Blue Heaven,* 1990; *L.A. Story,* 1991; *Father of the Bride,* 1991; *Grand Canyon,* 1992; and *Housesitter,* 1992. Also appeared in short subject *The Absent-Minded Waiter,* 1977; and in *Sergeant Pepper's Lonely Hearts Club Band,* 1978; *The Kids Are Alright,* 1979; and *The Muppet Movie,* 1979. Executive producer of show *Domestic Life,* CBS, 1984.

Member: Screen Actors Guild, American Guild of Variety Artists, American Federation of Television and Radio Artists.

Awards: Co-winner of Emmy Award for "outstanding writing achievement in comedy, variety, or music series," 1969, for *The Smothers Brothers Comedy Hour;* Emmy Award nomination for writing, 1975, for *Van Dyke and Company;* Georgie Awards from American Guild of Variety Artists, 1977 and 1978; Grammy Awards for best comedy album, 1977, for *Let's Get Small,* and 1978, for *A Wild and Crazy Guy;* Academy Award nomination for best short subject, 1978, for *The Absent-Minded Waiter;* named best actor by the National Society of Film Critics and New York Film Critics Circle, both 1984, both for *All of Me.*

Sidelights

Steve Martin—for years the very name conjured up the image of a daffy comic wearing rabbit ears, bellowing "well, excuuuuuuse me!" and cavorting as a "Wild and Crazy Guy." Those days are behind him now, and Martin has retired his old routines in order to embark on a film career of equal, if not greater, renown. The star of such hit movies as *The Jerk, All of Me, Roxanne, Parenthood,* and *Father of the Bride,* Martin has tapped a deeper comic vein, one that often combines both frolic and pathos in a single performance.

Miami Herald correspondent Ryan Murphy described Martin as "the Fred Astaire of comics, a performer who has evolved into opting for the quiet, bittersweet stumble over the broad guffaw almost every time." Martin's brand of humor has indeed changed dramatically, but the work he is doing now more closely resembles the man he is privately—and is thus a source of pride for him. "I think it's apparent that you can't continue to act stupid into your forties," the actor told *Film Comment.* "I feel real confident of my potential in movies in the future. I can play a pretty good range."

> *"The usual theory in comedy is that setting up a joke creates tension, and telling the punch line breaks the tension. My theory was, 'Let 'em break their own tension."*

Martin quit stand-up comedy at the very height of his career because he realized he had exhausted his material for that genre. He turned to writing screenplays and starring in movies—a daring decision that might have spelled the end of his career. After a string of film failures, including *Pennies from Heaven, The Man with Two Brains, Dead Men Don't Wear Plaid,* and *The Lonely Guy,* his stardom indeed seemed tarnished. He rebounded with the poignant and popular *Roxanne,* the physically-demanding *All of Me,* and *Planes, Trains, and Automobiles*—his first outing as straight man to another comic, John Candy. Subsequently he has become one of Hollywood's hardest-working actors, appearing in as many as two or three films each year.

"Martin may be the most all-American of comedians because of his nose-to-the-sawdust work ethic and his ambition," wrote *Gentleman's Quarterly* correspondent Elvis Mitchell. "From his first starring role, in *The Jerk,* in which he threw a saddle over his stage

shtick and rode it to box office-champeen status, to *All of Me,* in which he married pinpoint concentration to a grown-up movie star's performance, to *Parenthood,* in which he fully entered the adult world, you can see Martin steadily working his way through level after level of accomplishment."

In interviews, Steve Martin is reluctant to talk about his past or his current private life. He told one reporter that he finds such anecdotes boring and often beside the point. Asked about his childhood and his family relations, he told *Time* magazine: "I didn't grow up in a whorehouse [as fellow comedian and actor Richard Pryor did]. We were not close-knit—not a lot of hugging and kissing, not vocal or loud. We were middle class. When frozen food came in, we were right in there buying frozen food."

Martin was born in 1945 in Waco, Texas. He describes his youth there as 'ordinary." The pivotal moment for young Steve Martin came in 1955, when his family pulled up the stakes and moved to Garden Grove, California. Suddenly the star-struck boy found himself living just two miles from Disneyland. "I just loved the idea of Disneyland," the comic told *Time.* Martin promptly sought work in the theme park despite his tender age, and he was hired to sell guidebooks at the entrance. "The norm was about 50 books a day," he told *Time.* "One day I sold 625. I think it was a record."

An interest in magic earned him a performing job in Merlin's Magic Shop when he was only 15. He proved so popular there that he began accepting engagements at parties and Kiwanis Club banquets. At 18 he was a regular at the Bird Cage Theater in Knott's Berry Farm, performing four shows a day, five days a week. "Basic training," he called it in *Time.* Martin added: "I was aiming for show business from early days, and magic was the poor man's way of getting in." Martin also taught himself to play the banjo, bluegrass-style, and he incorporated the instrument into his stage act.

Never an enthusiastic student in public school, Martin was not planning to attend college. Stormie Sherk, a fellow performer at Knott's, persuaded him to change his mind. She gave Martin novels to read and introduced him to philosophical ideas that he found intriguing. Martin enrolled at California State University, Long Beach, with a major in philosophy. "I was romanticized by philosophy," he told *Time.* "I thought it was the highest thing you could study. At one point I wanted to teach it."

The academic honeymoon came to an end when Martin read the works of Ludwig Wittgenstein, a philosopher who redefined and reduced the scope of the discipline. "As I studied the history of philosophy, the quest for ultimate truth became less important to me, and by the time I got to Wittgenstein it seemed pointless," the comic told *Time*. "I realized that in the arts you don't have to discover meaning, you create it. There are no rules, no true and false, no right and wrong." Martin returned to his first love—comedy, and began to pursue the career with more ambition.

In 1967 Martin enrolled in a television writing course at the University of California in Los Angeles. He was also doing stand-up work at the time, but his audiences often were not responsive to his act. He was more successful finding work writing for other performers. By 1968 he had won a shared Emmy for comedy writing on the controversial *Smothers Brothers Comedy Hour,* and he went on to produce material for such varied entertainers as Glen Campbell, John Denver, Sonny and Cher (also see this issue of *Newsmakers* for sketch on Sonny Bono), and Dick Van Dyke.

Writing for others never satisfied Martin. He was still possessed with the idea of stage success on his own terms. In 1973 he left Los Angeles, based himself in Aspen, Colorado, and took his act on the road. "I was in my middle years and just needed some freshness," Martin said in the *Los Angeles Times.* "I needed to get out. It was a good thing, as it turned out, because my career started happening out of [Los Angeles]...in San Francisco and Miami—the Coconut Grove, of all places. In Hollywood, I was regarded as just another act."

About the same time, Martin sensed a mood change in the nation at large, and he restructured his act to fit the new mood. He gave up the conventional stand-up act of one-liners and honed sheer stupidity into an art form. "I developed a philosophy of never admitting to the audience that what I was doing wasn't working, never admitting that I wasn't the greatest thing in the world," he noted in *Rolling Stone.* "The usual theory in comedy is that setting up a joke creates tension, and telling the punch line breaks the tension. My theory was, 'Let 'em break their own tension,' the idea being that after wondering, 'What the f—- is this guy doing?' everyone starts to laugh because they're nervous."

He pulled out the rabbit ears and the fake arrow-through-the-head. He skidded across the stage on "happy feet." He gave the 1970s its mantra with "well, ex-cuuuuuse me." The audiences loved it. By 1976, television had found him.

Martin hosted *Saturday Night Live* for the first time in the fall of 1976. He was invited back numerous times thereafter, so often in fact that he and Dan Aykroyd developed a series of running skits on the "Wild and Crazy Guys," based on a pair of Eastern European immigrants. During the same period, Martin also hosted *The Tonight Show* frequently, and he recorded several best-selling albums at live concerts. He even had a Top Ten single hit with the novelty song "King Tut."

By 1980 Martin was packing the largest concert halls in the nation and starring in prime-time network television specials. He was also beginning to feel a strain. His routines were becoming tired and predictable, he was running out of new material, and he was especially annoyed by fans who expected him to be silly in public. Late in 1981 he gave up live comedy forever. "I was tired," he told *Rolling Stone.* "I didn't feel I had a choice about giving up the stage; it was just over."

It was not an end for Steve Martin, but a new beginning. His first motion picture, *The Jerk,* was a top-drawing movie in 1979. The film essentially offered the same absurdist Steve Martin humor as did his stand-up work. "*The Jerk* came at the crest of TV-induced Martin-mania," wrote Jack Barth in *Film Comment.* "It was the first chance to hear the Wild and Crazy Guy swear, and the first chance to pay to see him up close, since his concert venues by that time were too large for his own good. The film was stuffed with sight gags; a car towing a church or driving with no tires, Martin 'wearing' two dogs or dancing like Jerry Lewis in *The Nutty Professor.* The sheer density of the humor combined with the truth-in-advertising title put this one over the top."

Encouraged by the success of that film, Martin proceeded to make four others that simply died at the box office. He starred in a musical, *Pennies from Heaven,* and then turned out *Dead Men Don't Wear Plaid, The Man with Two Brains,* and *The Lonely Guy.* Although Barth noted that all of these movies "have had moments of mirth worth the price of admission," Martin tends to view them now as his apprenticeship in the motion picture business. "I see that whole stretch of time now as learning how to make movies," he told *Gentleman's Quarterly.* "That was actually my transition period. By *All of Me,* I started to get a footing. I was insecure about doing *All of Me,* but only because I was insecure about my movie career. I thought the script was funny, but I really didn't know what to do. But I got on a plane, reread this script and said, This is funny. This is what I want to do. It was the beginning of the second phase."

That "second phase" has assured Martin's film stardom and brought him a substantial amount of respect as a screenwriter. In *All of Me*, released in 1984, Martin portrays a lawyer whose body becomes partially inhabited by the spirit of one of his female clients. Martin was co-author of the script, with Rob Reiner. In 1986 Martin earned good notices for his cameo as a sadistic dentist in *Little Shop of Horrors*. The best was yet to come, however.

Roxanne, Martin's 1987 comedy, is based on the classic story of Cyrano de Bergerac, a love-smitten soldier with an oversized nose. In the movie, Martin appears as a fire chief—with a veritable banana for a nose—who helps a handsome co-worker woo a beautiful young woman. "The script challenges its star to be at once noble and fatuous, strong and swooning, utterly in control, and desperately in love—all of which Martin handles as gracefully as if he'd written it himself (which he did)," remarked *Time* correspondent Richard Corliss.

Martin's surge at the box office continued with hits such as *Planes, Trains, and Automobiles* (1987), *Dirty Rotten Scoundrels* (1989), *Parenthood* (1989), and *Father of the Bride* (1991). Ironically, the last two vehicles found Martin playing parts far removed from his life. He is childless, but in *Parenthood* he convincingly portrays an anxious father of younger children, and in *Father of the Bride* he appears as the beleaguered dad in the midst of massive wedding preparations. Martin told the *Chicago Tribune* that he chose the two family-oriented roles because "they were warm and funny and touching." He added: "The emotions involved in rearing children or feeling about children, you don't have to have the experience to have them. It's just the emotions of life. It's like missing someone or caring for someone. It's not impossible to get to."

The Steve Martin of the 1990s promises to be as ambitious and unpredictable as the Steve Martin of earlier decades. He continues to write screenplays— 1991's *L.A. Story* being one more recent example— and he is considering starring roles in several more comedies. Another challenge awaits him in serious drama. He played a cameo role in the Lawrence Kasdan film *Grand Canyon* in 1992, and he is telling reporters that he will not rule out other non-comic roles. Martin told the *Miami Herald* that his goals are quite simple. "I have two of them," he said. "I want to have a filmography, to make five or six movies you can say at the end of your days, 'Yeah, that was really good.' And the other thing is I want to have fun while I make them. Earlier in my career, I would go through hell to make movies. Now, I just say, 'Ah, whatever,' and try and enjoy it."

Martin and his wife, actress Victoria Tennant, live in Los Angeles. The comedian guards his privacy, saying little about his marriage or about his fine collection of modern American art. "People always expect me to, you know, do something funny when they see me," he told the *Miami Herald*. "They think I'm funny or outrageous all the time. But I can't show off, it's not bred in me.... It's embarrassing! But I just cannot be on." Except, of course, when the cameras are rolling. Then Steve Martin is ready to shine.

Selected writings

Screenplays

The Absent-Minded Waiter, Paramount, 1977.
(With Carl Gottlieb and Michael Elias) *The Jerk*, Universal, 1979.
(With Rob Reiner and George Gipe) *Dead Men Don't Wear Plaid*, Universal, 1982.
Easy Money, Orion, 1983.
(Coauthor) *The Man with Two Brains*, Warner Bros., 1983.
(With R. Reiner) *All of Me*, Universal, 1984.
(With Lorne Michaels and Randy Newman) *Three Amigos*, Orion, 1986.
Roxanne, Columbia, 1987.
L.A. Story, Tri-Star, 1991.

Books

Cruel Shoes, Putnam, 1979.

Selected discography

Let's Get Small, Warner Bros., 1977.
"King Tut" (single), Warner Bros., 1978.
A Wild and Crazy Guy, Warner Bros., 1978.
Comedy Is Not Pretty, Warner Bros., 1979.
The Steve Martin Brothers, Warner Bros., 1982.

Sources

Books

Contemporary Theatre, Film, and Television, Volume 5, Gale, 1988.

Periodicals

Chicago Tribune, January 2, 1992.
Film Comment, September 1984.
Gentleman's Quarterly, July 1990.
Los Angeles Times, February 3, 1991; February 10, 1991.
Miami Herald, February 10, 1991.

Newsweek, April 3, 1978; June 22, 1987.
People, May 1, 1978.
Rolling Stone, December 1, 1977; November 8, 1984.
Saturday Evening Post, November/December 1989.
Time, August 24, 1987.

—Anne Janette Johnson

Marlee Matlin

AP/Wide World Photos

Actress

Born August 24, 1965, in Morton's Grove, IL; daughter of Don (a used car dealership owner) and Libby (a jewelry store employee). *Education:* Attended William Rainey Harper College.

Addresses: *Home*—Los Angeles, CA. *Publicist —* Bragman, Nyman, and Cafarelli, Inc., 8693 Wiltshire Blvd., Penthouse Suite, Beverly Hills, CA 90211.

Career

Actress appearing in motion pictures, including *Children of a Lesser God*, 1987, and *Walker;* in television films, including *Bridge to Silence;* and in television series *Reasonable Doubts*, 1991—.

Awards: Golden Globe Award and Academy Award for best actress, both 1987, both for *Children of a Lesser God;* nominated for a Golden Globe Award for best actress in a television drama, 1992, for *Reasonable Doubts.*

Sidelights

NBC took a risk by featuring in its show *Reasonable Doubts* a hearing impaired assistant district attorney, Tess Kaufman, played by Marlee Matlin. Though few television viewers know sign language, Matlin, who is also deaf, signs her lines, while she clashes with a handsome detective—played by Mark Harmon—and solves cases. The show is predictable, critics say, but notable because of Matlin's presence and luminous acting. "I'm a lot like Tess in some ways," Matlin noted in an interview in the *Detroit*

Free Press. "I'm straightforward. I'm honest. I'm sensitive. If I don't like something I say I don't like it."

Matlin's outspokenness has landed her in hot water many times during her seven-year Hollywood career. She has been criticized for not being an appropriate role model for deaf people, but she counters such attacks, pointing out that she is an individual, not a symbol. At the same time, she's constantly struggling to overcome the obstacles of being deaf in a hearing world.

"It's hard for me to sell myself, because there's not enough people out there who are willing to accept me as a hearing impaired individual," she said, as quoted by the *Detroit Free Press.* "They let it get in the way." Matlin's blossoming television career is a fortunate path for the woman who won a best actress award from the Academy of Motion Picture Arts and Sciences at age 21, then found herself on top of the mountain with nowhere to go but down.

Born into a suburban Chicago family in 1965, Marlee Matlin had normal hearing until the age of 18 months, when she contracted a form of childhood measles called roseola. Her parents took her by plane to visit her grandmother in California, unaware of the damage the flight would cause to her hearing.

When they returned to Morton's Grove, a doctor diagnosed her as profoundly deaf. Matlin has no hearing in one ear and only 20 percent in the other.

Her childhood was tumultuous, for no other reason than Matlin was angry about her disability. "I wanted to be perfect," she revealed in *Ladies' Home Journal*, "and I couldn't accept my deafness. I was so angry and frightened." According to the *New York Times*, Matlin recalled that, as a result, she "fought." "I never held anything in," she continued. "I grew up thinking that I'm going to be independent, deaf or not, that no one's going to control me." But, *U.S. News & World Report* quoted her as also saying, "I couldn't accept it when people stared at me. I was so paranoid about being deaf."

Acting would become Matlin's emotional outlet. At age seven, she played Dorothy in *The Wizard of Oz* at the Children's Theater at the Center for Deafness in Chicago. She later attended a combination of private and public schools, extending her love of acting to summer camp.

As an adolescent, Matlin narrowed her career choices to acting or law enforcement. A short stint at a junior college, however, convinced her that opportunities in police work were limited. A friend talked her into auditioning for the Chicago production of the Mark Medoff Broadway play, *Children of a Lesser God*; she won a supporting part, the biggest small role she ever had. Luck was on her side when a Hollywood casting agent for the motion picture version of the play saw a videotape of the Chicago production and spotted Matlin. The agent cast Matlin into the lead role of Sarah, believing she would perform better than the actress who starred in the play.

After an audition in Los Angeles, Matlin was given the part. Her chemistry with co-star William Hurt was explosive. In the film, Matlin plays a deaf cleaning woman at a school for the hearing impaired; her character is so filled with rage about being disabled, she refuses to speak. Hurt plays a hearing teacher at the school who takes it upon himself to teach her to speak, whether she wants to learn or not. "There are deeper questions arising from the use or non-use of language to oppress, hurt or reward others," wrote Jim Neubacher in a review of *Children of a Lesser God* in the *Detroit Free Press*. "In her feature film debut, the hearing-impaired Matlin is sensitive and poised.... The sexual energy between [Matlin and Hurt]—however it is created—is fierce and bright."

With the popularity of the film, the world discovered Marlee Matlin, who was only 21 years old at the time. On Academy Awards night in 1987, she wore her hair back with a sprig of baby's breath and donned a pair of glasses and a prim evening dress. The award she won for best actress was delivered by her co-star and boyfriend Hurt, and her achievement was met with tumultuous applause. A graceful Matlin delivered her acceptance speech through sign language. "To tell you the truth," Matlin said simply, "I didn't prepare for this speech, but I definitely want to thank the academy."

Backstage, reporters mobbed her, asking her how it felt to be the first deaf actress to win an Oscar. Through her interpreter, she told them what some believed to be words coached by the intensely private Hurt: "I'm an actress who just doesn't happen to hear. I have my own hearing; it's not the way you hear. I'm a human being. That's the only way to respond to that question," she said.

"It's hard for me to sell myself, because there's not enough people out there who are willing to accept me as a hearing impaired individual."

Meanwhile, Matlin's life had turned into a celluloid fantasy story. During the filming of *Children*, she and Hurt had developed an off-screen relationship. Her parents were surprised when she moved to New York to share an apartment with Hurt, but Matlin and Hurt remained together for two years. After Matlin's Oscar, however, Hurt's ardor cooled, and the couple broke up in 1987. "It really shocked him when I won the Oscar," Matlin recalled in a *New York Times* interview. Some critics, too, were shocked that she had won. One reviewer felt that she was given the award only because she was a deaf person playing a deaf person.

"Another critic said I would never work again," Matlin remarked in the *New York Times*. "And he's not the only one who said that." But with the recognition of her acting peers, Matlin found doors opening. Her social life picked up. In 1987, she was listed as one of America's Ten Most Beautiful women by *Harper's* magazine. That same year, Matlin addressed acting students at her former school, the

Center on Deafness in Des Plaines, Illinois, telling them to not be afraid or give up. She also expressed that her original belief that there were no opportunities for deaf people in acting was wrong.

In 1988, after splitting up with Hurt, Matlin was spotted at the Olympics in Calgary with Jeffrey Moore, son of actor Roger Moore. Her name was also linked with that of actors Richard Dean Anderson and Rob Lowe. She explained in *Ladies' Home Journal* that she had no trouble communicating with boyfriends. "I charm them," she said. Matlin is an excellent lip reader, and "many men find her so fascinating they learn how to sign," LouAnn Walker wrote in *Ladies' Home Journal.*

Also becoming involved in politics, Matlin testified in 1988 before the U.S. Senate on the need for a national institute on deafness. She appeared on the television interview program *Nightline* during the controversy at Gallaudet, a university for the deaf that hired a hearing president who knew no sign language. In addition, she demanded that the television programs she appeared on contain closed-captions for deaf viewers. Turning to other causes, she taped a public service announcement for AIDS awareness and volunteered at the Starlight Foundation, which grants wishes to terminally ill children.

Matlin's career, which began at the top, gradually took a dive. Contrary to what she had told students at her old school, there were simply no suitable roles for her, even though she possessed an Oscar. In 1988, a more sophisticated Matlin presented the award for best actor on Academy Awards night and for the first time on television, she spoke words instead of signing them, after training with a speech therapist. "Although her graceful speech brought tears to the eyes of many audience members, it also sparked criticism from some hearing impaired viewers, who felt she was abandoning her own by not signing as she spoke," observed Walker. "But then, provocation is only par for the course for the mercurial, stubborn actress." Matlin defended her action to Walker: "It was a great accomplishment for me . . . . I understand their opinions. But why don't they understand my value? Why don't they understand my qualities?"

Also in 1988, Matlin got a taste of the other Hollywood: she starred in the film *Walker,* which was a box office flop. She played the wife of William Walker, an American who helped lead a takeover of Nicaragua in 1855. Though the motion picture was not poorly reviewed, it never reached a large audience.

In 1989, Matlin decided to try acting on television. She starred in a TV movie, *Bridge to Silence,* about a deaf woman rebuilding her relationship with her mother, who was played by the late actress Lee Remick. The movie was panned by Susan Stewart of the *Detroit Free Press:* "If you like your emotions overwritten, your hysteria overwrought and your script unencumbered by subtlety," the movie "is for you."

With her career in motion pictures at a virtual standstill—Matlin worked in two more films, *The Man in the Golden Mask* and *The Linguini Incident,* both of which were never released—the actress decided to stick with television in the hope of obtaining more steady work. She turned down one script that had her starring opposite a dog. Then, she was asked by producer Robert Singer to take a role in his new cop/attorney drama, *Reasonable Doubts.*

In the series, Matlin plays an attorney at odds with a police detective who happens to know sign language. The script required a certain amount of rewriting, and Harmon would often find himself speaking out loud the words Matlin signed. "At first, I could see that the writers were caught off guard," Matlin related in the *New York Times.* The actress soon put them at ease, and most of them learned to sign simple words like "cut" and "roll."

Reasonable Doubts garnered some popularity and has been renewed at least through 1993. On the whole, television has been kinder and steadier to Marlee Matlin than movies ever were. Though she was nominated for a Golden Globe Award for best actress in 1992, Matlin still gets criticisms that she should be a better role model for deaf people, but she refuses to let it bother her. "I got a letter from a guy . . . who told me I should stop swearing and I should stop using sexual connotations on my show because hey, deaf people don't swear, deaf people don't have sex, deaf people don't get involved with violence," the actress told the *New York Times.* "Well, there are plenty of deaf people who do, and why can't I represent that?"

Matlin has an interpreter, Jack Jason, whose parents are deaf. He makes her phone calls and translates for her at work and at home. In 1992, Matlin was sharing a house in the Hollywood Hills with former *L.A. Law* producer David E. Kelley. Describing the actress, a *New York Times* reporter declared: "When [Matlin] props her feet on the desk, two things are immediately evident. First they are constantly in motion, continually fidgeting, as if they were the repository of nervous energy the way other people's hands are. Second, they are covered by a pair of

suede Guccis small enough to form the mold of
Cinderella's glass slipper....She carries on her
conversation, sometimes signing, sometimes speaking, sometimes pantomiming, peppering it all with
the unprintable, but always meeting her visitor eye to
eye."

Sources

Detroit Free Press, October 5, 1986; February 2, 1987;
    March 31, 1987; April 1, 1987; April 13, 1987;
    August 24, 1987; December 27, 1987; April 9,
    1989; January 29, 1990; June 24, 1990; August 5,
    1991; September 26, 1991; January 1, 1992; Janu-
    ary 6, 1992.
Glamour, January 1988.
Ladies' Home Journal, April 1989.
Maclean's, October 7, 1991.
New York Times, January 5, 1992.
People, October 20, 1986; April 10, 1989.
Time, October 20, 1986.
U.S. News & World Report, November 10, 1986.

—*Ellen Creager*

Dawn Mello

Photograph by Jeanne Strongin

Fashion industry executive

Born c. 1938; grew up in Lynn, MA; daughter of Anthony Mello (businessman and inventor). *Education:* Attended Modern School of Fashion and Design.

Addresses: *Office*—Based in Milan, Italy, and New York, NY.

Career

B. Altman retail chain, began as assistant in fashion department, 1959; general merchandise manager and executive vice-president of May Department Store Co., 1960-71; returned to B. Altman as vice-president and fashion director, 1971-75; Bergdorf Goodman retail stores, vice-president, 1975-89; Gucci International, director of worldwide corporate image and product development, 1989—.

Sidelights

Most of the names people associate with high fashion are those of the designers—the Saint Laurents, the Halstons, the Guccis. But someone has to choose what styles to sell in the upscale New York-based department stores where people go to find these fashions. To that end, Dawn Mello may be one of the most influential, if not exactly famous, names in the fashion industry. She has built a career out of running the high-fashion offices of such stores as Bergdorf Goodman and B. Altman. In 1989 she was lured away to assume the creative directorship of the faltering Gucci International, thus initiating its turnaround.

Known as a "low-key, careful woman, at once cordial and distant," as Helen Dudar described her in a *Working Woman* article, Mello came by her ambition early. Her father, a Portuguese immigrant, started out "virtually shoeless and achieved middle-class status," according to Dudar. As Mello explained to Dudar, "I was raised by a father who insisted that I keep my eye on a career and raised me as if I were a man. And we're talking about the 1940s." Mello has equally high praise for her mother, who coped with Dawn's unusual height (she reached six feet tall before graduating high school) by telling her daughter "that I was average and everybody else was short," as Mello recalls.

After attending Boston's Modern School of Fashion and Design, Mello found a job at May Department Stores as a buyer. "There she met Ira Niemark, who was learning retailing at a May store in Hartford," reports Dudar. "When he left May to update B. Altman's flagship store in New York, he invited Mello along. They would prove to be a notable professional team for the next 17 years: Niemark, one of the shrewdest of financial managers, and Mello, who can shine without outshining, a woman able to sense the next season's trend even before it appears on the horizon."

That skill proved to be Mello's strongest talent, and it all but solidified her reputation in fashion. By the time she had joined Bergdorf Goodman, Mello was known as a woman who could dictate style. Niemark, speaking to Carrie Donovan in a *New York Times Magazine* profile in 1986, credited Bergdorf's fashion success to the fact that "it is not so much *what* we have as it is what we *don't* carry because Dawn Mello won't let it in the store."

If one manufacturer were in need of Mello's talents, it was the Gucci International of the late 1980s. "In its prime, back in the late 1950s and '60s, Gucci defined chic," noted *Time*'s Barbara Rudolph. "By the 1980s, however, the label had become tattered and worn, a victim of sloppy manufacturing, countless knockoffs and feuds among members of the Gucci clan."

Enter Mello, named a director of worldwide image and product development. Among her first duties was to oversee the overhaul of Gucci style. Rudolph cited a return to sophisticated fun with a "new line of leather goods [boasting] a rainbow palette of splashy colors." A line of $500 knapsacks, "aimed at a younger and hipper clientele, ranges from scarlet suede to bronze satin," as Rudolph continued. At the same time, she noted, "Mello's concept of a Gucci for the '90s takes many cues from bygone decades"— witness the return of a $565 hobo bag, "which had not been manufactured since 1975," and became a big seller once again.

Though she is surrounded by top designers and experts in the fashion field, Mello finds her inspiration from "moving around, from fantasies, from identifying with customers," as she remarked to Donovan. One customer provided a particularly valuable input, Rudolph added. "While she was eating dinner in a Florence restaurant, a man Mello had never met before showed her a worn-out pigskin Gucci briefcase that he had held on to for 25 years. Gucci no longer sold the case, he told her. Would they consider bringing it back? Mello admired the case, and Gucci," as Rudolph noted in the 1990 article, "will soon manufacture it."

Sources

New York Times, October 4, 1989.
New York Times Magazine, September 14, 1986.
Time, December 24, 1990.
Working Woman, April 1991.

—*Susan Salter*

Kiichi Miyazawa

AP/Wide World Photos

Prime minister of Japan

Born October 8, 1919, in Tokyo, Japan; married; wife's name, Yoko; children: Hiro (son), Keiko (daughter). *Education:* Imperial University of Tokyo, law department, graduated 1941. *Politics:* Affiliated with Japan's Liberal Democratic Party.

Career

Served in Japan's finance ministry, 1941-53; elected to upper house of Parliament (Diet), 1953-67; elected to lower house, 1967, and served concurrently as minister of international trade and industry, foreign minister, deputy prime minister, and finance minister, until 1991; selected by Liberal Democratic Party leaders as prime minister in 1991.

Sidelights

Kiichi Miyazawa's first four months in office as Japan's prime minister, beginning in November of 1991, were more nightmare than honeymoon. The 50th anniversary of the Japanese attack on Pearl Harbor came just days after he took office—forcing him to field U.S. demands for an apology. A month later, visiting South Korea, Miyazawa had to apologize for the 10,000 South Korean women forced into prostitution during World War II. In January of 1992, a leading member of his political faction was arrested on bribery charges—a ghostly reminder of a similar scandal that sent Miyazawa into political exile just four years earlier. Also around that time, at a formal state dinner in the midst of a highly charged summit meeting on trade, President George Bush collapsed

against Miyazawa and became ill. And in early February, Miyazawa, during a nationally televised debate, said that Americans "lacked the work ethic," setting off a new round of American indignation and threats of trade wars. Miyazawa was forced to issue a "read-my-lips" sort of apology, claiming he was also critical of Japanese workers. Days later, a right-wing activist armed with a samurai sword and handgun burst into Miyazawa's party office, fired at least one shot, and demanded the prime minister's resignation before ending a seven-hour standoff with police.

It was hard to believe that the job of prime minister was what the *New Republic* had once called Miyazawa's "lifetime dream." Miyazawa became prime minister at the age of 72 after having sought the post for years. He is, according to the London *Times,* "one of the last bureaucrats-turned-politicians still active who played a key role in the national transformation from postwar ruin to economic superpower." As a member of the Liberal Democratic Party (LPD), which has ruled Japan continuously since 1955, Miyazawa assumed leadership when he was elected the party president, succeeding Toshiki Kaifu. That election was no accident. His faction of the LDP, one of three, spent $7.8 million on the campaign to elevate Miyazawa. "Miyazawa himself, who is said to have cried when he failed four years ago to become prime minister, has pursued his goal with naked cupidity," according to the *New Republic.* That Miyazawa would ever achieve that goal seemed remote after he resigned as finance minister in December of 1988. He was implicated in a messy bribery scandal involving payments from the Recruit Corporation to leading LDP politicians, including a gift of stock to one of his top aides. Miyazawa first denied involvement, then waffled, then was forced to resign.

Miyazawa graduated from the Imperial University of Tokyo during World War II and took his first government job, with the finance ministry. Though living in Tokyo, in 1953 he inherited the same rural district near Hiroshima that his father (and even earlier his grandfather) had represented, according to the *Washington Post.* He attended the creation of the LDP in 1955, and has held most important cabinet posts for the party, including that of foreign minister.

According to the *Washington Post,* Miyazawa "is known in Japanese politics as an intellectual power-house but also as a man with a 'tall head,' a slang phrase that means haughty or conceited." The fact that he speaks fluent English—and flaunts it by reading American magazines on the floor of the Diet, Japan's parliament—doesn't win him friends, either. But Miyazawa is no lone wolf. His basic beliefs reflect Japanese political preference for consensus: no rice imports, no military role abroad (a precedent dating to Japan's defeat in World War II), and sustained economic growth.

He visited the United States as a student on the eve of World War II in 1939 and liked what he saw. It was all so different from the decadent America portrayed in his textbooks back home. "My first impression of my American friends was that they were so free, so dynamic, so spontaneous. The American boys and girls were their own masters. I was so impressed." And, later, he said he also had the chilling realization that America would prevail in the coming war because of the way American students could freely criticize their government. He told the *Los Angeles Times* in 1991: "So I thought: 'This is what democracy is... If we ever went to war with this country, we would lose...' Japan's leaders thought that, because America [was] in such disarray, they could beat America. That was a mistake."

After the war, Miyazawa, then with the finance ministry, served as a liaison officer with the U.S. Occupation Forces. But it was here that he also may have developed some of his less positive impressions of the United States. The *Boston Globe* quoted a close associate of Miyazawa as saying he "has a certain

disdain for America's pushiness in the world. He belongs to the old school that still feels strongly the humiliation of losing the war and American arrogance during the years of occupation."

Kazuo Aichi, a legislator in Miyazawa's party, told the *Washington Post,* "He can be pretty darned stubborn, but he's strong and confident and extremely well-informed and that will show up when he deals with America." And Masaya Itoh, a well respected commentator, told the *Los Angeles Times,* "He understands America but would be independent of America." The paper also noted that when Miyazawa's daughter married an American diplomat, he didn't attend the ceremony "and suggested their different cultural backgrounds would make the union difficult."

Miyazawa's actual political relationship to the United States has been a mixed bag. In 1970, as trade minister, Miyazawa halted talks over a textile pro-

> *"Japan's prime ministers are seldom chosen for their leadership qualities, vision, statesmanship, or ethics."*
> —New Republic

posal because of what he considered unreasonable U.S. demands. His successor completed the pact. But by the late 1980s, Miyazawa, then finance minister, was working so closely with then-U.S. Treasury Secretary James A. Baker III (see *Newsmakers 91*) on international finance issues that analysts began calling the Group of Seven—leaders of the seven biggest industrial democracies—the "Group of Two," according to the *Los Angeles Times.*

Miyazawa's posturing since becoming prime minister, in relation to the United States, has often sounded more like pity than trade policy to American ears. "That," wrote the *New York Times,* "is the message underlying Prime Minister Kiichi Miyazawa's recent spate of condescending-sounding speeches saying Japan must now show 'compassion' for a 'great country' struggling to solve AIDS, street crime, homelessness and a moribund education system." Even the apparent agreement to increase imports of American autos and parts that followed his January, 1992 meeting in Japan with Bush and U.S. auto company officials unraveled once the

Americans got back home, much to the horror of a White House facing a reelection campaign. Miyazawa quickly backpeddled and said, yes, there was an agreement after all. For a time, Miyazawa seemed unaware that messages meant for home consumption could still affect Japan-U.S. relations. Miyazawa's critical comments about American "work ethics" touched a sore spot on the U.S. psyche, prompting even talk show host Johnny Carson to joke that when he drove up to a Japanese restaurant soon after the prime minister's remark and tried to give his car keys to the valet, he was told, "Park it yourself, you lazy Yankee."

But the United States is just one sphere where Miyazawa and a more powerful Japan hope to assert new influence. Japan wants Moscow officials—or whoever is calling the shots in the former Soviet Union—to return the four Kuril Islands, which were seized after World War II, as a precondition to badly needed economic aid for former Soviet republics. Still, his early months in office produced little progress in that five-decades-old dispute. Former Soviet officials may have been put off by the blatant carrot-and-stick approach: Russian president Boris Yeltsin ducked a meeting with the visiting Japanese foreign minister in early 1992, saying he had business away from Moscow. The relationship between Miyazawa and the former Soviet Union had always been as icy as the Sea of Japan. "At one stage," wrote a reporter for the *Los Angeles Times*, "[Miyazawa] pointedly returned invitations to receptions marking the anniversary of the Soviet Union by replying: 'I do not celebrate events such as revolutions.'"

If the rest of the world (especially the United States) is ambivalent about Japan taking a leading role in world affairs, then so is Miyazawa. In an interview with the *Los Angeles Times* just before taking office, he said: "The question of leadership is a problem. It is better to look at Japan as a contributor. Being a leader, taking initiative and doing something—that kind of thing is not part of this country's culture. We are more the kind of country where everybody gets together and says let's move in this direction. Collective leadership is comfortable to Japan. As a country, we are a team player."

Domestically, too, Miyazawa has gotten off to a slow start. In a January 24, 1992, speech to the Diet—a sort of American-style State of the Union address—Miyazawa again called for a greater Japanese role in international affairs and for making Japan a "great place to live." But both opposition party leaders and members of his own party seemed distracted by the unfolding political bribery scandal and lack of reform

efforts, according to the *Japan Times*. Miyazawa called the arrest of his aide, Fumio Abe, "quite regrettable." The prime minister's response wasn't enough for most Diet members. Makoto Tanabe, chairman of the Social Democratic Party of Japan, said in the *Japan Times*, "Miyazawa failed to show a determined attitude in pursuing a thorough investigation of the scandal. While citing a long list of problems, Miyazawa failed to show the people where the urgent issues actually lie." Miyazawa did, however, call for a commission to regulate political donations. Any reforms he backs in the future will be a balancing act: the interests of his fellow LDP members versus dissatisfied voters in the Diet's upper house elections expected by mid-1992.

Miyazawa's hold on power may not be altogether firm. As the *New Republic* noted: "Japan's prime ministers are seldom chosen for their leadership qualities, vision, statesmanship, or ethics. Instead, the byzantine nature of the LDP means that they are selected on the basis of interfactional horse trading, often carried out in the seclusion of exclusive Tokyo restaurants." Miyazawa, wrote a reporter in the *New York Times*, "is not widely popular, and has a reputation as an aloof, autocratic backroom maneuverer."

His future may have been brighter without the Recruit Corporation scandal. Miyazawa was rehabilitated almost solely because so many other top LDP leaders were also tainted. Nine of his closest advisers had ties to the Recruit episode. The *New York Times* reported that "all the opposition parties criticized Mr. Miyazawa for installing once-tainted politicians to power, saying he had neglected the 'ethical code.'" In his early months in office, Miyazawa also fumbled chances to install a tax program that would have paid for international projects and a measure that could have allowed Tokyo to send Japanese troops on United Nations peacekeeping missions, according to *Newsweek*. "At a crucial moment in its history, Japan's lack of leadership is acute. Critics portray the country as a rudderless ship, a nation that pursues economic advantage almost mindlessly, with few internal political restraints."

Sources

Boston Globe, October 28, 1991.
Business Week, October 28, 1991.
Japan Times, February 3, 1992.
Los Angeles Times, October 12, 1991; October 13, 1991; October 28, 1991.
New Republic, November 4, 1991.
Newsweek, January 13, 1992.

New York Times, October 28, 1991; November 6, 1991; January 26, 1992; February 4, 1992.
Time, November 11, 1991.
Times (London), October 28, 1991.
Washington Post, October 28, 1991.

—Harvey Dickson

Scottie Pippen

Professional basketball player

Born September 25, 1965, in Hamburg, AR; son of Preston (a factory worker; deceased) and Ethel Pippen. *Education:* Central Arkansas University, B.A., 1987.

Career

Forward for Chicago Bulls basketball team, 1987—. Draft rights traded by Seattle Seahawks on June 22, 1987, for draft rights to Olden Polynice and other options.

Awards: Member of NBA All-Star team, 1990.

Sidelights

Scottie Pippen is a miracle superstar, a top-ranked basketball player who rose to greatness from almost complete obscurity in Arkansas. Pippen, who averaged 17.8 points, 6.2 assists, and 7.3 rebounds per game for the 1991 national champion Chicago Bulls, was not even recruited to play basketball on the collegiate level. Instead he began his college days as a team manager, little dreaming that he would one day command all the lush salary and endorsement opportunities of a well-known professional athlete.

"Pippen is one of the rare athletes in professional basketball, which features the most athletic players in sport," wrote Sam Smith in the *Chicago Tribune.* "He's tall yet both strong and quick. He can jump with big men and outrun smaller ones . . . . He fills numerous roles for the Bulls. He's a playmaker and a rebounder, a scorer and defender. He is one of the few players in the game who can take the ball off the backboard on one end, travel the length of the court and finish with a score on the other end." Paired with Michael Jordan (see *Newsmakers 87*), Pippen has helped to make the Chicago Bulls the best team in the NBA. *New York Times* correspondent Harvey Araton noted that the 6'8" Pippen "has grown into the prototypical N.B.A. small forward without surrendering the instincts and skills of a guard."

Some professional athletes grow up with the expectation of greatness—often they are the offspring of former players, or at least are privileged to compete in high-visibility arenas. Scottie Pippen had none of these advantages. The youngest of 12 children born to Preston and Ethel Pippen, he grew up in Hamburg, Arkansas. Hardly any town in America would be better qualified to be called "the middle of nowhere." Hamburg, with its population of little more than 3000, is located in the southeastern corner of Arkansas. One of its principal employers is a paper mill company, where Pippen's father worked much of his life.

Pippen had five brothers, so together they formed their own basketball team at the local playground. Life became difficult for the family when Pippen was a freshman in high school. That year Preston Pippen suffered a severe stroke, leaving him confined to a wheelchair and unable to talk. As the family struggled with this devastating illness, Scottie joined the high school basketball team. He held few expectations for his talents. At 15 he was still not as tall as his mother, and, as he told *Sports Illustrated*, "I didn't have any big plans for basketball."

Pippen got so little court time as a sophomore at Hamburg High that he decided to skip the basketball team's off-season conditioning program and serve as manager of the football team. "I was responsible for taking care of the equipment, jerseys, stuff like that," he told *Sports Illustrated*. "I always enjoyed doing that, just being a regular manager."

Pippen enjoyed it so much, in fact, that he was almost cut from the basketball team during his junior year. It took a vote from the other players to convince the coach to reinstate him. He warmed the bench that season, but by his senior year he had grown some, and he was given the point guard position as a starter. Still, at an inch under six feet and 145 pounds, he was hardly the kind of athlete that attracts college recruiters. Pippen did not receive a single scholarship offer. South Arkansas University in Magnolia sent him home after a tryout, and the nearest state campus, at Monticello, reported no vacancies.

Pippen's high school coach, Donald Wayne, had played basketball for Donald Dyer, the basketball coach at Central Arkansas University. Wayne persuaded Dyer to give Pippen a chance at least to attend the college with some sort of assistance. All Dyer could offer the frail point guard was a Basic Education Opportunity Grant and a work-study job—as manager of the basketball team. "I wasn't really that interested in playing," Pippen told *Sports Illustrated*. "I had gone through some hard times not playing in high school, but my coach had it in his mind that basketball was the way I would get an education."

What Pippen didn't realize was that he would continue growing taller all through college. He did not spend many months as the manager of the Central Arkansas team. By the middle of his freshman year he was 6'3", and by the beginning of his sophomore year he had grown an additional two inches to become a leader on the team and the recipient of a full athletic scholarship. He played point guard, forward, and center, moving around to confound the opposition. In his senior season for Central Arkansas, he averaged 23.6 points, 10 rebounds, and 4.3 assists a game, while shooting almost 60 percent from the field and the three-point range. "Best evaluation of talent I ever made," coach Dyer told the *New York Times*.

Word of Pippen's abilities began to leak out to professional scouts. Central Arkansas was not in the prestigious NCAA, however, but instead was in the lesser-known NAIA. Chicago Bulls assistant manager Billy McKinney told *Sports Illustrated* that competition in the NAIA is every bit as daunting as "amateur night at the Y." Few scouts were willing to venture into Arkansas to see Pippen, even though the NBA's director of scouting, Marty Blake, touted the young player as a hot prospect. "I advised as many teams as I could to go see him play," Blake told *Sports Illustrated*, "but when you're dealing with a player they've never heard of from a small college, the trick is to make people believe that he's bona fide. Some believe, and some don't." The few scouts who did make the trip were skeptical of Pippen's abilities because his opponents played so poorly.

> *"I had gone through some hard times not playing in high school, but my coach had it in his mind that basketball was the way I would get an education."*

By the time Pippen earned his degree in industrial education, he at least was convinced that he could be a professional basketball player. He finally proved himself to the doubters at a series of tournaments staged each year for the benefit of pro scouts. Playing against ever-stiffer competition, Pippen excelled in two such tournaments. Suddenly he was no longer an obscure prospect from a rural college, but rather a promising athlete who was certain to be selected high in the first round of the 1987 draft. Jerry Krause, the Chicago Bulls' vice-president for basketball operations, was particularly impressed with Pippen, especially when the young player did not fold up in competition with top NCAA prospects.

Realizing that Pippen would draft in the top ten, Krause struck a deal with the Seattle Seahawks, who had the fifth pick. The Seahawks chose Pippen, then promptly traded him to the Bulls for center Olden Polynice and some other options. Pippen still remembers his selection so high in the 1987 draft as the proudest moment of his life. When he called home, he told the *New York Times*, his mother said:

"Your daddy watched you on TV. He's got tears running down his face."

The first NBA game Scottie Pippen ever saw in person was the one he played in. He reported in *Sports Illustrated* that he was not overawed by the competition with seasoned professional players. "I guess guys who play on national TV get a lot of publicity," he said. "I was expecting more from them." If they were expecting less from Pippen, a rookie, they were soon put straight. Pippen showed consummate skills on both offense and defense, and his skills, combined with those of Michael Jordan, helped to push the Bulls into playoff contention for the first time in years.

The only cloud on Pippen's horizon has been injuries. During his first season with the Bulls he underwent surgery to repair a disc in his spine. After he healed, he became a starter and established himself as the team leader in rebounds, steals, and blocked shots, while being second only to Jordan in scoring. He helped the Bulls to the conference finals against the Detroit Pistons in 1989, but Chicago lost after Pippen suffered a concussion in a collision with

Scottie Pippen (number 33) goes over former Los Angeles Laker Kareem Abdul-Jabbar to score in a March, 1989 game. AP/Wide World Photos.

Piston Bill Laimbeer. Even more devastating to Pippen was a mysterious migraine headache that completely undermined his play in a crucial conference playoff game in 1990. Minutes before the seventh game in the hotly-contested playoff, Pippen began to have trouble with his vision. This was followed by a throbbing headache. "I thought maybe I'd eaten something and gotten poisoned," he told the *Chicago Tribune.* Pippen played in the game, but he was ineffectual, and the Pistons won the conference championship.

Well into the 1991 season Pippen was still enduring questions about "the migraine." He feels that one bad performance kept him from being voted onto the 1991 All-Star team. Worse, it undermined his confidence in himself and his game. "It stayed with me a long while, long into this season," he told the *Chicago Tribune* after the 1991 championship win. "I'd come to games and sit there and wait sometimes, almost like I expected it to happen. And then it wouldn't. But I always had that fear. Nothing like that had ever happened to me before." After a somewhat slow start in the 1990-91 season, Pippen overcame his anxieties and turned in his best year to date. He averaged 17.8 points, 7.3 rebounds, and 6.2 assists per game, while shooting at better than 50 percent from the field for the first time. The Bulls practically waltzed into the playoffs and won the national championship in four games straight.

Pippen told the *Chicago Tribune* that the Bulls' phenomenal 1991 season helped him to overcome his disappointment about his postseason play in 1990 and 1989. "It does make it better," he said. "That gave us an opportunity to redeem ourselves, and I, and my teammates, all got back into a position where we thought we should be last year. We've had a lot of guys step up their efforts to get us here [to the championship]. It's just been a great season."

Success has brought lucrative product endorsements to Pippen, including a Nike television commercial that sets the superstar inside a black-and-white 1940s basketball game. At the end of the commercial, Pippen strolls into the distance with a "scout" who promises him, "You could make hundreds of dollars playing professional basketball, son." The joke is glorious—a recent contract extension guarantees Pippen $18 million for the next five years as a Chicago Bull. That is strictly salary—any product endorsements provide extra income. Pippen has also earned an honor that goes beyond mere dollars and cents. He was chosen to play on the first United States Olympic basketball team to be manned by professionals. His selection to future NBA All-Star teams is assured, provided he stays healthy.

No one has described Scottie Pippen's career more poignantly than his former college coach, Don Dyer. "It's just an amazing story," Dyer told the *Washington Post.* "He started from zero. Nobody recruited him, nobody wanted him . . . . You couldn't have written a better script." As for Pippen himself, he told the *Chicago Tribune* that he sees room for improvement even now. "I feel like people are always going to be looking at my play, especially in big games. There will be no letting down because of my past. But I'm just approaching the game that I'm playing to win it, and whatever I've done doesn't really matter."

Sources

Chicago Tribune, May 24, 1991; June 17, 1991.
New York Times, October 27, 1991.
Sports Illustrated, November 30, 1987.
Washington Post, July 19, 1987.

—Mark Kram

Queen Latifah

Rap singer

Born Dana Owens, c. 1970, in New Jersey; daughter of Lance (a policeman) and Rita (a schoolteacher) Owens. *Education:* Attended Borough of Manhattan Community College.

Addresses: *Home*—Wayne, NJ. *Record company*—Tommy Boy Records, 1747 First Ave., New York, NY 10128.

Career

Began performing in high school as human beat box in rap group *Ladies Fresh;* signed with Tommy Boy Records in 1988; solo recording artist, 1989—. Recorded re-mix of the single "Fame" with David Bowie, 1990; contributed to remake of the O'Jays song "For the Love of Money." Has appeared on the television programs *Fresh Prince of Bel Air, In Living Color,* and *The Arsenio Hall Show.* Appeared in motion pictures *Jungle Fever,* 1991, *Juice,* 1992, and *House Party 2,* 1992. Owner of video store and Flavor Unit Management.

Awards: Named Best New Artist of 1990 by the New Music Seminar in Manhattan; named "Best Female Rapper" in the 1990 *Rolling Stone* readers' poll; nominated for a Grammy Award in 1990.

Sidelights

Queen Latifah has proven to be one of the most notable young artists in the rap music field. As a female who dresses in African-print outfits, she certainly distinguishes herself from the male-domi-

nant, sweatsuit-clad rap establishment. But it's not only because she physically stands out from the rest that she is significant. Latifah's genius lies in intelligent lyrics that promote female self-respect, African-American cultural pride, and the virtues of being positive. She also has an enigmatic, charming personality that impresses her audiences. With her albums, Latifah has won a multicultural, multigenerational following, bringing rap to a larger listenership than many of her fellows.

Latifah was born in New Jersey around 1970 and given the name Dana Owens. When she was eight, a Muslim cousin nicknamed her Latifah, which means "delicate and sensitive" in Arabic. She added 'Queen' when she got her first record contract. Ostensibly, it wasn't to denote rank, but to let black Americans know they are descendants of African kings and queens. "She is very culturally oriented," commented Latifah's mother, Rita Owens, to Peter Watrous in the *New York Times.* "And there are a lot of kings and queens from Africa."

Both of Latifah's parents had musical talent. Her father played drums, and frequently held jam sessions in the house. Latifah and her older brother would hit pots and pans to join in the mood. She also sang in the church choir. One example of her talent came when she won the role as Dorothy in *The Wiz* at Saint Anne's Roman Catholic school. Because of the popularity of the production in auditions, two casts were assembled, including two Dorothys. Latifah's mother, Rita Owens, told Dinitia Smith in *New York* that "She was the only person who got a standing ovation. When she sang 'Home,' people were crying."

When Latifah was still young, her parents separated and were eventually divorced. She, her mother, and the rest of the family moved into a housing project in East Newark, New Jersey. "It wasn't as bad as you might imagine," Latifah admitted to Watrous. "But a project can only get so good, because you're dealing with people with a different mentality, who may not care as much as you might about where you live." Latifah, however, felt a sense of community and camaraderie with the other people there. They all worked together to rid the place of drug dealers and to help each other.

Rita Owens showed the incredible strength that seemed to carry over to her daughter during these years. While working full-time during the week as well as holding a part-time job on the weekends, Latifah's mother also attended college, eventually getting a degree in education. Within two years, she succeeded in moving the family out of the projects. A bright child, Latifah was allowed to skip a grade in elementary school. Owens also managed to find enough money to send her daughter to a parochial school.

In 1980 Rita Owens was teaching art at Irvington High School while Latifah was a student there. Latifah was very active in school, playing as a power forward on the girls basketball team (which won two state championships during her time with the team), earning a high grade point average, and being voted Most Popular, Best All Around, Most Comical, and Best Dancer in her senior year. "In high school I was popular but I wasn't the type of popular other people were," she admitted to Bridgette Davis in the *Chicago Tribune*. While many won popularity for their looks or flirting ability, Latifah continued that "I was just popular for being me. I was popular with the coolest people and the nerds and the introverts."

Latifah hung out with a group of girls who would do rap music in the school bathrooms. She learned how to do the human beat box (making rhythm noises by blowing into a cupped palm)—much like the improvised rhythm of her father's jam sessions. She and friends Tangy B and Landy D heard that there was another female rap group in the area. They joined together to form the group Ladies Fresh and tried out

their act at the Irvington High School talent show. Latifah wrote the songs while her brother Lance served as the DJ. Soon, the ambitious group was performing in any venue they could land. Also, during basketball games, Latifah would perform a little rap to keep the morale high.

Latifah's mother was in charge of getting talent for the high school dances. She was up on the musical trends of the day and she invited Mark James, who was known as D.J. Mark the 45 King, to perform. Latifah and her friends began hanging around James, listening to music in his parents' basement. James began doing some original demos, and the group started calling themselves the Flavor Unit. According to Smith, in rap slang flavor means "something or someone has 'character' or 'a personality all his or her own.'" Eventually, the loosely-formed group would be organized into Flavor Unit Management, a business handling some of the major talents in rap, including Latifah and Naughty by Nature.

> *"We're living in an age when people need to talk. They don't communicate. That's why we have racism."*

After high school Latifah seemed content to attend college and work toward a broadcasting degree. Fate had something else in store for her, however. James took a demo of Latifah's called "Princess of the Posse" to Fred Brathwaite, host of *Yo! MTV Raps*. Brathwaite played it for some people at Tommy Boy Records, and they signed Latifah immediately.

In 1988 Latifah released her first single, "Wrath of My Madness," which sold an acceptable 40,000 copies. It was successful enough to introduce her to the musical community. With the video production of "Ladies First"—which showcased Latifah and other female rappers in an anti-apartheid message— Latifah had arrived. An exciting European tour, and the release of her first album, *All Hail the Queen*, followed. James produced most of the tracks on it.

The album was instantly acclaimed. The Detroit *Metro Times* noted that it "was received with open arms by both the public and critics. The 21-year-old New Jersey rapper broke the male-dominated boundaries of the business with her Afrocentric, woman's point-of-view rhyming and lyricizing." Ultimately, *All Hail the Queen* hit the Number 6 spot on *Billboard*'s rhythm and blues charts. Latifah was also praised for her courage in mixing rap with straight singing—something other rappers didn't do.

The album established her not only for her music ability, but also for her intelligent lyrics. Her theme song, "Ladies First," promoted both chivalry and the idea that women must take a stand for themselves and display self-respect. "We should treat each other like we're first and stop thinking we can't do rap or anything else as good as men," Latifah told Davis. Other songs looked at the issues of homelessness and African-American pride. Within a short time, *All Hail the Queen* proved that Latifah was not just a novelty act in the virtually all-male world of rap. She had established herself as a talented, intelligent musician with something important to say.

As a consequence of her debut effort, according to Watrous, "the Queen became a spokesperson for a neglected constituency—young black women—and for a media hungry for someone articulate, political and savvy about feminism but not confrontational." Fans all over the world looked up to Latifah. Twice she was invited to air her views on feminism at Harvard University. However, in spite of the topics of her songs, Latifah has shrugged off the label of feminist. "I have a fear of feminism," she told Smith. "To me, feminists were usually white women who hated men . . . . I don't want to be classified with them." What she prefers her ideology to be about is "womanism—feminism for black women, to be natural, to have our sisterhood."

Latifah has also become known for her graciousness and generosity toward other female rappers. This is unusual in the rap world, where infighting and competitiveness run rampant. In her own queenly way, Latifah invited female rappers Monie Love, Shelly Thunder, Harmony, Ice Cream Tee, and Ms. Melody to be in her "Ladies First" video. Her feelings about other female rappers has been one of healthy competition. "I'm proud of everybody, and I feel there's room for everybody," she told Alan Light in *Rolling Stone.* "So I don't feel threatened when other girls put out good records—I feel motivated to make a good record as well."

In terms of the other controversies in the world of rap, Latifah still remains supportive of her fellows. She has defended other rappers who use obscenities and see women as playthings in their music. Although she disagrees with their style, she defends their right to artistic expression. "A lot of what these guys are saying needs to be heard . . . They're bring-

ing reality—the reality of the black culture—to a lot of people . . . . I have to defend their right to say these things—even things I don't like," Latifah told Hunt in the *Los Angeles Times.*

Ultimately, this ideal of hers ties into how she feels about the role of rap music in society. "We're living in an age when people need to talk," she told Light. "They don't communicate. That's why we have racism." She feels strongly about the socially-conscious messages of rap music, concluding that "our problems are all about communication, and that's what rap is."

Latifah worked on various projects before releasing her second album; she landed television and movie roles and recorded a re-mix of David Bowie's song "Fame" in a rap format. She then released her eagerly awaited follow-up, *Nature of a Sista,* in 1991. Again, critics commended the rapper's intelligent lyrics as well as her musical ability. After the album was finished, she launched an exciting concert tour of the United States with reggae star Ziggy Marley (see *Newsmakers 90*).

Latifah had high hopes for *Nature of a Sista,* in terms of commercial success. "I really want [it] to go platinum," she told Watrous. "I want to sell a million records. A lot more doors open up if I get that status. Not to mention the money." Latifah, for all her liberal attitudes, is not above making material gains. "I could do a lot more," she claimed, citing numerous companies for which she could make commercials. "I want money, but I only want to endorse things I like."

Without her directly trying to endorse it, Latifah's unique way of dressing has nearly created a fashion trend. Shunning the high heels and tight dresses of her female contemporaries, Latifah opts for African garb—kufi hats, turbans, dashiki shirts, and print pants. "Being Afrocentric and proud of my heritage, that's something I grew up with. My mother always taught me that. When I started rapping, I wanted to make it part of my image," Latifah told Hunt. Besides, she remarked to Davis, "The African gear was the most comfortable. And it's always been that way." Yet she is not so entrenched in her image that she has become rigid. "I want people to know I'm human. Like I make sure I don't dress like this all the time.

Although glad to be in the spotlight, Latifah was ambivalent about her status as a spokesperson. "Being considered a leader can be a hassle," she told Hunt in the *Los Angeles Times.* "Some people put you on a pedestal and don't let you be human. It's like they see themselves in you—they see their best self in you and they expect perfection from their best self....You're forced into feeling you should be perfect. That's not a comfortable thing.''

Latifah surrounds herself with close friends from high school—called ''the posse''—to shield herself from some of the loneliness and isolation that can come from fame. ''I like having people around me who do for me as much as I do for them,'' Latifah commented to Watrous. Latifah returns the favors for them, and also keeps close to many of her friends who are rappers—forming a musical support group, so to speak. So far it seems to have worked—Latifah is remarkably well-balanced considering her quick rise to fame.

Positivity is the key to Latifah's message. She wants to say positive things and make money as well. Overall it has been a successful package for her. With many fans sampling her uplifting and powerful messages, she is enjoying a position of prominence musically and spiritually. Latifah concluded to Hunt that ''it's a great feeling to know that people listen to you—that what you say makes a difference to them.'' However, in the final analysis, Latifah doesn't want to be known solely for her messages; ''I don't use music for politics,'' she commented to Watrous. ''I do not preach...I don't talk about catching dolphins in nets. I just want to speak common sense.''

Selected discography

All Hail the Queen, Tommy Boy, 1989.
Nature of a Sista, Tommy Boy, 1991.

Sources

Books

Contemporary Musicians, volume 6, edited by Michael L. LaBlanc, Gale, 1991.

Periodicals

Chicago Tribune, July 4, 1990.
Detroit Free Press, August 30, 1991.
Ebony, October 1991.
Entertainment Weekly, December 28, 1990.
Essence, May 1991.
Interview, May 1990.
Los Angeles Times, January 28, 1990; September 8, 1991.
Metro Times (Detroit), August 23-September 3, 1991.
Mother Jones, September/October 1990.
Nation, April 16, 1990.
New York, December 3, 1990.
New York Times, August 25, 1991.
People, September 30, 1991.
Rolling Stone, February 22, 1990; October 17, 1991.
Time, May 27, 1991.

—*Nancy Rampson*

Herb Ritts

Lavine/Savu/Archive Photos

Professional photographer

Born c. 1954; son of Shirley Ritts (an interior designer). *Education:* Bard College, B.S. in economics, c. 1975.

Career

Sales representative for his family's Lucite furniture and accessories design company in Los Angeles, CA, c. 1975-79; professional photographer, 1979—. Works have been exhibited in gallery shows in Los Angeles, New York City, London, and Tokyo.

Sidelights

Master photographer Herb Ritts is arguably the hottest thing going in scintillating portraits of superstars. He has captured the likes of Kim Basinger, Madonna, Jack Nicholson, and Don Johnson in unexpected poses. "Drawing from a wide range of classic and pop references, his portraits are both distanced and intimate, playful and studied, and it may be this synthesis of opposites that gives them their contemporary urgency," appraised James Truman in *House and Garden*. Ritts has also distinguished himself in his original studies of nudes, many of which are of males. Marlena Donohue described his work in the *Los Angeles Times* as "a study of light, texture and innately erotic lines."

Oddly enough, Ritts did not set out to become a professional photographer. With a degree in economics from Bard College in hand, he embarked on a sales career for the Ritts family Lucite furniture and

accessories design company in Los Angeles. It was the middle of the 1970s, and Ritts had a talent for sales. Little did he know at the time that he had a far greater latent ability.

This gift surfaced one day when Ritts was out with his up-and-coming actor friend, Richard Gere. While waiting for a tire to be repaired at a desert gas station, Ritts pulled out his new—and first—camera. Taking advantage of sunlight and an automatic light meter, Ritts snapped Gere at various angles. The impromptu shoot wasn't over until three rolls of film were used up. Gere later handed the portraits over to his publicist who promptly convinced *Esquire*, American *Vogue*, and *Mademoiselle* to print them. Ritts's unexpected career in photography was subsequently launched as top-notch assignments started rolling in. His first official free-lance shoot was of actress-model Brooke Shields for *Mademoiselle*.

Ritts appears to have an uncanny ability for being in the right place at the right time. It's no wonder he was voted "most likely to succeed" both in junior and senior high schools. For example, a visit to a friend in New York yielded the opportunity to show the friend's girlfriend his portfolio of fashion shots. The girlfriend happened to be on the payroll of the Italian edition of *Harper's Bazaar* and was impressed with his work. Before long, cases of chic Italian clothes arrived from Milan for Ritts to photograph. As it luck would have it, Matt Collins, a male model, was boarding in Ritts's house in Hollywood Hills. Ritts shot photos of Collins, who looked smashing in the new Italian styles, under the pier in Santa Monica without any of the typical photographer paraphernalia or assistants.

Ritts's career continued to thrive, leading to contracts in the early 1990s with *Rolling Stone* and *Vanity Fair*, to name a few major magazines. Top record companies, movie studios, and ad agencies became his major clients. Ritts's daily rates grew from $750 a day in 1979 to a whopping $20,000 in 1990. Since most outstanding photographers command an average of $5,000 a day, he "could be the highest-paid commercial photographer working in the United States today," observed a writer for the *Los Angeles Times*.

In *W*, Aileen Mehle called Ritts "the brilliant photographer who makes beautiful stars look beautiful and ugly ones look sort of beautiful." This talent, apparently, has translated to television as well. Image-maker Ritts directed one television commercial in which Kim Basinger peddled pantyhose, but it has only been shown in Japan. He then guided an "Equal" sweetener advertisement featuring spokeswoman Cher.

While commercial photography is Ritts's bread and butter, his fine art sales are anything but meager. "He has a very big following from students who get together their pennies to [buy from] major collectors," revealed New York gallery owner Etheleen Staley in the *Los Angeles Times*. The photographer's exhibitions have been held at galleries in Los Angeles, New York City, London, Tokyo, and other major cities. No less than 15,000 visitors viewed Ritts's work at the Parko Gallery in Tokyo in April, 1989. And nearly 2,000 aficionados squeezed into the one-person show that opened on January 13, 1990, in Los Angeles.

Since Ritts has begun showing his work at gallery shows, the prices of his photographs have risen sharply as the demand for his work increases. The very event of an exhibition drives the photographer's prices up. As art dealer David Fahey explained in the *Los Angeles Times*: "I make them reasonably priced until 20 of the 25 are sold, and the last five are way up there." Some of Ritts's works have increased in value considerably. For example, his nudes and portraits shown in a 1985 group exhibition ranged in price from between $400 and $600. One of the popular shots from that show was *Fred with Tires*, which is now priced at $6,000. Other photographs

from the same collection are now worth between $2,500 and $4,000.

Nudes appeared in the photographer's first two exhibitions, while his third show was devoted to them entirely. Fahey was quoted in the same article as describing Ritts's vision as "not manipulated or structured, just more or less focusing on the lines and reinterpreting the nude in a romantic, traditional way . . . . They're beautiful photos by an important emerging photographer who has done well in establishing himself."

Ritts has also published two books of his work, and is secretive about two more upcoming tomes. *Duo*, which features black-and-white duotone photos in high contrast, was published in 1991 and features poses of former Mr. Universe and current bodybuilder Bob Paris with model Rod Jackson, taken in Baja California and the photographer's studio in Los Angeles. According to Drew Hopkins in *Interview*,

> *"The reason it's fun to work with Herb is that it feels like hanging out with a boy who lives down the street."*
> —Madonna

Ritts "has invoked a pure and often stark meditation on the male form, while at the same time maintaining a strong subtext of tenderness and intimacy." Ritts described the photographs in *Duo* as the "visual imagery" of the relationship between the two subjects, who were married in a Unitarian church ceremony in 1989. An edition autographed by Ritts, Paris, and Jackson is also available. All royalties earned from the $60 book are earmarked to further AIDS research through the organization AmFAR. Two volumes make up Ritts's second book, entitled *Men/Women*, and the price tag is $65. Sales on the two works have "rivaled that for Cabbage Patch dolls," publisher Jack Woody told Barbara Isenberg of the *Los Angeles Times*.

Some dealers have disparagingly remarked that Ritts's meteoric rise in the world of photography is a result of the controversy surrounding the work of the late photographer Robert Mapplethorpe, whose homoerotic compositions sparked heated debate over public funding for artists whose works are considered by some to be obscene. Ritts refuted this accusation and explained to Isenberg that he has been most influenced by George Platt Lynes, whose heyday was the 1940s and 1950s.

Ritts achieves his desired effects with texture and form rather than color. As an artist, his "special talent comes in using tightly grained paper and controlling light so as to eliminate surface detail to get huge, broad planes of tone to age the look of an amazing array of textures," observed Marlena Donohue in the *Los Angeles Times*. He also manages to get uncanny poses from superstars. In *House and Garden*, Madonna explained that "the reason it's fun to work with Herb is that it feels like hanging out with a boy who lives down the street." "But don't let the Beaver Cleaver facade fool you," the pop diva advised in *Interview*. "He's a barracuda with a sweet countenance."

In the late 1980s Ritts painstakingly transformed his turn-of-the-century, Hollywood Hills house into the contemporary home of his dreams. Mirroring the owner's artistic style, the house is "spacious, monochromatic, and bathed in natural sunlight, and it advertises a grand vision with quiet understatement," wrote James Truman in *House and Garden*.

Madonna's *True Blue* album cover was shot by Ritts against his garden wall. And while Ritts designed a wrought iron table for his sitting room, there is a paucity of furniture around the house. Richard Gere pointed out in *House and Garden:* "You go around and there isn't even anything to sit on. Most of us buy what we need and replace it [with better pieces] later. Herb won't allow furniture in the house unless it's exactly the right piece."

But the spirited perfectionist didn't have to wait to decorate his walls with the works of great photographers such as Cartier Bresson and Man Ray— artists who occupy a place in the relatively short but glorious history of photography, artists whose ranks Herb Ritts has no doubt joined.

Sources

House and Garden, June 1988.
Interview, October 1988.
Los Angeles Times, December 15, 1989; February 11, 1990.
New Statesman and Society, February 9, 1990.
W, February 3-10, 1992.

—*Victoria France Charabati*

Don Shula

Professional football coach

Full name, Donald Francis Shula; born January 4, 1930, in Grand River, OH; married Dorothy Bartish, July 19, 1958 (died, 1990); children: two sons, three daughters. *Education:* Attended John Carroll University, Cleveland, OH, 1950. *Religion:* Catholic.

Career

Professional football player (defense), 1951-57, began with Cleveland Browns, traded to the Baltimore Colts, 1953, and to the Washington Redskins, 1956; assistant football coach at University of Virginia, 1958; member of coaching staff at University of Kentucky, 1959-61; defensive coordinator for Detroit Lions, 1961-62; head coach of Baltimore Colts, 1963-70, led Colts to Super Bowl III in 1968; head coach of Miami Dolphins, 1970—, led Dolphins to Super Bowls in 1972, 1973, 1974, 1984, and 1985; earned 300th career victory with defeat of Green Bay Packers, September 22, 1991.

Awards: Named NFL Coach of the Year 1964, 1967, 1968, 1971, 1972, and 1973; named NFL Coach of the 1970s, 1980.

Sidelights

Don Shula is what coaching is all about," wrote Mike Freeman in the *Washington Post.* As leader of the Miami Dolphins football team, Shula is a grizzled veteran of three decades of head coaching in a professional sport that hires and fires on the slightest whim. At 61 he began his 28th season in 1991 with credentials that will surely waltz him into the Football Hall of Fame: 300 career victories—100 coming in his first decade of coaching—three consecutive Super Bowl appearances, six visits to the Super Bowl overall, and being the only coach ever to guide a team to a perfect season (the Dolphins went 17-0 in 1972). It is not surprising that *Miami Herald* sports editor Edwin Pope dubbed Shula "the best coach in the history of pro football."

Shula is the winningest active coach in the NFL today, and the secret of his success is hardly a secret at all. For years he has demanded intelligent play from his team members, using brutal and even humiliating tactics to exact perfection. *Tropic* magazine correspondent Dave Barry wrote: "To describe [Shula] as 'intense' would be like describing the universe as 'fairly large' .... He is not, never ever, just one of the guys. This is Don Shula. This is the man who coached Johnny Unitas, won back-to-back Super Bowls, went an entire season without losing a game and has an expressway named after him. And if you say something he thinks is stupid—he hates mental errors—he might just decide to make you writhe like an insect." All-pro defenseman Bubba Smith, who played under Shula in Baltimore, put it another way. Smith told the *Washington Post:* "If a nuclear bomb were to be dropped, the only two things I bet would survive would be Astro-Turf and Don Shula."

Shula is indeed a survivor. Some of the opposing coaches he faces today were still in high school and college when he began his professional career. His longevity in pro football has been sustained by only one factor: winning. In almost 30 years as a head coach, he has had only two losing seasons. His teams have earned berths in post-season play 16 times. All this has been accomplished by a man who has made some of the world's dictators seem benign. "I shoot from the hip and try to be as honest as I can," Shula told the *Tropic.* "Finesse is not part of my game. But in the long run, I've found that players, and family, are more appreciative. They may not like it at the time, and I don't expect them to. But if it helps them in the long run, that's how I'm judged, and that's how I hope that they finally evaluate the situation."

> *"The game has not passed me by. I still enjoy every phase of coaching. I still get excited on game day."*

Few people have shown a stronger commitment to football than Shula. That devotion to the game dates back to his early childhood. He was born in 1930 in Grand River, Ohio, the very cradle of football enthusiasm. He donned spikes as a youngster and earned his first serious injury—a bad cut on the nose—at the tender age of eleven. The cut was so severe that his parents forbade him to play any more football. He was devastated.

The following year, 1942, he forged his parents' signatures on the permission card that would enable him to play football. A bout with pneumonia just before the season began left him weak and unable to play, but an assistant coach encouraged him to return as soon as he could. He did eventually rejoin the team, but kept his participation secret from his family until he became a starter. Only then did his parents relent and agree to watch him perform. In his first game he returned a punt 75 yards for a touchdown. Overnight his parents became his biggest fans.

In 1946 Shula was named All-Ohio quarterback as a senior at Thomas W. Harvey High School. Like many other talented athletes, he enjoyed participating in other sports, and he excelled in basketball, track, and baseball, where he played second base and outfield. After graduation he went on to John Carroll University in Cleveland and continued to make news as a football star. One memorable game saw him gain 125 yards in a 21-15 upset over Syracuse University. Not surprisingly, several professional teams expressed interest in him.

Shula began his pro career in his home state, with the Cleveland Browns. There he was put on defense, and he showed a talent for intercepting passes—including one he ran 96 yards for a touchdown, only to see the play nullified by a penalty. In 1953 Shula was part of a 15-player trade to the Baltimore Colts. He spent three years on the roster with that franchise and then had his contract sold to the Washington Redskins. His playing career ended without great fanfare in 1957.

Newly married to Dorothy Bartish at the time, Shula was reluctant to leave football behind permanently. He was therefore quite pleased when the University of Virginia offered him an assistant coaching job in 1958. The following year he moved to the University of Kentucky as part of that team's staff. Where he had been an average player at best, Shula showed uncanny skill as a coach, and his work at Virginia and Kentucky quickly drew the notice of the professionals. By 1961—after only three years on the college level—he joined the Detroit Lions as defensive coordinator.

His rise after that was no less meteoric. In 1963, with just two years of professional coaching experience to his name, he was asked to become head coach of the Baltimore Colts. He was only 33 at the time, the youngest head coach in NFL history. The Colts had a proud tradition in Baltimore, but even so, few were prepared for the era Don Shula launched in that city. In his second season with the franchise he led the Colts to a 12-2 record and earned the first of six "Coach of the Year" awards. The Colts went 10-3 in 1965 and 9-5 in 1966 before exploding in 1967 with an 11-1-2 record. Still the post-season honors eluded Shula, and he was determined to get to a Super Bowl by any means necessary.

Shula became famous for his sideline tantrums and practice-session tirades. A number of his former players swear they would never *ever* play for Don Shula again, that he could be ruthless and humiliating. Dave Barry wrote in *Tropic:* "I think just about anybody who ever played any kind of sport is afraid of [Shula], on some level. He's the ultimate Coach Figure, and he evokes feelings of inadequacy, memories of having your butt chewed out for failing some long-ago testosterone test by striking out or quitting the team or not getting back into the game when your leg is only broken partway through for God's sake and the trainer put a whole roll of tape on it, what are you some kind of fairy? That's the way Shula makes you feel, without even seeming to try.''

These tactics alone would not win ball games, however. What Shula showed from his earliest years was an unusually intelligent approach to the game, a dizzying array of plays that made the best use of some extremely talented players. Shula finally got his Super Bowl bid with the Colts in 1968. His team went 13-1 during the regular season and was highly favored to beat the New York Jets. Unfortunately for Shula, the Jets handed the Colts an upset in Super Bowl III.

After one more season with the Colts, Shula moved south to Miami in 1970 to coach the Dolphins. The year before he arrived, the Dolphins had compiled a 3-10-1 record, but Shula was undaunted. In the middle of a Florida summer, he instituted four-a-day practices and demanded that his players shave and keep short haircuts. In just one season he turned the team around, bringing it to a 10-4 record and earning a spot in the playoffs. Then the Shula era in Miami *really* began.

By 1971 the Dolphins had become a potent force in the American Football Conference (AFC). They advanced to the 1972 Super Bowl on a 10-3-1 record, only to be beaten 24-3 by the Dallas Cowboys. Chastised bitterly by Shula, the Dolphins returned the following year and turned in a legendary season. They went undefeated through 14 regular season games, then breezed into the Super Bowl and defeated the Washington Redskins 14-7. The perfect 17-0 year was Shula's tenth as a head coach, and it was also the year that saw him earn his 100th victory. He was 43.

Shula's Dolphins continued to set precedents in the 1973-74 season, when they returned to the Super Bowl for a third consecutive year. This time they beat the Minnesota Vikings, 24-7. The victory was just one part of a phenomenal four-year stint during which the Dolphins played 62 games without back-to-back losses and earned a 53-9 record. His temperamental outbursts notwithstanding, Shula was named Coach of the 1970s in 1980.

The Dolphins have only had two bad years—1976, when they went 6-8, and 1988, when they went 6-10. In between, Shula protected his career by returning to the Super Bowl in 1984, only to lose 27-

17 to the Redskins. In typical Shula fashion, the coach called off Miami's ticker-tape parade for the team, saying such celebrations were only for winners. The Dolphins tried again in 1984-85, advancing to the Super Bowl on the talents of quarterback Dan Marino. During that season—and into the playoffs— Shula pioneered the no-huddle offense, a series of plays run quickly in order to mystify the opposing defenders. Even so, the Dolphins lost a hard-fought game to the San Francisco 49ers, under 49ers coach Bill Walsh.

By the late 1980s, according to *Washington Post* correspondent Mike Freeman, "people were questioning if the game had passed Shula by. When the Dolphins suffered four straight non-playoff seasons, Shula was lumped in with legends Tom Landry and Chuck Noll as coaches who had possibly lost it." Shula admits he has mellowed—especially since the loss of his wife to cancer in 1990—but he still thinks he can outwit any other coach in the NFL, and he is out to prove it. His Dolphins made the playoffs in 1990 and brought Shula his 300th career victory early in the 1991 season. Don Shula's job in Miami is hardly in peril.

A father of five and a grandfather, Shula says he still feels every bit as enthusiastic about football as he did when he began coaching the pros in 1963. "One of the biggest things for me is . . . I still think of myself as a young coach," he told the *Washington Post*. "The game has not passed me by. I still enjoy every phase of coaching. I still get excited on game day." Shula told the *Miami Herald:* "I've been in Super Bowls in the '60s, in the '70s, in the '80s—I want to be in one in the '90s . . . . In Super Bowls, I've coached in more than anybody else, but I'm 2-4. I don't want to end with a losing record."

Shula also stands in good position to become the coach with the most wins in the history of football. George Halas, the only other NFL coach to win more than 300 games, won only 325 over 36 seasons. Shula could beat that record in a total of 30 seasons or less. Shula told the *Washington Post* in 1991 that the numbers mean very little to him, though. "I've never thought about 300 the way other people are [thinking about it]," he said. "I've always been a today and tomorrow kind of guy. Really, I think about Sunday and then the next Sunday. The most important thing is this year. We have to win ball games this year. That's what's really important."

Asked in the *Tropic* what he likes best about his job, Shula had a quick reply: "I don't think that there's anything that rivals what happens after a ball is kicked off—the excitement, the emotional highs and lows. It's unreal. I don't think it can be duplicated in any [other] job in that short a period of time.''

Sources

Miami Herald, November 29, 1983; October 28, 1984; January 8, 1985; July 10, 1988.
Tropic (Miami, Florida), September 11, 1988.
Washington Post, September 22, 1991.

—Mark Kram

Paul Simon

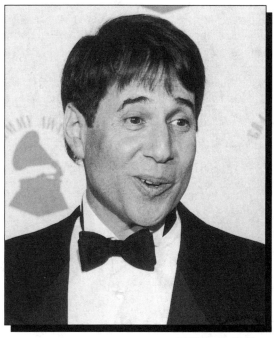

Singer and songwriter

B orn November 5, 1942 (some sources say 1941), in Newark, NJ; son of Louis (a college professor and musician) and Belle (an elementary schoolteacher) Simon; married Peggy Harper, 1969 (divorced, 1975); married Carrie Fisher (an actress and writer), 1983 (divorced, 1983); children: Harper (son). *Education:* Received B.A. from Queens College; briefly attended Brooklyn Law School.

Addresses: *Home*—New York, NY. *Office*—c/o Warner Bros. Records, 3300 Warner Blvd., Burbank, CA 91510.

Career

S inger and songwriter, 1956—. Performed with Art Garfunkel as Tom and Jerry, 1957-59, and as Simon and Garfunkel, 1964-71; solo performer, 1971—. Has appeared in numerous cable television concerts and in several commercial television specials, including *Simon and Garfunkel*, CBS-TV, 1969, and *Paul Simon*, NBC-TV, 1977. Producer of and actor in film *One Trick Pony*, 1980. Has made several appearances on television show *Saturday Night Live*.

Awards: Numerous Grammy Awards, including (with Garfunkel) for best album, 1969, for *The Graduate;* (with Garfunkel) for best performance by a pop vocal group, 1969, for "Mrs. Robinson"; (with Garfunkel) for best album, 1970, for *Bridge Over Troubled Water;* (with Garfunkel) for best single, 1970, for "Bridge Over Troubled Water"; (with Garfunkel) for best performance by a pop vocal group, 1970, for "Bridge Over Troubled Water"; for best album, 1975, for *Still Crazy After All These Years;* for best album, 1987, for *Graceland;* Emmy Award, 1977, for musical special *Paul Simon;* United Negro College Fund Frederick D. Patterson Award, 1989; 1990 inductee (with Garfunkel) into the Rock and Roll Hall of Fame. Holds nine platinum and fourteen gold records.

Sidelights

T he thing that happens to musicians in middle age," Paul Simon told *Newsweek* in 1991, "especially if you've had a lot of success, a lot of attention, is that there comes a point when you either rediscover why you love music or it just becomes slick." Simon, one of the most successful folk-rockers of the 1960s, has been able to sustain his prominence through more than two decades and through a number of fleeting musical fads. As a member of Simon and Garfunkel, and later as a solo performer, the singer-songwriter seems to have stayed in style precisely because he is continually "rediscovering" musical styles—from folk-influenced rock ballads to rollicking gospel, blues, jazz, and reggae-fueled tunes to an eclectic brand of "world music."

A *New Yorker* contributor noted that Simon's collected body of works "form[s] one of the most original and moving bodies of pop music in America." Addressing himself to the lyrics Simon has written, *Saturday Review* essayist Bruce Pollock claimed: "Simon's songs mirrored the alienation, malaise, and despair of the [1960s] era, but did so melodiously, with a good beat, so you could dance to them.... Like the rest of us, Paul Simon has finally passed through adolescence, long considered a terminal condition not only of rock 'n' roll but also of the generation that came to majority in the Sixties. That generation became hooked on rock music as a way of receiving its essential data. And today these same listeners, older and somewhat wiser, continue to respond to Simon [who has] arrived at a more mature perspective and [is] able to mirror in [his] works something beyond pop platitudes."

> "I feel that you should use fame and wealth to make some kind of contribution to the community that you live in and the world at large."

Simon grew up in Forest Hills, a middle-class section of Queens, New York. The son of educators, he has described himself as a happy child who had a keen interest in sports. He discovered popular music at the same time that rock and roll was discovering itself—in the early 1950s. At this time he became friends with Art Garfunkel, a tall, gangly youth who lived in his neighborhood. Virtually inseparable, the two boys would spend their days listening to the radio, playing their Elvis Presley and Bill Haley and the Comets records, and attending local rock concerts. Accompanied by Simon's acoustic guitar, the pair began singing together in the mid-1950s, performing at private parties and school dances. Encouraged by their growing local popularity, the duo decided to cut a demonstration record at a Manhattan recording studio. The demo so impressed a producer from Big Records that he offered the pair a recording contract.

While they were still in high school, Simon and Garfunkel, then dubbed "Tom and Jerry," had their first success—a single entitled "Hey, Schoolgirl," which sold more than 100,000 copies. Thanks to the success of this single, they were invited to sing on

American Bandstand and several other rock and roll television shows of the time. Simon recalls these early days with mixed feelings. "I must have been very angry, probably about not growing [tall]," he told *People*. "I was doing well. When I was fifteen Artie and I played on *American Bandstand*. I batted first on the baseball team. I had a school jacket with letters and everything on it. I was popular. But I was a real angry guy. I spent a lot of time by myself playing guitar."

Tom and Jerry did not follow up their first hit song with others. Instead, Simon and Garfunkel went their separate ways, Simon to study English literature at Queens College, and Garfunkel to enter the architecture program at Columbia University. They were, however, eventually reunited in the early 1960s, at which time Simon was unenthusiastically taking classes at Brooklyn Law School. During their separation Simon had never given up music entirely; in fact, he had been working as a backup musician and songwriter for several New York recording studios and had even traveled briefly to England, where he performed in folk clubs. Upon their reunion he and Garfunkel began performing original folk tunes at outdoor concerts and small clubs, soon attracting a regional following. Their big break came in 1964 when they were offered a recording contract with the Columbia label.

Their first album, *Wednesday Morning, 3 A.M.*, was influenced by the work of such established folk artists as Bob Dylan and Joan Baez and combined traditional as well as original folk pieces. Although *Wednesday Morning* attracted little attention, in late 1965, more than a year after the album's debut, Columbia—without Simon's knowledge—overdubbed a rock accompaniment to one of the album's songs, "The Sounds of Silence." Released as a single, the remixed version of the song shot to the number one spot on the *Billboard* Top 100 chart. A string of hits followed for the duo, including "I Am a Rock," "Mrs. Robinson," "Scarborough Fair/Canticle," "The Boxer," and "The 59th Street Bridge Song (Feelin' Groovy)," most of which are still staples of "classic rock" radio stations. With songs such as these, which subtly combined Simon's meditative but hard-hitting and ironic lyrics with Garfunkel's softly expressive voice, the pair went on to become the most commercially successful urban folk performers of the day.

According to Dave Marsh in the *Rolling Stone Record Guide*, Simon and Garfunkel's "socially relevant but gentle folk rock . . . quietly bridged the Sixties generation gap." Marsh added that Simon's "elliptical, imagistic writing soon became very big on the rock-lyrics-are-poetry circuit, but he was really an expert popular-song craftsman, influenced by both folk and rock but owing allegiance to neither." Simon was largely responsible for the arranging, recording, and mixing of the duo's songs, but it was Garfunkel—whose clear tenor voice and gentle appearance charmed audiences—who frequently received credit for the group's success. This conundrum became painfully clear soon after Simon and Garfunkel released their best-known hit, "Bridge Over Troubled Water," in 1970. The song and the album of the same title sold more than nine million copies in two years, yet even that level of achievement failed to save the musical relationship. Though they had become inseparable in the public eye, the two performers had highly divergent personalities and, after years of strained relations, Simon and Garfunkel split in 1971 to pursue solo careers. It was thought by some that Garfunkel's budding career as an actor (he was to appear in such films as *Catch-22* and *Carnal Knowledge*) was in large part responsible for the pair's disbanding at the peak of their popularity. Concerning their split, Simon remarked to Jan Hodenfield in the *New York Post*, "It ended, and I sort of didn't

want to be a partner. I didn't want to be always half of something . . . . I think we were both in agreement that the end had come because it was too hard after it had been easy." Excluding a brief appearance at a political rally in 1972, the pair would not sing together again in public until they gave a highly acclaimed concert in New York City's Central Park in 1981.

Although critics issued dire predictions about Simon's viability as a solo artist, they greatly underestimated the singer-songwriter's talent for incorporating various musical styles into his repertory while continuing to issue his poetic and introspective lyrics. In fact, the music that Simon produced during the course of his solo career is considerably more complex and varied than his work with Garfunkel. As Janet Maslin argued in *The Rolling Stone Illustrated Guide of Rock and Roll*, "Paul Simon and Randy Newman are virtually alone among singer/songwriters in their capacity for accompanying highly polished lyrics with music of comparable sophistication." Simon's first solo album, *Paul Simon*, for example, impressively combined jazz, reggae, Latin, and rock in a cosmopolitan mix. Released in

Paul Simon performs his first South African concert in Johannesburg's Ellis Park in January of 1992. Reuters/Bettmann.

1972, this album included the reggae-flavored hit "Mother and Child Reunion" and every Simon album since has contained at least one memorable single.

Following his debut solo album Simon released a series of equally ambitious and eclectic works, culminating in *Still Crazy After All These Years*, which was awarded the 1975 Grammy Award for best album. Yet, while the songwriter's wistful, often wry lyrics and enthusiasm for experimentation remained, the subject matter of Simon's solo works tended to be rather narrow in scope, examining the artist's highly personal views on love and life resulting in such bittersweet hit songs as "Love Me Like a Rock," "Late in the Evening," "Fifty Ways to Leave Your Lover," and "Slip Slidin' Away."

Although by the mid-1970s Simon had firmly established himself as one of rock music's premier craftsmen, after the release of his 1983 *Hearts and Bones* album, the songwriter experienced a deep sense of artistic anxiety. This was due in part to the poor airplay his most recent album had received. As Simon told *Esquire*, "I was just a blank. I had done *Hearts and Bones*, and [radio stations] didn't play it. I don't know why. My first reaction was that I had done something bad, I was being punished . . . . I had come to assume, gradually, that I would write ten songs, and one of them would be a hit, usually not the one I thought." Moreover, not only was he burnt out musically, Simon was also experiencing the pain of his recent divorce with actress Carrie Fisher, with whom he had lived for seven years prior to their marriage. The songwriter was eventually saved from his creative crisis by a friend who introduced him the "township jive" songs of black South African musicians. So impressed was he with this music that in 1985 Simon traveled to Johannesburg and there recorded several partial tracks with prominent South African musicians. Although he was not aware of this at the time, these tracks would form the basis for what was to become Simon's most highly acclaimed album to date, *Graceland*.

With the release of *Graceland*, Simon moved away from the introspective stance of earlier solo albums, searching for new forms of musical expression and demonstrating what *Rolling Stone*'s John McAlley called "a willingness to explore a world of ideas and feelings outside the labyrinthine complexity of his own psyche." Winner of the 1987 Grammy Award for best album, *Graceland* is a frankly experimental record mixing the distinctive *mbaquanga* beat of South African musicians with Simon's haunting lyrics. Deemed by McAlley "a spirited, cross-cultural

masterpiece," *Graceland*, though it was to receive little airplay outside of its hit "Call Me Al," was a commercial as well as critical success, becoming Simon's first million-selling album in over a decade.

Graceland was also an important album for the music industry as a whole because it introduced large numbers of listeners to South African variations of "world music," a label loosely referring to any non-English-speaking musician singing in his or her native language. Although such artists as the Talking Heads and Peter Gabriel had previously experimented with pan-world rhythms in their music, it was the release of *Graceland* that afforded Western audiences the opportunity to hear such world musical acts as Ladysmith Black Mambazo, Hugh Masekela, Youssou N'Dour, and Miriam Makeba. Considered by Robert Browning, director of the World Music Institute, a "milestone," *Graceland* and its accompanying tour—in which Simon served as more of an emcee and backup musician than headlining artist—exposed enormous audiences to decidedly non-Western music and culture.

Simon followed the huge success of *Graceland* with *The Rhythm of the Saints* (1990), his first collection of new songs in four years and an album that extended his foray into world-beat music. Blending Brazilian drums and African guitars with his typically subtle, understated lyrics, this album introduced its audience to the ritual rhythms of *candomble*, an Afro-Brazilian cult that mixes African spirits with Roman Catholic icons. More inherently spiritual than Simon's previous works, *The Rhythm of the Saints*, according to McAlley, examined "with visionary beauty and brooding intensity the viability of faith in a corrupt, heartless and sometimes merely predictable world."

As he had done in putting together *Graceland*, Simon approached the making of this album in a rather unorthodox manner. Whereas most singer-songwriters write their songs first and then assemble musicians to record these songs, Simon inverted this process in the making of *The Rhythm of the Saints*. That is, without any songs in mind Simon journeyed to Brazil, where he recorded local drummers playing traditional rhythms. Taking these tracks back to his New York studio, he improvised melodies and lyrics until the songs gradually emerged. Describing such a process to *Newsweek*, he remarked, "When the groove is there you have the heart and the body going. When you start to add the brain [the chords, melodies, and lyrics], the editing process tells you what's right and wrong." In making *The Rhythm of the Saints* in such a manner, Simon produced a unique, hybrid mixture that *Maclean's* Brian D.

Johnson described as "hot tropical roots meet[ing] the cool breeze of a cerebral pop sensibility." Although Simon's last two albums have consciously broken down musical and cultural barriers, the artist does not feel that his recent experimenting with world music has caused him to turn away from his roots. As he explained to *Maclean's*, "I don't think I've left my own Northern Hemisphere permanently. I know that every artist is always looking to come home. And the further out there you get, the more interesting the route home."

While critics have occasionally accused his songs of being overly nostalgic and at times even despairing, Simon has never apologized for the somber tone of his lyrics—noticeable since his earliest songs. "I'm investigating...all the time, asking what is the problem, what is it," he told *Esquire*'s Jennifer Allen. "Part of my personality keeps pushing at what hurts, what hurts." Moreover, in spite of the angst his songs frequently contain, Simon resents the image many have of him as a melancholy artist. "They always ask me if I'm happy when I'm finished with my work," he told Allen. "Happy? Who's happy? What's happy? It's a dumb question."

Simon's personal life has frequently provided material for his introspective lyrics. Twice married and divorced, he admits to having difficulties sustaining close relationships. He has reconciled with Garfunkel to the extent that they occasionally play and record together (they shared a 1975 hit "My Little Town," for instance), but he prefers solitude or the company of his son Harper, an aspiring musician. Completely ambidextrous, as a child Simon dreamed of becoming a professional baseball player and, though he has learned to deal with the fact now, early in his career he was so sensitive about his height that he preferred to be photographed from below. A perfectionist and perpetual self-improver, Simon has taken voice lessons, composition lessons, and even juggling lessons. Intensely private—he rarely grants interviews—Simon dislikes talking about his personal life, although he candidly acknowledges that *Still Crazy After All These Years* in part chronicles the dissolution of his marriage to Peggy Harper and admits that certain lyrics in the title song to *Graceland* cathartically address his painful divorce from Carrie Fisher.

In spite of his penchant for privacy, Simon believes that his status as an artist carries with it a social responsibility. As he told *Maclean's*, "I feel that you should use fame and wealth to make some kind of contribution to the community that you live in and the world at large." Yet, he adds, he avoids using his songs to preach messages: "When I find myself

[preaching] I always pull back. I like the subtext better—which doesn't mean that I don't think concern should be expressed about the rain forest or repression in Central or South America. But a song is a very fragile form." Simon's contributions to numerous charitable causes attest to his willingness to act upon issues he feels are important, whether they involve preserving the Amazonian rain forest, providing housing for New York City's homeless, or restoring a crumbling lighthouse near his Long Island, New York, summer home. Simon has also worked with the Children's Health Fund in Manhattan, a group bringing medical attention to poor and underprivileged children, and has raised money for the Fund for Detained and Imprisoned Children in South Africa. In recognition of his fund-raising efforts, the United Negro College Fund in 1989 awarded the songwriter its highest honor, the Frederick D. Patterson Award.

In addition to lending his musical talents to various charitable causes, Simon has also been one of the music community's most politically active members. The songwriter's activism is not a recent phenomenon, however, as one of his earliest compositions, "He Was My Brother," a song Simon calls his "first serious song," was written to commemorate the death of his college classmate, Andrew Goodman, a civil rights worker slain in Mississippi in 1964. Yet it was his *Graceland* project that thrust Simon into the political spotlight when it was learned that a number of the album's tracks were recorded in South Africa. Viewing Simon's use of South African musicians as a refutation of United Nations cultural sanctions against South Africa, single-issue groups attacked the singer's actions. Further exacerbating the situation was the fact that exiled South African musicians Hugh Masekela and Miriam Makeba joined Simon in a 1987 concert before a racially mixed crowd in Zimbabwe. Arguing that he had turned down a number of offers to play in South Africa, Simon wrote a letter to the United Nations Special Committee Against Apartheid explaining that he had refused to perform there and that he unequivocally supported the boycott.

More recently, however, Simon has again aggravated certain groups within South Africa with his decision to bring his 1992 tour to Johannesburg. Although the United Nations General Assembly had lifted the cultural boycott against South Africa, the Azanian Youth Organization (Azayo), a radical black consciousness group, warned Simon not to perform in the politically turbulent country. Feeling that genuine political reform in South Africa had not yet begun, Azayo, backed by the Pan Africanist Congress, threatened violence, if needed, to stop Simon from performing. Supported by Nelson Mandela's African National Congress (ANC) and the predominantly black South African Musician's Alliance, Simon nevertheless performed in Johannesburg, even after a grenade attack on the office of the concert's promoters. Despite the controversies caused by this tour, Simon refused to back down under outside pressures, even violent ones. As he once explained to *Esquire*, "By nature I'm a tenacious person."

When not fulfilling his role as pop music's premier globetrotter, Simon spends his time composing songs in his New York City apartment. The singer has written more than 250 songs and, since he has retained the rights to all of them, is very wealthy. He told *People*: "Entertainers are paid disproportionately high sums of money for their contribution to society. I used to feel guilty, but now I accept that gratefully. When someone tells me, 'You've given me a lot of pleasure in my life,' it all seems like a gratifying, very pure way of earning money." Undaunted by the fact that he is almost 50 years old, Simon plans to continue composing and performing his musically rich and emotionally complex music as long as he has an audience that wants to hear him. "If I'm healthy," he told *People*, "I'll still be doing what I've done since I was 13—writing songs. It's as exhilarating now as ever. I get a very satisfied feeling that I never get in any other part of my life."

Selected discography

With Art Garfunkel

Wednesday Morning, 3 A.M., Columbia, 1964.
The Sounds of Silence, Columbia, 1966.
Parsley, Sage, Rosemary and Thyme, Columbia, 1966.
Bookends, Columbia, 1968.
The Graduate (soundtrack), Columbia, 1968.
Bridge Over Troubled Water, Columbia, 1970.
Simon and Garfunkel's Greatest Hits, Columbia, 1972.
Concert in Central Park, Warner Bros., 1981.

Solo recordings

The Paul Simon Songbook, Columbia, 1965.
Paul Simon, Columbia, 1972; reissued, Warner Bros., 1988.

There Goes Rhymin' Simon, Columbia, 1973; reissued, Warner Bros., 1988.
Live Rhymin': Paul Simon in Concert, Columbia, 1974; reissued, Warner Bros., 1988.
Still Crazy After All These Years, Columbia, 1975.
Greatest Hits Etc., Columbia, 1977.
One Trick Pony, WEA, 1980.
Hearts and Bones, Warner Bros., 1983.
Graceland, Warner Bros., 1986.
The Rhythm of the Saints, Warner Bros., 1990.

Sources

Books

Contemporary Musicians, volume 1, edited by Michael L. LaBlanc, Gale, 1989.
The Rolling Stone Illustrated History of Rock and Roll, edited by Jim Miller, Random House, 1976.
The Rolling Stone Record Guide, edited by Dave Marsh, Random House/Rolling Stone Press, 1979.
Simon, George T., *The Best of the Music Makers*, Doubleday, 1979.

Periodicals

Detroit Free Press, January 7, 1992.
Esquire, June 1987.
Guitar Player, February 1991.
High Fidelity, May 1982.
Jet, March 20, 1989.
Maclean's, November 12, 1990.
Melody Maker, November 26, 1977.
Newsweek, January 14, 1991.
New Yorker, September 2, 1967; April 29, 1972.
New York Post, May 26, 1973.
New York Times, February 27, 1972; February 28, 1982.
New York Times Magazine, October 13, 1968.
People, November 3, 1980; September 5, 1983; October 6, 1986.
Rolling Stone, May 28, 1970; October 30, 1980; October 15, 1981; July 2, 1987; November 15, 1990.
Saturday Review, June 12, 1976.
Time, January 31, 1972.
Variety, March 22-28, 1989.

—*Robert F. Scott and Anne Janette Johnson*

Barbra Streisand

Singer, actress, and film director

Born Barbara Joan Streisand, April 24, 1942, in Brooklyn, NY; daughter of Emanuel (a literature teacher) and Diana (Rosen) Streisand; married Elliot Gould (an actor), March, 1963 (divorced); children: Jason. *Education:* Graduated from Erasmus Hall High School, 1959; attended Yeshiva of Brooklyn.

Addresses: *Home*—New York, NY; and 5775 Ramirez Canyon Rd., Malibu, CA 90265.

Career

Worked as a singer in nightclubs around New York City, including the Lion and Bon Soir, 1960-61; made professional theatrical debut in Off-Broadway production *An Evening With Henry Stoones*, 1961; made Broadway debut in the musical *I Can Get It For You Wholesale*, 1962; star of musical comedy *Funny Girl* on Broadway and in London, 1964-67; recording artist with Columbia Records, 1962—; star of numerous television specials, including *My Name is Barbra*, 1964. Films include *Funny Girl*, 1968, *Hello, Dolly*, 1969, *The Owl and the Pussycat*, 1970, *What's Up, Doc?*, 1972, *Up The Sandbox*, 1972, *The Way We Were*, 1973, *For Pete's Sake*, 1974, *Funny Lady*, 1975, *A Star Is Born* (also co-producer), 1976, *The Main Event*, 1979, *All Night Long*, 1981, *Yentl* (also director and producer), 1983, *Nuts* (also producer), 1987, and *The Prince of Tides* (also producer and director), 1991.

Awards: Winner of eight Grammy Awards, including best female pop vocalist, 1963, 1964, 1965, 1967, 1977, 1986, and special Grammy Award, 1992; Academy Award for best actress, 1969, for *Funny Girl*; Academy Award for best song of the year (with Paul Williams), 1976, for "Evergreen"; Academy Award nomination for best picture, 1992, for *The Prince of Tides*; numerous Golden Globe awards, including best musical/comedy and best director, 1983, for *Yentl*; recipient of special Tony Award, 1970; recipient of Emmy Awards; nominated for Directors Guild Award for best director, 1992, for *The Prince of Tides*.

Sidelights

Over the course of her long career, Barbra Streisand has defined the word "superstar" by her excellence in many areas of the entertainment industry. She was still a teenager when she was first acclaimed for her powerful singing, and within a few years, her electrifying performances on Broadway had also won her the titles of actress and comedienne. By the time she was 25 years old, she had gone west to take Hollywood by storm, proving herself in motion pictures first as an actress, then as a producer, and most recently as a director.

Streisand's determination to be something special arose early in her less-than-happy childhood in Brooklyn, New York. Her father died when she was just over a year old, leaving his family in difficult financial and emotional circumstances. Her mother remarried five years later, but Barbra was alienated by her cold, distant stepfather. By the age of 14 she was full of an intense longing to escape Brooklyn and its "baseball, boredom and bad breath," as she was quoted as saying in *Premiere* magazine. At 16 she graduated with honors from high school and immediately left Brooklyn for Manhattan, where she hoped to realize her dream of becoming an actress.

In her earliest days of searching for stage work, Streisand carried a folding cot under her arm and squatted in the apartments and offices of friends. Within a few months she had her own studio apartment, was enrolled in several acting classes, and had parts in a few obscure off-Broadway productions. In one of these, she befriended a cast member

---

"When I came to Hollywood in 1967, I was intimidated by the movie stars....[The day after a Hollywood party] I read in the columns that I was arrogant and aloof. The truth is, I was absolutely frozen to my seat."

---

who owned a sizable collection of recordings by famed vaudevillian Fanny Brice. The two young actors listened to Brice for hours at a time, and were inspired to create a nightclub act for Barbra—one that included singing. She knew that her untrained voice was special, but she hadn't given much consideration to singing professionally. As Kevin Sessums noted in a *Vanity Fair* profile, "Streisand always considered herself an actress, and from the beginning used her singing talent as a means to an emotive end. But it was the Voice, more than anything else, that catapulted her show-business career."

Streisand's singing won her a loyal following at such New York nightclubs as the Showplace, the Ninth Circle, and the Lion. She began getting bookings in mainstream clubs after winning a talent contest at the Lion in 1961. She had a long engagement at the Bon Soir, a chic Manhattan nightspot, and that

exposure led to appearances on local television programs and a stint on the road as Liberace's opening act. While Streisand enjoyed the publicity her singing brought her, her sights remained fixed on acting. One of the biggest obstacles she had to overcome was her own distaste for casting practices, which she considered humiliating. "I always had too much pride to knock on people's doors and say, 'Give me a job,'" Streisand told *Ladies' Home Journal* contributor Paul Rosenfield. "I would have given up the career if I had not gotten the job in [her first Broadway musical] *I Can Get It For You Wholesale*. I would have become a hat designer."

In *I Can Get It For You Wholesale*, Streisand stopped the show in the supporting role of Miss Marmelstein, a brash and homely secretary. The show ran for nine months; when it closed, Streisand was a bona fide star. She signed a recording contract with Columbia, and her very first recording, *The Barbra Streisand Album*, became the top-selling record released by a woman in 1963. She was a unique talent, a Broadway powerhouse in an era dominated by folksingers and English rock bands. At the age of 20, she had the opportunity to headline her first show when she auditioned for the lead in *Funny Girl*, a musical based on the life of Fanny Brice. She coveted the part, which would allow her to showcase her flair for comedy, drama, and song. But the show's producers were concerned that she was too young to be convincing as the matron she would have to play in the second act. They subjected Streisand to seven grueling auditions while considering Anne Bancroft, Carol Burnett, and Mary Martin as alternate candidates for the Brice role. After the producer gave Streisand the part, she took *Funny Girl* through triumphant runs in both New York and London. The show "thrust her permanently into the cultural consciousness," stated Sessums, and she became inexorably identified with her role.

When producer Ray Stark began planning a film version of *Funny Girl* in 1967, there was no question that anyone but Streisand would star in it. Her formidable stage presence translated well to film. A *Newsweek* reviewer called her portrayal of Brice "the most accomplished, original and enjoyable musical comedy performance ever put on film," and she won an Academy Award for best actress in 1969. To the disappointment of her fans in New York, she chose to remain on the West Coast after completing the film, rather than return to Broadway. Through the late 1960s and early 1970s, she released a steady string of films that demonstrated the amazing scope of her talents. *Hello, Dolly* found her carrying another blockbuster musical; *The Owl and the Pussy-*

cat and *What's Up, Doc?* emphasized her comic abilities; and in *The Way We Were*, a bittersweet romantic drama, she was a convincing partner for the favorite leading man of the day, Robert Redford.

Although Streisand is commonly perceived as an extremely confident person, she considers herself "very shy"; she told Rosenfield: "When I came to Hollywood in 1967, I was intimidated by the movie stars." Early in her career, at a party given in her honor, she was awed by guests such as Marlon Brando and Cary Grant. "The next day I read in the columns that I was arrogant and aloof. The truth is, I was absolutely frozen to my seat," she remembered. That incident marked the beginning of a longstanding antagonism between Streisand and some elements of the Hollywood press. She was frequently reported to be temperamental and very difficult to work with. When she began producing some of her own films, she was portrayed as one obsessed with control. "People see [producing] as some ego trip, and it's the weirdest thing," she commented to Rosenfield. "What does producing mean? It means getting it on the screen, watching over it like it's my baby. What's wrong with a woman doing that? How could anyone *not* want to be in control of their work? It's a very anti-feminist thing we're talking about here."

During the mid-1970s, the direction of Streisand's career was partially influenced by Jon Peters, a Hollywood hairdresser with whom she was romantically involved. Their relationship increased the negative press about Streisand; detractors felt that Peters's guidance had compromised her artistic integrity. He ran her production company, co-produced two of her movies, produced her album *ButterFly*, and reportedly urged her into recording music with more poprock appeal than her standard repertoire. Many of the projects on which Peters and Streisand collaborated—such as the films *A Star Is Born* and *The Main Event*—were fairly popular with the public, but not with most reviewers.

In time, Streisand became weary of the personal and unprofessional manner in which the entertainment industry reviewed her work. For that reason and several others, she slowed her working pace considerably during the late 1970s and into the 1980s. Her live performances were already very rare, after anti-Semitic death threats at a concert left her with a severe case of stage fright. Since she had already made a fortune and proved herself on so many levels in doing so, there was simply no longer any need for Streisand to involve herself with any project that didn't passionately interest her.

The film *Yentl* was such a project. As early as 1979 Streisand began background research on the story of a young Jewish girl whose love for learning is so great that she adopts a male identity in order to study the Talmud and continue her schooling—prerogatives traditionally open only to men. The story resonated for Streisand on many levels. The tale of a woman struggling to steer her own destiny in a patriarchal society meant a great deal to her, and the emphasis on education in the story captured her imagination because of the idealized memory of her father, who had been a teacher. "Barbra's family was fractured by the death of her father so early," Streisand's friend Marilyn Bergman was quoted as saying in *Vanity Fair*. "*Yentl* was an homage to her father and the coming to terms with that loss." Besides producing, starring in, and singing for the soundtrack of *Yentl*, Streisand also made her debut as a director. The movie was five years in the making, and audiences responded warmly to the care and effort its creator had put into every frame. At the Golden Globe Awards, which are voted on by the general public rather than industry insiders, *Yentl* was chosen as best musical/comedy, and Streisand was named best director.

Directing proved deeply satisfying for Streisand, but it was some time before she found a motion picture property that seemed appropriate for her follow-up effort. In the meantime, she released *The Broadway Album*, a collection of fresh renditions of classic show tunes; it became her most popular album in years, with her version of "Somewhere," from *West Side Story*, climbing high on the 1986 pop charts. Also in that year, she gave a rare live performance. The occasion, a fundraising concert staged at her Malibu ranch, brought in $1.5 million in support of Democratic presidential hopefuls. In 1987 she won praise for her performance in *Nuts*, a gritty drama about a woman fighting to prove her mental competency. It was also about that time that she read something that inspired her to direct again: Pat Conroy's best-selling novel, *The Prince of Tides*.

Conroy's sweeping story chronicles a South Carolina family's struggle to come to terms with their past traumas and their dysfunctional relationships with each other. The central character, Tom Wingo, is summoned to Manhattan by psychiatrist Susan Lowenstein after his twin sister Savannah attempts suicide. Lowenstein probes Wingo's childhood memories, looking for clues as to how to best resolve Savannah's psychological torment. Perhaps the greatest challenge Streisand faced as director was compressing Conroy's lengthy tapestry of memories into the time limitations of a feature film. Her skill in doing so was widely praised. *New Yorker* reviewer Terrence Rafferty faulted the book as being "bloated," but credited Streisand with improving on the original. "Her direction is smooth and canny: she sets up the fundamental dramatic conflicts clearly and economically, and she keeps the narrative moving along at a satisfying pace," he wrote. "*The Prince of Tides* plays better on the screen than it does on the page partly because Streisand is such a skillful director."

Reviewers who loved Conroy's book were equally enthusiastic about the film adaptation. "That the movie version of Pat Conroy's novel remains so true to its source is the achievement of Barbra Streisand, who directs, produces and stars in it as psychiatrist Susan Lowenstein," reported Wolf Schneider in *American Film.* "Her poignant translation of the property takes strength from Conroy's screenplay, along with a tour-de-force turn by [Nick Nolte, as Tom Wingo] . . . The resulting crash of emotion, intellect and humor has 'Oscar' written all over it." Schneider added that any "paring down" of the characters in the screenplay was "brilliantly compensated for with flashbacks and narration that add depth." *Vogue* writer Joan Juliet Buck applauded Streisand's "painstaking care for detail and metaphor," and noted that "as a director, Streisand shows gusto and style . . . . And she has elicited a staggering, brilliant performance from Kate Nelligan, as Tom's mother." Despite its popularity and critical acclaim, however, *Prince of Tides* failed to garner an Academy Award nomination for best director—an Oscars night omission that several stars present for the awards ceremony decried—but did receive a nomination for best picture.

Directing *The Prince of Tides* was, for Streisand, one of the great achievements in a remarkable career. Her voice alone would have assured her place in entertainment history, as her 1991 vocal release—a four-CD, three-decade retrospective entitled *Just for the Record*—clearly demonstrated. But Streisand has never been comfortable resting on her laurels. Projects she may tackle in the future include a second Broadway album, a sequel to *The Way We Were,* a live concert tour, and directing a film version of Larry Kramer's play about the AIDS epidemic, *The Normal Heart.* Her hunger for new challenges has always been the driving force behind her work. "I think nothing is impossible," she told Rosenfield. "I think you can be whatever you want to be . . . . I don't accept the word no easily. I've always been fighting it my whole life."

Selected discography

The Barbra Streisand Album, 1963.
The Second Barbra Streisand Album, 1963.
The Third Barbra Streisand Album, 1964.
Funny Girl, 1964.
People, 1965.
My Name Is Barbra, 1965.
Color Me Barbra, 1966.
Simply Streisand, 1967.
Stoney End, 1971.
Barbra Joan Streisand, 1972.
The Way We Were, 1974.
ButterFly, c. 1975.
A Star Is Born, 1976.
Streisand Superman, 1977.
Wet, 1979.
(With Barry Gibb) *Guilty,* 1980.
Yentl, 1983.
Emotion, 1984.
The Broadway Album, 1986.
Just For the Record, 1991.

Sources

American Film, January-February 1992.
Cosmopolitan, October 1991.
Esquire, October 1982; April 1985.
Harper's Bazaar, November 1983.
Ladies' Home Journal, August 1979; January 1988; June 1988; February 1992.
Newsweek, January 5, 1970.
New Yorker, January 27, 1992.
New York Times, October 28, 1991.
People, January 3, 1983; December 12, 1983; March 12, 1984; March 10, 1986.
Premiere, December 1991.
Saturday Review, January 11, 1969.
Vanity Fair, September 1991.
Vogue, December 1991.
Working Woman, March 1986.

—*Joan Goldsworthy*

Aung San Suu Kyi

Copyright by Dominique Aubert/Sygma

Activist, political prisoner, and Nobel laureate

Surname pronounced "Soo Chee"; born c. 1945; daughter of Aung San (founder of modern Burma); married Michael Aris (a college instructor); children: Alexander, Kim. *Education:* Attended Oxford University.

Career

Secretary-general of the National League for Democracy, a Burmese political group.

Awards: Sakharov Prize, 1990; Nobel Peace Prize, 1991.

Sidelights

The winner of the 1991 Nobel Peace Prize may well not know of her honor. Aung San Suu Kyi, leader of the democratic opposition party in her native Burma (also known as Myanmar), has been under house arrest since July 1989. She is allowed no contact with the outside world, including that with her husband and two sons.

But for Suu Kyi, who was born into a political family—her father, assassinated by a rival when the girl was two, is credited with being the founder of independent Burma—danger has become something of a way of life. And when it comes to promoting her cause, the nonviolent democratic revolution of her homeland, she will not be swayed. So fearless is Suu Kyi, according to Dorinda Elliott in a *Newsweek* piece, that she "once led a protest past kneeling soldiers

who were aiming their guns directly at her. Only a last-minute cease-fire order saved her life."

Suu Kyi received her education in the West, attending Oxford University, but, noted Elliott, "the high-spirited politics graduate seems to have always known she was destined to return to her homeland." Leaving her family in Britain to aid her ill mother back in Yangon in 1988, Suu Kyi had immersed herself in the country's political turmoil within months. A military junta had overtaken Burma (renaming it Myanmar); but even before that the Asian nation had been virtually sealed off from the rest of the world, according to Elliott. "Mismanagement has reduced it to one of the 10 poorest [countries], with a per capita annual income of $210."

Between 1988 and mid-1989, Suu Kyi hit the campaign trail, inciting cheering crowds with her National League for Democracy (NLD), preaching the cause of nonviolent revolution through political pressure. "We have a Fascistic government in power," Suu Kyi was quoted as saying *Interview*. "Like all Fascists, the only language they understand is confrontation." Nonviolence, she added, "does not mean we are going to sit back weakly and do nothing." Her voice was silenced when she was taken prisoner in 1989, but her influence could not be stifled.

"Although she was already under house arrest at the time," wrote *Time*'s Bruce W. Nelan, Suu Kyi's party "won a landslide victory in the May 1990 parliamentary elections, taking 392 of the 485 seats. But the generals refused to surrender power. Instead they arrested scores of elected parliamentarians and hundreds of Buddhist monks."

Meanwhile, Suu Kyi continued living in seclusion in her mother's house, reportedly spending her time reading, studying Japanese, and practicing aerobics and meditation. The junta government soon ordered soldiers to surround the home; "a sign tells passersby not to come near," stated Elliott. "When neighbors stopped hearing her play Mozart on her piano, they speculated that she had sold it to pay bills. The government offered to let her leave the country, provided she stayed out of politics. She declined, demanding the release of political prisoners and the transfer of power to the NLD."

After winning the 1990 Sakharov Prize, Suu Kyi was nominated for the Nobel Peace Prize by Czechoslovakian president Vaclav Havel (see *Newsmakers 90*). Soon after, the Nobel committee granted the gold medal and cash award to the courageous opposition leader, citing her quest as "one of the most extraordinary [recent] examples of civil courage in Asia," as *People* quoted the committee. The announcement of Suu Kyi's win brought a "predictably unimpressed" reaction by Burma's military government, Nelan

related. "The cool reception the award was given in other Asian states was hardly more encouraging," he continued, offering the view that some Asians see the Peace Prize as "a form of interference in Burma's domestic affairs, even of neocolonial badgering."

Meanwhile, Suu Kyi has become a heroine to the cause of Burmese democracy. Contrary to the wishes of the junta, the NLD leader's presence "is everywhere—on T-shirts, posters; in popular songs," according to *Interview*. On the occasion of Suu Kyi's birthday, more than 1,000 people worldwide signed a card for her, reported *People*. Its message read: *Like the candles/On this birthday cake/The bars of repression/Will one day burn down/and set free your dream of democracy*. It is not reported whether Suu Kyi ever received the card.

Selected writings

Aung San of Burma (a biography of Suu Kyi's father), Seven Hills Books (U.S.) and Kiscadale Publications (U.K.).

Sources

Interview, July 1991.
Newsweek, October 28, 1991.
People, October 28, 1991.
Time, October 28, 1991.

—Susan Salter

Clarence Thomas

Supreme Court justice

Born June 23, 1948, in Pin Point, GA; son of M. C. and Leola (Anderson) Thomas; one of three children; married Kathy Grace Ambush, 1971 (divorced, 1984); married Virginia Lamp, 1987; children: (first marriage) Jamal. *Education:* Graduated from Holy Cross College, Worcester, MA, 1971; received law degree from Yale University Law School, 1974. *Politics:* Republican. *Religion:* Born Baptist, raised Catholic.

Career

Held summer jobs in legal aid and at Hill, Jones & Farrington (law firm), c. 1971-74; staff member for Attorney General John Danforth, Missouri, 1974-77; legal counsel for Monsanto Corporation, St. Louis, MO, 1977-80; head of Equal Employment Opportunity Commission, 1980-89; appointed to federal appeals court, 1990; confirmed as Supreme Court Justice, 1991.

Member: Advisory board of the *Lincoln Review.*

Sidelights

The appointment of Clarence Thomas as a justice of the U.S. Supreme Court in November of 1991 followed perhaps the greatest furor over such an event in modern history. A conservative jurist with experience in the education department under President Ronald Reagan, Thomas had also headed the Equal Employment Opportunity Commission and, while there, allegedly sexually harrassed a staff member, Anita Hill. Hill's accusations surfaced only after Thomas's nomination to the nation's highest court by President George Bush; Hill was by this time a law professor. The Senate confirmation hearings that dealt with these charges had enormous political and social ramifications above and beyond Thomas's suitability for the Supreme Court. The judge's appointment was a watershed for the Bush administration, which needed to replace retiring black justice Thurgood Marshall. The choice of a black conservative effectively stymied Democratic opposition to Thomas, who suspended his lifelong criticism of racial politics long enough to call his confirmation hearings a "high-tech lynching." That remark is representative of the many contradictions embodied by this controversial figure. Indeed, *Newsweek* noted that "Thomas is an intense opponent of affirmative action, yet has benefited from it throughout his life . . . . the very reason he was named to succeed Thurgood Marshall on the Supreme Court is because of his race."

At the same time, Thomas's confirmation left in its wake a number of simmering conflicts: Many women felt Hill's charges weren't taken seriously enough by an all-male Senate panel, advocates of abortion rights and affirmative action feared that Thomas would be a hostile voice on the increasingly conservative Court, and many blacks felt they had been subject at once to tokenism and racist manipulation. For a figure whose "humble beginnings" were a high-profile calling card among his Washington sponsors, Thomas had already made an impression that was anything but humble.

Thomas was born in 1948 in Pin Point, Georgia, a tiny coastal hamlet named for the plantation that once stood there. His mother Leola was 18 at the time of his birth; his father M. C. Thomas left the family two years later. Leola, her two children—Clarence and his sister Emma Mae—and her Aunt Annie Graham occupied what *Newsweek* described as "a one-room wooden house near the marshes. It had dirt floors and no plumbing or electricity." Their destitute life was struck by further misfortune five years after M. C. walked out on the family, ostensibly headed for Philadelphia: the house burned

> "Race-conscious remedies in this society are dangerous. You can't orchestrate society along racial lines or different lines by saying there should be 10 percent blacks, 15 percent Hispanics."

down, so the family moved near Leola's parents, Mr. and Mrs. Myers Anderson. Having in the meantime married a man who didn't want to raise the children—there was now a third child, a son, who went by the name Peanut—Leola agreed to let the Andersons care for the two boys and sent Emmie Mae to live with Aunt Annie in Pin Point.

Myers Anderson exercised a huge influence on Clarence's life. A devout Catholic who created his own fuel oil business in Savannah in the 1950s, he provided the example of self-motivation in the face of segregation that would inspire his grandson. Through hard work and a refusal to submit to the poverty and degradation of menial work, he "did for himself," as one of his favorite expressions went. He fed and cared for Clarence and Peanut and paid for their education at St. Benedict the Moor; at this all-black grammar school, white nuns exercised firm discipline. The racist vigilante group known as the Ku Klux Klan often threatened the nuns, who rode

on the backs of buses with their students and demanded hard work and promptly completed assignments. Clarence's grandfather once took him to a meeting of the National Association for the Advancement of Colored People (NAACP), of which Anderson was a member, and read the boy's grades aloud. "The most compassionate thing [our grandparents] did for us was to teach us to fend for ourselves and to do that in an openly hostile environment," Thomas noted in a 1987 speech before the Heritage Foundation, published in *Policy Review* in 1991.

The young Thomas graduated from St. Benedict's in 1962, spent two years at St. Pius X High School, and then transferred—at his grandfather's insistence—to a white Catholic boarding school called St. John Vianney Minor Seminary. Clarence did well in school, but experienced for the first time the hostility of racism. His schoolmates' derisive remarks came as a shock—his segregated youth had ironically provided some insulation from everyday racism—but he kept his composure. Following St. John's, Clarence went to Immaculate Conception Seminary in Conception, Missouri, to study for the priesthood. As one of only four blacks there, Thomas was again made acutely aware of the double standards of white Christian society. One incident, however, caused him to give up on the seminary for good: the voice of a fellow seminarian cheering the news that black civil rights leader Martin Luther King, Jr., had been shot in 1968. "I knew I couldn't stay in this so-called Christian environment," he remarked later.

In 1968 Thomas began his studies at Holy Cross, a Jesuit college in Worcester, Massachusetts. This period saw an intensification of Thomas's struggle with his identity, his background, and the politics of race. He joined the Black Student Union, a militant group on campus that succeeded in using its political and rhetorical energies to make some changes, including an all-black dormitory, more courses relevant to black students, and increased financial aid. The atmosphere of questioning and empowerment was exhilarating for Thomas, though unlike many of his contemporaries he never abandoned his earliest sources of strength: "Thomas still spoke the conservative maxims of his grandfather and the nuns far more often than the chic of the left," reported *Newsweek*. Though he adopted some of the language, style, and arguments of the radical Black Panther Party's leaders, he remained a skeptic and was often the sole dissenter among his revolutionary circle. This tendency would serve him in good stead as he learned what he would later call "the loneliness of the black conservative."

During his sophomore year Thomas met Kathy Grace Ambush and began a relationship that would lead to their 1971 marriage. In 1973 their son, Jamal, was born. Thomas had registered for the draft in 1966, at age 18, but had a student deferment; when he graduated in 1971, and his number in the conscription lottery was low, he seemed a likely candidate for military service in Vietnam. However, he failed his physical examination. He had applied to Yale, Harvard, and the University of Pennsylvania law schools—all of which had accepted him—and decided on Yale because of the financial support it offered him. Thomas was a beneficiary of Yale's new affirmative-action policy, which offered opportunities to minority students. Though he benefited from this policy, it raised in Thomas—perhaps for the first time–doubts about whether he had succeeded on his own merits. These doubts would trouble him throughout his career and would motivate a deep distrust of what conservatives like to call "entitlements" or "handouts."

Thus he strained to demonstrate his qualifications, to prove that something other than his blackness had brought him into the Ivy League. While at Yale he held some summer jobs; he assisted a small legal-aid establishment, which brought him into contact with welfare cases, and spent a summer at the law firm of Hill, Jones & Farrington. Yet when he began to look for work as his graduation drew near, he found that few law firms were interested in him. The pay they offered was demonstrably lower than what white graduates would have been offered, and they tended to assume Thomas wanted to do social rather than corporate law. Once again, he found himself pigeonholed by race.

Rather than accept what he considered an insufficient salary from the firm where he'd done his summer work, Thomas accepted a position on the staff of John Danforth, attorney general of Missouri. Danforth had attended Yale himself and, as an Episcopal minister and Republican, he saw in Thomas a promising young conservative. Thomas worked hard under Danforth and specialized in tax law. He achieved a victory when he appealed a decision against the state—it regarded the governor's banning of personalized license plates—and won in a higher court. Danforth's office felt that the case was unwinnable since many wealthy, influential people had these so-called vanity plates; Thomas felt it necessary to prove that the privileged few couldn't control the law.

Yet Thomas himself was allegedly status-seeking; he bought a BMW automobile while working in Danforth's office, though he told fellow workers that a Mercedes-Benz was the car for a "gentleman" to drive. This affection for status symbols no doubt grew out of Thomas's fondness for the ideology of self-help. He took a large step in the direction of greater financial stability when Danforth left Missouri to take a Senate seat; Thomas landed a job as legal counsel for the Monsanto Corporation. There, as *Time* phrased it, he "shepherded pesticides through government registration."

Monsanto's chemical empire supported him comfortably until he decided to move on to Washington. He returned to Danforth's staff and worked on energy and environmental issues, but was at the same time struck by the work of a handful of black conservatives. The writings of right-wing black economists Thomas Sowell and Walter Williams, as well as the black conservative journal, the *Lincoln Review*, had a galvanizing effect on Thomas. He joined the advisory board of the *Review*, which has created waves in the black community by taking some very unpopular— some would say reactionary—stands. The journal's editor, Jay Parker, argued on behalf of the government of South Africa, while the journal itself opposed a holiday for Martin Luther King, Jr.; questioned the extent, if not the existence, of racial discrimination; and referred to abortion as a plot to "slaughter" blacks. Parker and Thomas chatted on the phone in 1980; the controversial editor would soon be looking for interested black conservatives to join the administration of President Ronald Reagan.

Thomas's first offer from Reagan's camp was a position as a policy staffer on energy and environmental issues, but he turned this job down, accepting—in spite of his previous aversion to such matters—a place at the head of civil rights under the secretary of education. Ten months later he was put in charge of the Equal Employment Opportunity Commission (EEOC), an agency charged with enforcing civil rights laws. Why Thomas accepted these jobs remains unclear, since they are the sort of classically "black" appointments he had resolutely avoided in the past. Some observers have speculated that Thomas merely took the positions with the highest political visibility, while others suggested that his recent infatuation with ultraconservative black thinkers like Sowell and Parker had awakened in him a new political enthusiasm, and that he wished to tackle affirmative action and other issues head on.

In any case, Thomas's years at EEOC were fraught with conflict. He has been described as a demanding supervisor, who often dealt with employees harshly. He allegedly settled petty scores in harsh ways, argued inconsistently on issues like hiring quotas for minorities—he both opposed and supported them over the course of his tenure—and reportedly avoided prosecuting thousands of age discrimination cases. Although less doctrinaire than "the other Clarence"—Reagan's fiery Civil Rights Commission chair Clarence Pendleton, another conservative black who alienated much of the civil rights community—Thomas made his self-help philosophy well known. He remarked to Lena Williams in a *New York Times* profile that "race-conscious remedies in this society are dangerous. You can't orchestrate society along racial lines or different lines by saying there should be 10 percent blacks, 15 percent Hispanics." He also made waves by remarking in 1984 that civil rights leaders just "bitch, bitch, bitch, moan and whine."

> *"He had the gall to present himself as a victim, a man who had been forced to endure the unspeakable agony of sitting comfortably in a chair for two weeks and being asked a series of facile questions to which he gave equally facile answers."*
> —Lewis Lapham

Despite the discontent he evoked from civil rights activists, Thomas was granted a second term at the EEOC in 1984. It was a difficult period for Thomas, who had separated from his wife, Kathy, in 1981; they divorced in 1984, and Clarence retained custody of Jamal. The circumstances of the marriage and the divorce remain a well-guarded secret, and allegations of abuse made at the time returned to haunt Thomas during his confirmation hearings years later. Thomas became a stern taskmaster at home, pressuring Jamal to succeed at school just as Myers Anderson had pressed him in his own youth. In 1986 he met Virginia Lamp, a white fellow law school graduate active in conservative causes. The two fell in love and married in 1987. Virginia was a Labor Department lawyer when Thomas was nominated for the Supreme Court.

In a critical 1987 speech before the conservative Heritage Foundation, Thomas articulated his feelings about the perils of "entitlement" programs, job quotas, and—most notoriously—welfare. He had some years earlier shocked listeners by criticizing his sister for her dependency on welfare, though, according to *Time*'s Jack E. White, "she was not getting welfare checks when he singled her out but [was] working double shifts at a nursing home for slightly more than $2 an hour." But in this Heritage Foundation speech he articulated more specifically his concern about the "welfare mentality." Though Reagan and others on the right had rankled blacks and civil rights proponents with derisive references to "welfare queens," Thomas's criticisms may have been harder for his opponents to dismiss—or so the administration hoped.

The Heritage Foundation speech also outlined Thomas's plan for bringing more blacks into the ranks of conservatism. "I am of the view that black Americans will move inexorably and naturally toward conservatism when we stop discouraging them; when they are treated as a diverse group with differing interests; and when conservatives stand up for what they believe in rather than stand against blacks," he proclaimed. He went on to suggest that the "unnecessarily negative" approach of the Reagan administration had been more alienating than its political philosophy toward welfare and affirmative action. (Thomas has long opposed affirmative action, but bases this opinion on a distrust of white institutions which he believes keep blacks begging for jobs and other economic opportunities.) Many critics have attacked Thomas for this ardent individualism. Bruce Shapiro represented many of Thomas's opponents when he wrote in *The Nation* of Thomas's "far-reaching commitment to unravel the fabric of community and social responsibility."

Perhaps the most important strand of the Heritage Foundation speech was Thomas's invocation of natural law. This discussion provided the most substantial evidence of his judicial philosophy, and was particularly worrying to civil rights advocates and many people concerned about the fundamental separation of Church and State. The alarm of these constituencies was magnified by Thomas's citing of Heritage trustee Lewis Lehrman's argument on behalf of the rights of the fetus as grounded in the Declaration of Independence as "a splendid example of applying natural law." In brief, natural law depends on applying a perception of God-given rights and rules—as, indeed, the Declaration and other founding documents of the American republic do, at least rhetorically—to human law. "Without such a notion of natural law," Thomas claimed in his speech, "the entire American political tradition, from Washington to Lincoln, from Jefferson to Martin Luther King, would be unintelligible." Thus, against what he perceives as the abstractions and inhumanity of the welfare state, Thomas promotes a philosophy that "establishes our inherent equality as a God-given right." Yet many critics have expressed grave reservations about the implications of such a belief.

The Republican party, however, which saw potential in Thomas early on, began to regard him as a good prospect for the nation's highest court. President Bush nominated him to the federal appeals court in 1990, and he was confirmed by the Senate in March of that year. The appeals court is a common stop on the route to the Supreme Court, and this was a route in which Thomas had expressed no uncertain interest. Bush nominated him to the United States's highest court in 1991. Still, his performance on the appeals court wasn't exactly impressive. "As Supreme Court nominees go," reported Margaret Carlson in a 1991 *Time* profile, "Thomas has little judicial experience. He is not a brilliant legal scholar, a weighty thinker, or even the author of numerous opinions." Bruce Shapiro was more blunt in the *Nation*, counting the judge "among the more scantily qualified Supreme Court candidates in recent memory."

The stage was set for an ideological battle over Thomas's appointment even before Anita Hill went public with her accusations. The NAACP, after lengthy discussion and much internal upheaval, voted to oppose Thomas's confirmation. The chairman of the organization, William F. Gibson, read a statement featuring a seven-point argument for opposing Thomas. Printed in its entirety in *Crisis*, the statement reasoned that "Judge Clarence Thomas' judicial philosophy is simply inconsistent with the historical positions taken by the NAACP." The criticisms centered on Thomas's performance at the EEOC and what Gibson characterized as the judge's "reactionary philosophical approach to a number of critical issues, not the least of which is affirmative action." Oddly enough, the NAACP stressed the importance of looking past race in this instance— though it believes fervently in the importance of having African-Americans on the Supreme Court— to focus on Thomas's record. Thus an organization traditionally affiliated with the "entitlement" sensibility Thomas so disliked had actually judged him on his merits and found him wanting. Similarly, the Congressional Black Caucus (CBC) voted 20-1 to oppose Thomas's confirmation. The lone dissenter was also the CBC's only Republican.

Jesse Jackson, perhaps the most vocal black activist in the United States, was particularly critical of Thomas. *In These Times* quoted Jackson's remarks to a Chicago meeting of his organization, Operation PUSH: "He is a prime beneficiary of our [civil rights activists'] work. He got public accommodations, the right to vote, open housing because of civil rights marches and activism; yet he stood on our shoulders and kicked us in the head."

George Bush expressed his support for Thomas largely on the basis of the judge's character. Thomas's life story, a real-world example of the conservative ideal, appeared in virtually every endorsement. Bush made no mention of the nominee's judicial temperament, nor of his decisions on the appeals court; it was clear that this appointment was a symbolic one. Strangely enough, Thomas's patron had chosen him because he was a successful *black* man. Whether Thomas privately considered himself a beneficiary of a White House "quota" remains unknown. In any case, Thomas's personal odyssey from Pin Point to the pinnacle of Washington, D.C., success, or some version of that odyssey, would always serve as an endorsement. Lena Williams's *New York Times* article concluded by referring to Thomas's "difficult childhood and his ability to succeed against the odds," an angle that the Bush administration would exploit to the utmost in its presentation of Thomas the judicial candidate.

The Senate's confirmation hearings appeared to be moving along smoothly when Anita Hill's allegations were made public. On October 8, Hill—a professor at the University of Oklahoma Law School—held a press conference in which she made public the main points of the testimony she had previously given the Federal Bureau of Investigation. The FBI report had been reviewed by the confirmation committee but not made public, and on the day of Hill's press conference the Thomas vote was scheduled to move to the Senate floor. By this time, however, the story had been exposed by National Public Radio legal affairs correspondent Nina Totenberg (also in *Newsmakers 92*). A wave of protest by women's groups and other activists arose, leading the committee, headed by Delaware's Joseph Biden, a Democrat, to review Hill's charges. Her testimony accused Thomas of badgering her for dates while she worked at the EEOC, and of accosting her with stories of pornographic film scenes and his own sexual prowess. The accusations fit the paradigm of sexual harassment in the workplace: the male superior uses sexual banter and other discomfiting tactics as a means of exercising power over a female underling. Hill claimed that Thomas's constant harassment made it difficult for her to do her job and even caused her anxiety that manifested itself in the form of physical distress.

The televised hearings, during which Hill, Thomas, and several witnesses on both sides testified about the allegations, were among the most widely-viewed political events in television history. Thomas denied any wrongdoing, but stopped short of calling Hill a liar. Most of Thomas's political allies on the committee—Republican senators Strom Thurmond, Arlen Specter, Alan Simpson, and Orrin Hatch—interrogated Hill mercilessly, and suggested that Hill was either being cynically manipulated by liberals or was lying outright. *Spy* magazine reported that numerous young researchers had been recruited by the White House staff to find embarassing or otherwise damaging disclosures about Hill and her testimony. The partisan battle over the confirmation became so vicious that following the vote, considerable press attention was devoted to the Congress's political game-playing and the painful divisions it left among various constituencies.

Thomas himself remarked during the course of the televised hearings that the process had been a harrowing personal ordeal for him and his wife. Indeed, he claimed, he would have preferred "an assassin's bullet to this kind of living hell," and he would have withdrawn from consideration earlier had he known what lay ahead. Lewis Lapham's column in *Harper's* the following month attacked Thomas as a hypocrite: "He had the gall to present himself as a victim, a man who had been forced to endure the unspeakable agony of sitting comfortably in a chair for two weeks and being asked a series of facile questions to which he gave equally facile answers." Lapham asserted that Thomas displayed "contempt for the entire apparatus of the American idea—for Congress, for the press, for freedom of expression, for the uses of democratic government, for any rules other than his own."

Many blacks had supported Thomas and followed the Republicans' theory that Hill was part of a campaign to smear him. Many women who opposed Thomas and believed Hill vowed to defeat Thomas's backers in the next elections. Another ramification of the Hill-Thomas debacle was the major attention suddenly afforded the previously neglected question of sexual harrassment; the phrase entered the mainstream political vocabulary almost overnight. In any event, the verdict—in the minds of the committee and in the press—was that both witnesses were credible and that determining the truth of what had taken place nearly a decade before was well nigh impossible. The president urged Congress to give Thomas the benefit of the doubt, arguing that he was innocent until proven guilty. Others pointed out that Thomas was not on trial for harrassing Hill, and that any doubt was sufficient to disqualify him. In the end, Thomas was confirmed by a 52-48 margin, the smallest—according to *Time*—by which any justice has been confirmed this century. To those who complained about the confirmation hearings' focus on these "personal" matters, the *New Republic* replied that "the Bush administration promoted Mr. Thomas's nomination as a matter of character, not of professional qualifications; and it has reaped a bitter reward."

Following the confirmation, Virginia Thomas told her story to *People*, recounting the tension of the confirmation fight and speculating that Anita Hill was in love with Clarence Thomas. She referred to the struggle to get Thomas confirmed as "Good versus Evil." Alisa Solomon, meanwhile, writing in the *Village Voice*, argued that Anita Hill was attacked for showing the same qualities for which Clarence Thomas was celebrated: her ability to argue, her aggressiveness, and her self-sufficiency. Thomas, Solomon wrote, "seems unable to see women as a class, and therefore unable to recognize the importance of rulings that affect us."

Clarence Thomas has made it to the top, and his defiant individual style and renegade opinions have left him with many admirers and many detractors. Whether he will distinguish himself on the Supreme Court remains to be seen. The question on most observers' minds is this: Will Thomas be the gadfly on a conservative court, or will he fall in line with its prevailing right-leaning tendencies? His experience prior to his confirmation guaranteed that he will be watched just as closely *after* donning his robes. What his celebrated triumph over hard circumstances will mean then, no one can predict.

Sources

The American Spectator, October 1991.
Crisis, August/September 1991.
Harper's, December 1991.
In These Times, July 24, 1991; August 7, 1991; October 23, 1991.
Nation, September 23, 1991; October 14, 1991; October 28, 1991; November 4, 1991; November 11, 1991.
New Republic, October 28, 1991.
Newsweek, September 16, 1991; October 21, 1991; October 28, 1991.
New York Times, February 8, 1987; October 8, 1991.
People, October 28, 1991; November 11, 1991.

Policy Review, Fall 1991.
Spy, December 1991.
Time, September 16, 1991; October 28, 1991.
U.S. News & World Report, October 21, 1991.
Village Voice, October 22, 1991.

—*Simon Glickman*

Nina Totenberg

AP/Wide World Photos

Journalist

Born January 14, 1944; eldest daughter of Roman (a Polish emigre and concert violinist) and Melanie Totenberg: married Floyd Haskell (former Democratic senator from Colorado), 1979. *Education:* Attended Boston University.

Addresses: *Office*—National Public Radio, 2025 M Street NW, Washington, DC 20036.

Career

Worked for *Boston Record American,* then *Peabody Times,* 1965-68; writer for *Roll Call,* and then *National Observer,* 1968-72; worked for *New Times,* 1972-75; legal affairs correspondent for National Public Radio, 1975—; legal affairs correspondent for the *MacNeil/Lehrer News Hour,* 1986—.

Awards: Alfred I. duPont-Columbia University Silver Baton Award for outstanding broadcast journalism, 1988; Breakthrough Award/George Polk Award from Long Island University, 1991. Honorary degrees from Gonzaga University, 1986, and Northeastern University, 1988.

Sidelights

When Nina Totenberg, legal affairs correspondent for National Public Radio (NPR), reported the contents of a confidential affidavit on October 6, 1991, her breakthrough story cut two ways. Totenberg made public the allegations of Anita Hill, a law professor at the University of Oklahoma, who claimed that she had been the victim of sexual

harassment as an employee of Clarence Thomas, Hill's former boss and then nominee for the U.S. Supreme Court. Throughout the nominating process, supporters of Clarence Thomas had downplayed his thin legal qualifications—of all Supreme Court nominees in history, Thomas's rating by the American Bar Association was the lowest—and promoted his character instead, so revelations like those Totenberg read on the air were a blow to his reputation and a setback for the tactics of his supporters. But Totenberg's story also damaged the Senate Judiciary Committee itself, whose members, despite their access to Hill's affidavit, had largely failed to investigate her claims.

In the week that followed, as faxes poured into Senate offices indicating the furor touched off by Totenberg's story, the Judiciary Committee postponed Thomas's confirmation vote and began a twelfth-hour investigation of Hill's charges. PBS coverage of the event—which Totenberg co-anchored with Paul Duke—went head to head with prime-time programming and baseball's World Series, in many cities capturing a greater share of the viewing audience. The proceedings made for riveting television, and the gavel-to-gavel coverage exposed the attitudes of the all-male committee on an issue—sexual harassment—whose political explosiveness they appeared unprepared for.

As national attention focused on Washington, the battle for political leverage grew. Conservative senators attacked Totenberg, saying that media exposure of these sensitive issues had ruined the lives of both Hill and Thomas, and that Totenberg was to blame. A Republican senator from Wyoming, Judiciary Committee member Alan Simpson, questioned Totenberg's journalistic ethics when the two were guests on television's *Nightline,* and when the show was over he followed her into the street. "He was in a complete rage. He was out of control," Totenberg told Ann Louise Bardach of *Vanity Fair.* Still, those who witnessed Simpson holding open the door of her limousine so she couldn't leave, report that Totenberg gave as good as she got. As she admitted to Bardach, "I certainly did use some choice epithets."

Nina Totenberg was born in New York City in 1944 to Melanie Totenberg and her husband, Roman, a concert violinist. Totenberg left her hometown of Scarsdale, New York, to attend Boston University but dropped out for a newspaper job at the *Boston Record American.* In 1968 she moved to Washington, D.C., where at the *National Observer* she gained her first battle experience against Washington powercrats. A profile of J. Edgar Hoover she wrote for the paper so infuriated the feared director of the Federal Bureau of Investigation (FBI) that he tried to pressure her employers into firing her. But the management stood by Totenberg's story and, to prove it, printed Hoover's letter. In 1972, when Totenberg switched to a second Washington journal, *New Times,* she scored another capitol coup with a story many elected officials were glad was not longer, her often-quoted article, "The 10 Dumbest Members of Congress."

But it was at her next job as legal-affairs correspondent reporting for NPR—a position she has held since 1975—that she gained the influence that enrages senators and can suddenly change the nation's TV programming. Media analyst Ron Powers, in an article for the December 1990 issue of *Gentlemen's Quarterly,* called her "one of the most admired and competitively feared reporters in Washington." This growing reputation came at some personal expense. After her frequent newsbreaks and sometimes startling connections to insider information, rumors began of an affair with the late Supreme Court Justice Potter. Totenberg told *People* magazine's Susan Reed and Sandra McElwaine in 1991 that such rumors were "silly and mildly slanderous," adding that, at the time the allegations were made, she was "a young female in an all-male environment, and I was doing reporting that they were not." Former *New York Times* editor Bill Kovach told *Vanity*

Fair's Bardach: "It's astounding to me how Nina becomes a lightning rod for other journalists. She is one of the most knowledgeable and aggressive reporters in the business, but whenever she breaks a story, the first reaction in the Washington press corps is 'What do you want? She's sleeping with a justice or someone else.' No one says these things about any male reporter, some of whom wouldn't think twice about sleeping with someone to get a story."

But whatever rumors have circulated during her years in the public eye, the reasons for her success are no secret to those who work with her. NPR's Washington bureau chief Bruce Drake told Scott Walton of the *Detroit Free Press,* "She's one of the best reporters I've ever worked with in print or broadcast journalism. First of all, she works very hard at making contacts around town. She knows

> *"When I walk into the Capitol every morning, I'm walking into the smallest town in America. And I know that at least 300 of the 535 key residents—the congressmen—have heard me fifteen minutes before I've arrived."*
> —Cokie Roberts

everybody in Washington. So it's very hard to keep anything from her. And she's an extremely methodical reporter. She runs every angle into the ground. It's a combination of those things that result in a payoff."

Totenberg's work gathering the Anita Hill story is a fine example of this persistence. She was aware of rumors of Thomas's sexual harassment months before she broke the story, but since she is notoriously strict about substantiating her stories, it wasn't until days before Thomas's scheduled confirmation that she had enough evidence to satisfy her own strict standards. For the February 1992 issue of *Mirabella,* Totenberg explained to Joyce Johnson that the story was not simply a matter of Hill's affidavit landing on her desk by means of a mysterious leak. "I'd heard rumors and then I started checking them. And then I started checking Hill. And then I got a corroborative witness—Judge Susan Hoerchner. And *then* I got

Hill's affidavit and then she agreed to talk to me. *So I had an interview and an affidavit and a corroborative witness. And then I delayed the story essentially a whole news cycle—one day—to get the Judiciary Committee's reaction as to why they hadn't looked into these stories."* To get the story in, Totenberg called Cadi Simon, senior foreign-desk editor for NPR, who left a family meal late that Friday to help Totenberg cut the tape for the next day's broadcast as well as transcribe the story to be faxed to newsrooms across the country.

In her *Mirabella* article called "Radio Dames," Joyce Johnson described this close cooperation of colleagues, the type of teamwork that helped Totenberg file her breakthrough story. This "old-girl network" has grown in power and influence right along with NPR. Ron Powers profiled the network's senior members, of whom Totenberg was one, in his *Gentlemen's Quarterly* media column. Both Johnson and Powers focus on the primary place of NPR's news team among the Washington media, and the influential presence of NPR's women in this "National Public Resource."

One of the women Powers profiled, Cokie Roberts, explained matter-of-factly the power NPR wields in D.C. "When I walk into the Capitol every morning, I'm walking into the smallest town in America. And I know that at least 300 of the 535 key residents—the congressmen—have heard me fifteen minutes before I've arrived. NPR's influence is spectacular not just because more people are listening to us, but because of *who's* listening." This power and the freedom that NPR gives its reporters to shape the news—the average NPR spot is four and a half minutes, as opposed to the forty-five second bites given to their network TV colleagues—does not come cheap: the salaries they earn on the radio are a fraction of what correspondents command on TV. Totenberg explained the tradeoff to Powers: "When I stand in any line of reporters at a big event that I'm covering, be it a big Supreme Court argument, a trial or an election campaign, *I am the star in the line, not* my colleagues from NBC, CBS and ABC. People recognize me because they see me on MacNeil/Lehrer—but they're NPR listeners above all. Those colleagues would love to trade places with me if NPR could pay them enough. They've gotten used to living richer, to the fact that their salaries are disgraceful."

Yet it may have been money, or the lack of it, that landed so many women at NPR in the first place. Since so few men are willing to contemplate a career on the salaries that public or listener-supported radio can offer, women took many of the available spots.

At NPR, they could occupy more than the token or—often literally—figurehead positions available to them on TV news. The success of the first generation of NPR's women reporters bred loyalty; where else could they find such power to shape their own stories? And the high profile of these women brought in further recruits. As Totenberg told Joyce Johnson, "It really is the old-girl network. Initially there were a lot of women here because they didn't pay much. But then it became self-perpetuating, in that we knew other women who would be interested. It's a very reinforcing place for women to work. You're not one of the few."

And Totenberg has thrived in this environment, filing her regular reports for NPR's *Morning Edition, Weekend Edition* and *All Things Considered.* In addition to breaking the Anita Hill story, which brought her the prestigious George Polk Award for radio reporting, she also derailed President Ronald Reagan's nomination of Douglas Ginsburg to the Supreme Court when she revealed his marijuana use—a fact that had escaped even the FBI's background check. That scoop brought her the 1988 Alfred I. duPont-Columbia University Silver Baton award for outstanding broadcast journalism, and, on the popular front, led *Esquire* to enshrine her as one of the "52 Women We Love." Totenberg had also been on the front line in the reporting of such stories as the Watergate trials, the Iran-Contra hearings, and the investigations into former Attorney General Edwin Meese's dubious dealings.

With her continual presence at the forefront of breaking news, it seems Totenberg might have been prepared for the firestorm that came down upon her personally after her October 6, 1991, report set off the Thomas-Hill controversy. Totenberg, in many interviews, claimed that the fallout was a "shoot-the-messenger" response. In addition to Senator Simpson's ad hominem attack on *Nightline,* she suffered a painful reopening of a 20-year old wound when a *Wall Street Journal* editorial reviewed Totenberg's dismissal for plagiarism from the *National Observer;* she countercharged that she was sexually harassed when she worked there. Totenberg had admitted taking quotes from a *Washington Post* article without attributing her source. A former *Washington Post* editor, Nicholas Von Hoffman, told *Vanity Fair's* Bardach that "it was an industry practice to borrow quotes, or quote quotes," while another *Post* employee told her that attributing quotes was, at that time, "almost considered wimpish." But Totenberg's personal exposure to sexual harassment was, she told *People,* something she didn't want to talk about. Comparing it to Hill's, Totenberg said, "Mine was a totally different kind of experience. Mine was physical, hers was not. It happened, and that's it."

Even months after Thomas's confirmation as a Supreme Court justice, senators still targeted Totenberg. Angered that Hill's affidavit was ever available to NPR at all, conservative senators initiated investigations to find the "leak." On February 3, 1992, they subpoenaed Totenberg and New York *Newsday*'s Timothy Phelps in an attempt to force the two to disclose the identity of the Senate staffer who gave the document to the media, thus setting up a first amendment battle from which Totenberg is unlikely to back away.

It would be hard for the Senators to choose a tougher opponent. While some claim that her marriage in 1979 to former Colorado senator Floyd Haskell has mellowed her, Totenberg herself believes she has become, as she told *People*, simply "older, wiser and nicer." Haskell has been her sounding board on sensitive political issues, however, and when she sought his advice before revealing the Anita Hill story he told her that the Judiciary Committee's failure to investigate the charges was "outrageous." She called Haskell her "barometer" in *People* magazine and also sounded a note Haskell's former colleagues might well consider as they prepare for Totenberg: "We're opposites in many ways. He is dignified and restrained."

Sources

Detroit Free Press, October 15, 1991.
Entertainment Weekly, October 25, 1991.
Gentlemen's Quarterly, December 1990.
Mirabella, February 1992.
People, October 28, 1991.
Time, October 28, 1991.
Vanity Fair, January 1992.

—*Kevin Conley*

Andries Treurnicht

AP/Wide World Photos

South African Conservative Party leader

Born Andries Petrus Treurnicht, February 19, 1921, in Piketberg, Cape Province, South Africa; son of Andries (a farmer) and Hester (Albertyn) Treurnicht; married Engela Dreyer; children: four daughters. *Education:* University of Stellenbosch, South Africa, B.A. and M.A. (theology), 1945; University of Cape Town, South Africa, M.A. and Ph.D. (philosophy).

Addresses: *Office*—Metropolitan Building, 159 Skinner Street, Pretoria 0001, South Africa.

Career

Minister of the Dutch Reformed Church, 1946-60, serving in Oudtshoorn, Rondebosch, Stellenbosch, and Pretoria, South Africa; editor of the Dutch Reformed Church's newspaper, *Die Kerkbode.* Served on the Dutch Reformed Church's General Synod, 1966. Appointed editor of the Pretoria newspaper, *Hoofstad,* 1967. Nationalist party member of South African Parliament in 1971 from Waterberg in the Transvaal. Chairman of the Broederbond, early 1970s. Broke with Nationalist party, 1982; formed Conservative party, advocating separate national areas based on race. Also author of numerous books.

Awards: Medals from Afrikaanse Studentebond, 1967, and the Students' Representative Council, University of Pretoria, 1976; Decoration of Meritorious Service presented by South African prime minister, 1982.

Sidelights

Andries Treurnicht, leader of the South African Conservative party, launched his party's "Freedom Manifesto" in May of 1990 before a crowd estimated at about 50,000 people. Accompanied by the widow of former South African prime minister H. F. Verwoerd, the architect of separate development, Treurnicht promised to fight to restore to Afrikaans-speaking whites what the government had "unjustly given away." He was referring to the restoration of the policies of separate development that legalized white supremacy and deprived blacks of basic political and civil rights.

Treurnicht warned the government of Nationalist party leader F. W. de Klerk (see *Newsmakers 90*) that "The ANC [African National Congress] hates the Boer people and the white nation. They demand our land. They reject our right to exist." The Boers (Afrikaans for farmer) are Afrikaners, people of Dutch descent. Of the five million whites in South Africa, approximately 60 percent are Afrikaans speakers. Confident that his party could win a whites-only election, Treurnicht called on the government in 1989 to hold a referendum to "put its integration and abdication politics to the voters."

Treurnicht's accusations of betrayal by the government followed the February 1990 release of ANC leader Nelson Mandela after 27 years in prison. With Mandela's and other nationalist leaders' release, the government began negotiating with black leaders to devise a democratic, multiparty system for all South Africans. Toward this goal, Parliament repealed legislation supporting apartheid—South Africa's system of government, which includes policies of racial discrimination against non-Europeans. For many South African whites, however, the apartheid legislation had guaranteed them advantages, and a repeal of the laws of apartheid threatened their economic and political superiority.

In response to this threat, whites—mostly Afrikaans speakers—formed about 25 right-wing organizations. Their politics range from those advocating a separate, all-white homeland within South Africa to those supporting ultra-right neo-Nazi terrorism. Despite their differences, these organizations share the spirit of Afrikaner nationalism that imbued the early Dutch settlers with determination against the British during England's colonization of the region. Afrikaners share an identity based on history, language, culture, and religion, as well as a desire for self-determination as individuals and as a group. They draw their support from government employees, small business owners, farmers, and semi-skilled clerks and mechanics, whose jobs and property will be the most threatened by a majority (democratic) government.

The Conservative party is one of the largest Afrikaner organizations and is the only one represented in the South African Parliament. The Conservative party was founded by Treurnicht in 1982 when he and 17 others left the Nationalist party over its policies of power-sharing with Indians and other non-whites. From its small base, the Conservatives attracted supporters and in the 1987 elections outpolled the Federal Progressive party to become the official opposition. In 1989 whites-only Parliament elections, the Conservative party won about 30 percent of the vote and nearly doubled its membership to 39 out of a possible 166 seats. No general election has been held since Mandela's release, but the party has won some important parliamentary by-elections.

According to sociologist Janis Grobbelaar, writing in the *South Africa Foundation Review*, the Conservative party's "performance reflects at the very least that the white right wing is well organized and established in the northern provinces and that Afrikaner nationalism has found a reinvigorated home. Given

these facts it is obvious that Afrikaner nationalism still has an important and significant role to play in the short- to medium-term as South African politics unfold." Treurnicht said in March of 1991 that the battle will be fought in Parliament, as long as the Conservative party believes government will give whites the opportunity to go to the polls. Grobbelaar has said that when the Conservative party believes "that the parliamentary road cannot or will not protect the promised land, [then] alternative routes are most likely to be sought."

As long as the Nationalist party continues to have the support of the police and armed forces, alternative routes involving violence are closed to the Conservatives. The police demonstrated their loyalty to the Nationalist government when they fired tear gas and buckshot on white right-wing AWB (Afrikaaner Weerstandsbeweging) demonstrators in Ventersdorp in August of 1991. Three AWB members were killed

> *"The ANC [African National Congress] hates the Boer people and the white nation. They demand our land. They reject our right to exist."*

and 58 other people injured. The police were preventing the demonstrators from entering a hall where State President F. W. de Klerk was speaking.

The reaction to the confrontation between police and the AWB underscored the possibilities of a united, extraparliamentary right. Treurnicht said that it could mark the beginning of the "Third Boer War," a reference to two previous occasions when Boers fought the British for their right to self-determination. Since the conflict in Ventersdorp, the moderate leadership within the Conservative party has been under pressure to adopt a more militant policy. A number of top Conservative party members have strong links with the AWB.

Treurnicht's religious and political career has been influenced by Dutch theologian/politician Abraham Kuyper, who stressed the importance of self-determination and sovereignty in individual social spheres. As described by Angus Gunn in *South Africa International*, separate development was a small step from Kuyper's world view that "the Creator recognized certain spheres of human activity that had identities and intrinsic organic orders that set them apart. These spheres, or creation ordinances as Kuyper called them, had a sovereignty of their own. They were supposed to evolve harmoniously and independently under the direct government of God."

Treurnicht was trained as a theologian and served as a dominee or minister for 16 years in the Dutch Reformed Church. He left the pulpit in 1960 to become editor of the church's newspaper, *Die Kerkbode*. As editor of the paper he played a major role in the Dutch Reformed Church's decision to withdraw its membership from the World Council of Churches, a move prompted by the 1961 meeting of the World Council of Churches at Cottesloe, Johannesburg, during which the Council concluded that there was no scriptural basis for apartheid laws. In a series of articles in *Die Kerkbode*, Treurnicht disputed the liberal findings of Council, arguing that two of the basic tenets of the church (and apartheid)—the essential unity of mankind and ethnic diversity—were provided for in the New Testament. Treurnicht's arguments persuaded the Dutch Reformed Church to break off relations with the international body and to continue its endorsement of the apartheid policies of the Verwoerd government. Twenty-eight years later, in 1989, the Dutch Reformed Church recanted its previous policies, calling apartheid a "heresy," and described the churches' former support of it "a sin."

With the conservative element ascendant in the church, Treurnicht rose quickly within its hierarchy. He became an assessor in the Cape Synod in 1965 and in the General Synod in 1966. In 1967 he was appointed editor of the new Pretoria daily, *Hoofstad*. As a member of the National party, he was an outspoken conservative. However, he did not join Dr. Albert Hertzog in 1969 when Herzog was dismissed from the Cabinet and left to form the Herstigte Nasionale Party (HNP). In 1971 Treurnicht ran as a National party candidate for Parliament for the seat in Waterberg. He defeated HNP candidate Jaap Marais. Much of the power and influence Treurnicht had in the party derived from his early 1970s role as chairman of the Broederbond—a secret Afrikaner society that wields power in government, industry, and cultural life for the promotion of Afrikaner interests.

In 1975 Prime Minister B. John Vorster appointed Treurnicht deputy minister of Bantu Administration and Education. His appointment came just a year before the black township of Soweto erupted in violence over his department's demand that Afrikaans be the language of instruction in the schools.

In 1978 the leadership post in the party for the Transvaal became vacant with the resignation of Connie Mulder. Treurnicht ran against minister of manpower S. P. Botha, who was responsible for the government's revamping and liberalizing labor legislation. Treurnicht beat Botha for the post of provincial leader by a substantial majority. In 1979 Treurnicht became minister of public works and tourism and the following year he was appointed minister of state administration.

Treurnicht opposed the constitutional reform package proposed by the Nationalists in 1977, which created separate elected parliaments for Indians and "coloreds," as well as for whites. His outspoken opposition to the new constitution, to integrated rugby competition, and to proposals for legalizing black labor unions earned him the nickname in the press of "Dr. No." Treurnicht became the spokesman for those dissatisfied with the fast pace of reforms in the new government of P. W. Botha. The conflict came to a breaking point in 1982 over the issue of power-sharing with Indians and "coloreds." Treurnicht saw the new system as a diminution of white political power because Botha insisted that all three of the Parliaments had to reach decisions by consensus. Treurnicht and 17 others walked out of the Nationalist party and formed the Conservative party.

The Conservative party increased its support from its first test at the polls in 1983. David Welsh of the University of Cape Town, who was quoted in the *Christian Science Monitor*, said of the 1988 by-elections that the appeal of the Conservative party, unlike that of the ultraright, was no longer confined to poorer Afrikaners. It has broken the "respectability barrier" and won support from the middle and lower echelons of the vast white bureaucracy as well as from sections of the the professional classes.

Apparently Treurnicht reaffirms the sense of urgency that he and the Afrikaner people feel at the efforts of the de Klerk government to negotiate with the black majority. According to Treurnicht, the freedoms, rights, and very existence of South African whites are at stake, causing the whites, Nationalists included, to reevaluate their future. Treurnicht has refused to take part in negotiations with the government and black groups unless the government accepts the right of whites to "self-determination." In an address to thousands of people at the Afrikaner monument in Pretoria in 1990 he said, "We are serious. There is no boat waiting for us in the harbour to take us away."

Sources

Books

Adam, Heribert, and Hermann Giliomee, *The Rise and Crisis of Afrikaner Power*, David Philip, 1979.
de Gruchy, John W., *The Church Struggle in South Africa*, Wm. B. Eerdmans, 1979.
Grastrow, Shelagh, *Who's Who in South African Politics*, Ravan Press, 1990.

Leach, Graham, *South Africa*, Methuen, 1986.

Periodicals

Christian Science Monitor, March 31, 1988.
South Africa Foundation Review, February 1990.
South Africa International, July 1991.

—Virginia Curtin Knight

Gus Van Sant

Photograph by Abigayle Tarsches, courtesy of Fine Line Features

Film director, producer, and screenwriter

Full name, Gus Van Sant, Jr.; born in 1952 in Louisville, KY; son of Gus (an apparel company executive) and Betty (Seay) Van Sant. *Education:* Rhode Island School of Design, B.S., 1975.

Addresses: *Home*—Portland, OR.

Career

Director of films, including *The Discipline of D. E.*, 1977; *Mala Noche* ("Bad Night"), 1985; *Switzerland*, 1986; *Five Ways to Kill Yourself* (short), 1987; *Ken Death Gets Out of Jail* (short), 1987; *My New Friends* (short), 1987; *Junior* (short), 1988; *Drugstore Cowboy*, 1989; and *My Own Private Idaho*, 1991.

Awards: Los Angeles Film Critics' Award for best independent film, 1987, for *Mala Noche*; Los Angeles Film Critics' Award, New York Film Critics Circle Award, and Independent Spirit Award, all 1989, all for screenplay (with Daniel Yost) *Drugstore Cowboy*; National Society of Film Critics Award for best screenplay, director, and film of 1989, for *Drugstore Cowboy*.

Sidelights

According to Terrence Rafferty, film critic for the *New Yorker*, filmmaker Gus Van Sant is "one of the few really original talents to emerge from the bleak landscape of American movies in the eighties." David Ansen of *Newsweek* concurred, deeming the emergence of Van Sant "the most heartening news from American 'independent' cinema since Steven (*sex, lies and videotape*) Soderbergh." Wedding gritty realism with a poetic imagination, Van Sant's films are set in the seamy, skid-row enclaves of the Pacific Northwest and explore the lifestyles of such social outcasts as illegal aliens, drug addicts, and male prostitutes. In films such as *Mala Noche* ("Bad Night"), *Drugstore Cowboy*, and *My Own Private Idaho*, Van Sant depicts the lives of these marginalized characters affectionately yet without sentimentality, demonstrating what Ansen described as "an unforced lyrical touch and a feel for low life that's free of both condescension and macho romanticizing."

Though his films depict the lives of outcasts and lowlifes, Van Sant himself comes from a wealthy background. The son of an apparel company executive, Van Sant was born in Louisville, Kentucky, in 1952. Due to his father's work as a salesman, the family moved often during the boy's childhood, living in Denver, Chicago, and Atherton, California, before settling down in Darien, Connecticut, when Van Sant was ten years old. The Van Sants lived in Darien until Gus was a senior in high school, at which point the family settled in Portland, Oregon. It was during his high school years in Darien that Van Sant's interest in filmmaking began; later, he would often go to the movies after his job at a Manhattan advertising agency, watching everything from classic comedies to avant-garde experimentalism. Although he continues to be an avid moviegoer, Van Sant told *Rolling Stone*'s David Handelman: "I'm not a film-historian type, like [Martin] Scorsese, who's seen everything. I'm influenced by what I happen to stumble across."

Upon graduating from high school in 1971, Van Sant enrolled at the Rhode Island School of Design with his good friend and subsequent collaborator Eric Alan Edwards. Van Sant, who at 16 had begun making dramatic movies with a Super 8 camera, intended to divide his time between painting and filmmaking. He soon realized, however, that he did not possess a dedication for painting and decided to focus exclusively on filmmaking. Pivotal in Van Sant's decision was seeing Stanley Kubrick's *A Clockwork Orange* during his freshman year, and his subsequent reading of Kubrick's unique screenplay. As Van Sant told *Rolling Stone:* "It had a completely different format. The descriptions ran down one side in a single-word column that read like a poem, but it came out the exact same number of pages as a traditional screenplay. I thought, 'This is wild; you can do anything you want!' It doesn't matter, because the movie is what counts."

Van Sant graduated from the Rhode Island School of Design in 1975 and moved to Los Angeles where he spent several years on the fringes of the film industry, including working as an assistant to *Groove Tube* director Ken Shapiro. During one of his occasional trips back East, Van Sant visited the New York apartment of Beat generation guru William S. Burroughs, whom he had located in the phonebook. After meeting with the iconoclastic author, Van Sant obtained the rights to film one of the Burroughs's short stories, "The Discipline of D. E. [Do Easy]." The aspiring director shot the film in black and white in 1977, and it was shown at the New York Film Festival. Burroughs himself would later appear in Van Sant's work as a defrocked junkie priest in *Drugstore Cowboy.*

Following a two-year stint as a commercials producer for the New York advertising agency of Cadwell Davis, Van Sant returned to Portland in 1983 and began work on his first feature film. Not only did he script, direct, and produce *Mala Noche*, Van Sant also financed the entire picture with his personal savings. Working out of a Volkswagen van with a crew of three, the director completed *Mala Noche* in 1985 and sent video copies of the 16mm black-and-white film

to numerous distributors, before ultimately finding an agent at William Morris.

Based on a short story by Portland street poet Walt Curtis, *Mala Noche* is set in skid-row Portland and tells the story of a gay convenience store clerk's obsession with a Mexican illegal alien, who repels his amorous advances. The clerk (Walt) tries to win over the young immigrant (Johnny) by giving him small gifts and letting Johnny and his friends use his car. Though Walt's romantic interest in Johnny is clear, the boy teases the clerk, accepting his handouts but deriding Walt as a "stupid faggot." As the movie unfolds, Walt's unrequited obsession for Johnny grows deeper and becomes increasingly hopeless. As Walt remarks at one point, "Johnny will never, never go anywhere with me; I find that sad and absurd." The film ends tragically with the police shooting Johnny's friend Roberto and a humiliated but undaunted Walt still pursuing Johnny.

> *"I really don't know the streets, don't know how they work....I'm the kind of person that just makes it up at home."*

Although the picture was not released to general audiences, *Mala Noche* marked an acclaimed critical debut for the Portland filmmaker. *New York Times* film critic Vincent Canby called *Mala Noche* "a very well-made movie, terse and to the point, nicely photographed by John Campbell and written and directed by Mr. Van Sant with sardonic humor." Deeming the film "a stunning debut," Terrence Rafferty praised the fluidity and technical assurance of Van Sant's direction, adding that "what made the picture particularly exciting was that he appeared to be using his skills in an unusually honest, exploratory way." Fellow *New Yorker* reviewer Pauline Kael similarly praised the film's cinematic qualities remarking that *Mala Noche* has "a wonderful fluid, grainy look—expressionist yet with an improvised feel. It has an authentic grungy beauty."

While *Mala Noche* was Van Sant's first full-length film, it exhibited several features that have now become trademarks of the filmmaker's work, including a dark comic minimalism, starkly poetic imagery, and quirky, keenly observed characters. The young director told *Interview* that he had initially thought of the film—which was produced for approximately $20,000—as "a long-shot bet on my future." Van Sant's bet was to pay immediate dividends, however, as *Mala Noche* won the Los Angeles Film Critics' Award for best independent film of 1987.

The critical success of *Mala Noche* led independent Avenue Pictures to finance Van Sant's next feature, *Drugstore Cowboy*. This film was also shot in the Portland area, with a crew of 70 and a budget of $5 million. Scripted with Daniel Yost and adapted from an unpublished novel by convict and lifelong drug addict James Fogle, *Drugstore Cowboy* chronicles the exploits of a heroin-addicted hustler (Bob Hughes) and his "crew," who satisfy their drug habits by robbing pharmacies. Set in the Oregon countryside during the early 1970s, *Drugstore Cowboy* is told from Bob's point of view and offers a sordid and often darkly humorous insider's view of an addict's life. The film unfolds in a long flashback as a wounded Bob—shot by a teenage drug pusher—looks back on his past adventures with his wife and their two younger companions. A self-professed "shameless full-time dope fiend," Bob (played by Matt Dillon) leads the foursome in a constant pursuit of the perpetual high, frequently just one step ahead of police.

For Bob, his wife Dianne, their friend Rick and Rick's teenage girlfriend Nadine, drugs offer an escape from an otherwise dead-end existence. Similar to *Bonnie and Clyde* in its depiction of a young outlaw couple, *Drugstore Cowboy* intersperses the petty disputes and elaborately planned robberies of this shabby, close-knit group with dreamy images of falling snowflakes and flying hats, visualizations of Bob's drug-induced fantasies. The film's turning point occurs when Nadine dies from an overdose and Bob leaves his wife and Rick in an attempt to go straight. Although the movie closes by returning to Bob's ambulance ride to the hospital when he is first shot, there is a slim measure of hope left by the mere fact that the reformed Bob is still alive.

Drugstore Cowboy was almost universally well-received, garnering a number of prestigious awards including the National Society of Film Critics Award for best screenplay, director, and film. Once more, critics praised Van Sant's originality and stylistic innovation. Terrence Rafferty called the movie "a funny and oddly moving low-life picaresque, with a daring mixture of tones and styles," while David Ansen noted, "Every minute of *Drugstore Cowboy* is vital and alive, even when its junkie protagonists seem barely to be breathing."

Reviewers seemed particularly impressed with Van Sant's straightforward, nonjudgmental presentation of drug addiction. Ansen, for instance, deemed *Drugstore Cowboy* "maybe the most honest movie about drug addicts ever made." Echoing Ansen, a *Variety* contributor remarked, "No previous drug-themed movie has the honesty or originality of Gus Van Sant's drama." In an era dominated by a "Just Say No" approach to drugs, Van Sant was taking a great risk in making a movie that presented anything but an entirely negative view of drug addiction. In fact, so graphic was the film's depiction of drug paraphernalia and abuse that Van Sant's distributor feared an "X" rating from the industry's ratings board. What *Drugstore Cowboy* addresses that other movies about drug addiction often seem to avoid is the very real attraction that drugs hold for users. As Bob remarks to a social worker, "I'm a junkie. I like drugs. I like the whole life-style." In *Drugstore Cowboy* Van Sant neither moralizes on the dangers of drugs nor glorifies his junkie characters. As one writer for *American Film* noted, "There are plenty of opportunities for preachment here, but the script offers insight instead."

Succinctly summing up Van Sant's first two features, Rafferty wrote: "In both pictures, the filmmaker's affection for his down-and-out characters and their mean Northwestern streets was obvious, but he didn't romanticize the people or their milieu. These movies were bracingly clear-eyed, unsentimental. Van Sant didn't condescend to his characters, and he didn't make apologies for them, either. *Mala Noche* and *Drugstore Cowboy* looked at a murky, threatening world with a level gaze, and Van Sant's vision of things as they are had a startling lucidity—a purity that transcended banal naturalism. In these pictures he gave the most abject people and places a kind of integrity; harsh circumstances and desperate needs took on a comic grace."

Despite the critical and commercial success of *Drugstore Cowboy*, Van Sant had difficulty finding financial backing for his next project. The problem was not that the director was without offers; the number of screenplays sent to Van Sant after the release of *Drugstore Cowboy* increased from one a month to ten a week. Rather, the new film's controversial subject matter (male prostitution) along with its proposed source and style (a retelling of William Shakespeare's *Henry IV* plays) caused many studios to shy away from supporting the project. Although he was offered several big-budget features with recognizable Hollywood stars, Van Sant maintained his intention to make his own film, not a studio product.

The director had become interested in male prostitution while trying to break into the movie industry in Los Angeles during the late 1970s. Describing to *Rolling Stone* how he used to watch "hustlers" on Los Angeles's Hollywood Boulevard, Van Sant remarked: "It was like watching another life that was as removed from my life as somebody in another country and yet it was happening simultaneously in our society. It suggested this otherworldly story, but filled with a lot of desperate, end-of-the-line, colorful characters." Though he had originally planned a low-budget production with cast of actual hustlers, Van Sant decided to use the $2.7 million budget New Line Cinema gave him to attract River Phoenix (*Running On Empty*) and Keanu Reeves (*River's Edge*), the two actors he had initially envisioned in the leading roles. As he had done in casting Matt Dillon in the lead of *Drugstore Cowboy*, Van Sant chose to employ teen idols in less than typical or glamorous roles.

More ambitious in style and scope than his two previous features, *My Own Private Idaho* veers widely from reality to fantasy and combines such disparate elements as pornographic magazine covers that come to life, documentary-like anecdotes told by real street hustlers, snippets of home-movies, and Shakespearean dialogue. Largely indebted to Orson Welles's 1966 film *Chimes at Midnight*, another reworking of Shakespeare's *Henry IV*, Van Sant had thought of the film's major conceit a number of years earlier. Described by *Village Voice*'s J. Hoberman as a "tragicomic account of a narcoleptic street hustler pathetically smitten with a slumming golden boy," *My Own Private Idaho* tells the story of two young male prostitutes, Mike Waters (Phoenix) and Scott Favor (Reeves), who drift through the back roads of the Pacific Northwest turning tricks and getting high. Virtually defying plot summary, the film essentially recounts how the lives of Mike, who is searching for his long-lost mother, and Scott, who is running away from his wealthy parents, dovetail. Told from Mike's point of view, the film occasionally blacks out when the narcoleptic young hustler does.

Critical response to *My Own Private Idaho* was generally positive, though perhaps more mixed than with Van Sant's two earlier movies. Donald Lyons in *Film Comment* called the picture "the best American movie of the Nineties" while J. Hoberman found the film "densely textured, beautifully shot (when not purposefully raw), and continually surprising." In a less laudatory response, Rafferty described *My Own Private Idaho* as "a beautiful disaster," remarking that, "for all the technical adventurousness of [the film, it] lacks the emotional complexity of *Mala Noche* and *Drugstore Cowboy*, and it's surprisingly humorless."

An aspect of the film that some critics panned was the director's use of Shakespearean elements, from the Falstaff beer ads and the Elizabethan-influenced costumes of the street people to the paraphrased passages of Shakespearean dialogue. "There's something glib and imprecise about Van Sant's appropriation of Shakespearean motifs" noted Rafferty. Lyons found the use of Shakespearean dialogue "oafish" and "shrill," adding that it would have been "better for Van Sant to have filmed the Shakespeare (with actors who could speak it) or reimagined the entire thing." In spite of such criticisms, a number of reviewers praised Van Sant's willingness to take chances in *My Own Private Idaho* as well as the director's ambitious attempts to expand upon his earlier successes.

Like *My Own Private Idaho*'s Scott Favor, Van Sant himself has rejected a wealthy background for the vitality of the Pacific Northwest's seamy corridors; both character and director share an upper-middle-class fascination with the lower depths. Frequently described as the "street poet of the cinema," Van Sant makes films that exhibit what Lance Loud of *American Film* called "an uncanny ability for making movies in which seemingly desperate characters are not so bad after all." Walt in *Mala Noche*, Bob in *Drugstore Cowboy*, and Mike in *My Own Private Idaho* are all figures whose lifestyles put them on the margins of society. However, in spite of their unsavory ways, Van Sant depicts these characters in an evenhanded manner. The reason for this objective treatment, according to Donald Lyons, lies in the fact that "Van Sant is like [Russian writer] Dostoevsky, so at home in the heart of the sinner." Clearly, though, the director's knowledge of streetlife is largely secondhand. As Van Sant remarked in *Rolling Stone*: "I really don't know the streets, don't know how they work. . . . I'm the kind of person that just makes it up at home. I mean, certain people who lived that life were around during filming [of *My Own Private Idaho*]. It's like if you're making a film about boating, you have some boaters around or else a storm's gonna come up and drown you. But half the time, you're right anyway."

Comparing Van Sant to such bohemian writers as Allen Ginsberg and William S. Burroughs, *Rolling Stone*'s Handelman claimed that the director "has a passion for the stories of seemingly dark and marginal worlds, finding in them a rich texture of poignancy, wisdom and hilarity . . . . His movies themselves exhibit a different way of looking at the world, an unromanticized appreciation of the vicissitudes of life as it passes by." Closely aligned to Van Sant's off-center subject matter is the director's nontraditional method of filmmaking. Employing a free-form approach, which opens itself to improvisation and experimentation, Van Sant often allows his actors to come up with their own lines or actions. This means that the composition of each shot is often decided on the spot. Commenting on the effects of the director's style in the *New Yorker*, Pauline Kael remarked, "Van Sant's films are an antidote to wholesomeness; he's made a controlled style out of the random and the careless. He rings totally unexpected bells."

In setting his films in the Pacific Northwest, Van Sant has been linked with another independent American filmmaker, David Lynch (*Blue Velvet*, *Wild at Heart*, and the TV series *Twin Peaks*). Comparing the two filmmakers, Lyons argued: "David Lynch knows the territory and in his best work—the *Twin Peaks* pilot—applies a satiric varnish to it, but he seems limited to, so to speak, uncovering the insects under the rocks on Ozzie and Harriet's lawn. How much tougher to dwell under the rock with the lowlife and crawl with them toward sky and cloud—which is what Van Sant does." Van Sant has lived in Portland since 1983 and clearly feels comfortable setting his films there. Claiming that the city's isolation gives it originality, the director told *Rolling Stone*, "It's free of a lot of the pigeonholing that goes on in big cities. There's a woodsy quality to the people, and a pride, whether you're a bank manager or a hired killer that shoots heroin."

Although his first three feature films have established him as a major voice in American independent cinema, not much is known about Van Sant's personal life since the filmmaker has a reputation for being reserved and elliptical, even among his friends. Candid about his homosexuality, Van Sant lives in a rambling three-story Victorian house in Portland that doubles as his studio, plays guitar in a rock band named Destroy All Blonds, and occasionally exhibits his paintings in Portland galleries. Since 1984 the director has been making an annual autobiographical short film that he ultimately plans to assemble into a cinematic diary. What is known about Van Sant is that he will remain busy for the foreseeable future. Among his upcoming projects are a screen adaptation of Tom Robbins's 1976 best-seller *Even Cowgirls Get the Blues,* a movie about the life of pop artist Andy Warhol, and possibly a film about Ken Kesey (author of *One Flew Over the Cuckoo's Nest*) and his band of Merry Pranksters. Whatever his plans will include, success does not seem to have dulled Van Sant's adventurousness. He may have arrived in the big time but this self-proclaimed "director for Sodom" has not forsaken his unique cinematic vision. As he told *American Film*, "There's lots of ways to make a movie. I like my own."

Sources

American Film, May 1990; November 1990; September/October 1991.
Film Comment, September/October 1991.
Interview, January 1990.
Newsweek, October 23, 1989; April 15, 1991.
New York, October 9, 1989.
New Yorker, October 30, 1989; October 7, 1991.
New York Times, May 4, 1988.
Rolling Stone, October 19, 1989; October 31, 1991.
Variety, August 30, 1989; October 11, 1989.
Village Voice, October 1, 1991.

—*Robert F. Scott*

Obituaries

Klaus Barbie

Born Nikolaus Barbie, Jr., October 25, 1913, in Bad Godesberg, Germany; died of leukemia, September 25, 1991, in Lyons, France. Former German Gestapo chief. Klaus Barbie was convicted of 177 counts of war crimes in 1987 in Lyons, France, a city that he terrorized as chief of the brutal Nazi Gestapo—the German secret police—during World War II. Between 1942 and 1944, Barbie rounded up Jews to be sent to concentration camps and tortured civilians believed to be in the Resistance—an underground force opposing Nazi occupation. In addition, he was believed to have helped torture to death Jean Moulin, a Resistance leader, as well as send a group of 44 Jewish children to camps in April of 1944 and another 650 two months later when the war was over. Never showing remorse, Barbie said in 1979, as quoted by the *Washington Post*, "I regret each Jew I did not kill."

Though Barbie left Germany after the war, he eventually returned, surviving as a thief until being captured by members of the U.S. Counter Intelligence Corps, which was part of the U.S. Army. Instead of turning him over to the French to stand trial for his crimes, the intelligence agency used him to learn Nazi secrets, some of which they hoped could be used against the Soviet Union. The intelligence agency, noted the London *Times*, "refused French demands to hand him over to justice, fearing that some of their own secrets might thus get back to Moscow."

Hidden by the U.S. Counter Intelligence Agency in Peru, Barbie soon made connections with right-wing military officers in Bolivia and became involved in drug and arms smuggling, terrorism, and political intrigue. In 1982 (one source says 1983), he was finally handed over to the French government, thanks in part to Nazi hunters Beate and Serge Klarsfeld. Throughout his trial five years later, and until his death, Barbie never renounced the oath he made as a Nazi party member to German chancellor Adolf Hitler when he joined in the late 1930s.

Refusing to attend his own trial in 1987, he was sentenced to life in prison on July 4th of that year.

Barbie's father was reputed to be a rough, abusive alcoholic who died of wounds he received fighting the French in World War I. His mother was not able to send him to school, and when Hitler was amassing membership for his party, Barbie joined, attracted to promises of financial security. An intelligent pupil and an efficient soldier, Barbie became renowned for his zealousness and was put to work in the SS (stormtrooper) divisions in Holland in 1940, and in Russia in 1941 and 1942. He was subsequently sent to Lyon, a zone as yet unoccupied by the Germans and thought to be a major center of activities for the Resistance. There he earned the nickname Butcher of Lyon, personally torturing Jean Moulin, a French hero chosen by French statesman Charles de Gaulle to unite the different anti-German forces into a cohesive and effective unit.

It was not until many years later that the missing Barbie was charged in France with war crimes. A death sentence was handed down in 1954, but the charges could not be brought against him in the 1980s because of a 20-year statute of limitations. There were plenty of other charges of inhumane behavior to be brought against him, however; in 1987, he finally received punishment. Barbie's wife, reported to be a faithful Nazi herself, died the year of his capture, and his son died in a hang-gliding accident two years earlier. The notorious Nazi criminal is survived by his daughter, Ute. **Sources:** *Chicago Tribune*, September 26, 1991; *Times* (London), September 27, 1991; *Washington Post*, September 26, 1991.

Frank Capra

Born May 18, 1897, in Palermo, Sicily; died of natural causes, September 3, 1991, in La Quinta, CA. Film director. Frank Capra was an imaginative motion picture director whose homespun philosophy found a wide appeal among American moviegoers.

"Movies should be a positive expression that there is hope, love, mercy, justice and charity," Capra once explained in the *Los Angeles Times*. "A filmmaker has the unrestricted privilege of haranguing an audience for two-hour stretches—the chance to influence public thinking for good or for evil.... It is, therefore, his responsibility to emphasize the positive qualities of humanity by showing the triumph of the individual over adversities." An immigrant who adopted a charismatic optimism about life in America, Capra survived unemployment during the economic Depression of the 1930s and discouragement later in his film career, when he believed he had lost his touch. Although movie critics sometimes faulted Capra for relying on sentimentalism, he tackled difficult subjects and made them inspirational.

The director's best known film was made in 1946. *It's a Wonderful Life* tells the story of a financially troubled family man who, on the verge of committing suicide, is given the opportunity to see what the world would be like if he had never been born. Most moviegoers during the years following the Depression, though, no longer yearned for the escapism the motion picture offered. Capra's film had to wait until the 1970s, when it was widely broadcast on television, for the American public to rediscover his magical idealism.

Capra's early years were marked by poverty, and only seven of his 14 brothers and sisters survived childhood. When the family moved to California, Capra went to work selling newspapers, picking fruit, and teaching himself to play banjo. At 16 he entered the California Institute of Technology, where he paid his own way and studied chemical engineering. After completing school, Capra was selected for military duty and served as a math teacher in a Fort Scott artillery school. "When [World War I] was over and I got loose," Capra once told the *Los Angeles Times*, "I found that the market for chemical engineers was at an all-time low. I was a complete flop at getting a regular job."

Capra worked various odd jobs and began his film career in 1922, when he met Walter Montague, a vaudeville actor who gave the inexperienced Capra his first break. Capra recalled in the *Los Angeles Times*, "I never really said I had film experience; I just let him assume that." His first stab at directing, *Fultah Fisher's Boarding House*, was made with one cameraman, amateur actors, and a budget of $1,700. He subsequently took a break from directing, writing vaudeville gags before making silent films. Critics have noted that his exposure to vaudeville influenced the way Capra would later direct his leading men.

"When a Capra hero started to get too lofty, you could be sure he'd trip over a trash can or get trapped in a phone booth before long," a *People* correspondent observed.

The 1930s was arguably Capra's most creative, active, and successful decade. He discovered actresses Barbara Stanwyck and Jean Harlow, casting them in movies that would make them household names, and paired Clark Gable with Claudette Colbert in the classic comedy *It Happened One Night*, a film that won several Oscars, including one for best director. Stories pairing innocent characters with cynical ones were perfect for the Capra touch, as evidenced by his other Oscar-winning projects, *Mr. Deeds Goes to Town* and *Mr. Smith Goes to Washington*. Though the films for which he remains best known were yet to come, Capra would never again be so adulated.

In the early days of World War II, General George C. Marshall, the U.S. Army chief of staff, asked Capra to join the service and help salvage morale. "General Marshall was working with undernourished, undereducated recruits," Capra once recounted in the *Washington Post*. "One day he said to me, 'I think these boys can do the job if they know what the hell it's all about... if they are given answers as to why they are in uniform, and if the answers they get are worth fighting and dying for. I want a series of documented films that will explain to our boys why we are fighting and the principles for which we are fighting.'" Capra took Marshall quite literally, making a seven-part series called *Why We Fight*, which the *Chicago Tribune* called "smoothly persuasive propaganda." Nevertheless, the series won Capra an Oscar for best documentary in 1942.

A discharged colonel with many military honors, Capra returned to his film career but never enjoyed the same popularity he had in the 1930s. With 1960's *A Pocketful of Miracles*, "I was losing my touch," he admitted, as quoted by the *Washington Post*. Capra also found himself losing the directoral control he once had over his films; after retiring from moviemaking, he became a champion of directors' rights, outlining his cause in his 1971 autobiography *Frank Capra: The Name Above the Title*. **Sources:** *Chicago Tribune*, September 4, 1991; *Los Angeles Times*, September 4, 1991; *People*, September 16, 1991; *Times* (London), September 5, 1991; *Washington Post*, September 4, 1991.

Miles Davis

Born Miles Dewey Davis III, May 25, 1926, in Alton, IL; died of pneumonia, respiratory failure, and a stroke, September 28, 1991, in Santa Monica, CA. Trumpeter, composer. Miles Davis, the legendary jazz trumpeter, released groundbreaking albums and performed in numerous concerts, emanating a sullen and ominous presence that earned him the nickname Prince of Darkness. After making several recordings with his bebop mentors, Davis formed a nine-piece band and recorded with Gil Evans, inspiring a cool jazz movement. He also popularized jazz based on modal scales, performing with Bill Evans on such LPs as *Kind of Blue*, and shook the jazz world with the rock and roll-influenced *Bitches Brew* of 1970. Each step in Davis's career spawned a creative and popular revolution. While he was never credited with inventing a jazz form, Davis had a sense of what was timely and provocative.

Few, however, could claim that Davis was an easygoing man; usually labeled arrogant by his fellow performers, Davis nevertheless helped launch the careers of several modern musicians. The trumpeter's own career was marked by several productive and successful pairings with various musical geniuses, including Charlie Parker, Gil Evans, and John Coltrane. On the other hand, audiences were sometimes put off by Davis's standoffish stage manner: he often performed with his back to them. Jazz great Herbie Hancock protested in *People*, "He never did that. He was looking at [the band]. He wouldn't focus on the audience, he would focus on the band, on the music."

More cerebral than instinctive, Davis could argue and explain his musical ideas and techniques brilliantly, as he did in his 1989 book, *Miles: The Autobiography*, which he wrote in collaboration with Quincy Troupe. As excerpted in the London *Times*, Davis wrote, "To be a great musician you've got to be open to what's new, what's happening at the moment. You have to be able to absorb it if you're going to continue to grow and communicate your music."

The son of a dentist and a music teacher, Davis took up the trumpet at age 13. By the time he was 18, he was playing with the Billy Eckstine band and attending the Juilliard School of Music. Though not a master of the intricacies of the instrument, "Davis was later to turn his technical limitations to his own advantage . . . he evolved a smoother, burnished sound rooted in the middle register," observed the London *Times*. Davis soon moved to New York City to be near the bebop movement, which was fathered by trumpeter Dizzy Gillespie and Charlie Parker, the

great saxophonist. Charlie Parker's innovations, in particular, provided an influence crucial to Davis's musical progression. The *New York Times* noted that his "unmistakable, voicelike, nearly vibratoless tone," was well suited to the cool jazz he helped develop in the late 1940s and early 1950s.

Davis eventually turned away from cool jazz and used his bebop background to inform the new hard bop style. His 1959 *Kind of Blue* album with pianist Bill Evans reflected the influence of modal jazz, a style based on modal scales rather than chords. The fusion genre would be Davis's next leap, and *Bitches Brew* walked the line between his earlier jazz music and the more rock-oriented recordings that would dominate his oeuvre in the 1980s. The LP sold exceptionally well for a jazz recording, and Davis earned a much wider audience. Jon Pareles described Davis's musical wanderlust in the *New York Times*: "every four or five years, sometimes even more frequently, he would destabilize his style and start again."

Davis's chilly persona can perhaps be partly attributed to poor health; he suffered from diabetes, sickle-cell anemia, and gallstones, illnesses which were no doubt aggravated by chain-smoking, a heroin addiction during the 1950s, and regular cocaine use. In 1957 Davis had nodes removed from his vocal cords and permanently lost full use of his voice several days later in a screaming match with record producers. He subsequently spoke with a raspy whisper; some critics compared his voice to the sound of his trumpet, which invited one to "lean closer to hear the cry at its center," remarked the *New York Times's* Pareles.

After a 1972 automobile accident in which both of his legs were broken, Davis was afflicted with leg infections, pneumonia, and bleeding ulcers and became addicted to painkillers. It was not until 1981, when he married his third wife, actress Cicely Tyson, and released *The Man with the Horn*, that he came out of the seclusion of his Manhattan brownstone. "I didn't feel like listening to music. Didn't want to hear it, see it, smell it, nothing about it," Davis once recalled in *People*. After his marriage to Tyson ended in 1988, he spent much of his time in Malibu, California, painting and entertaining at his home. His late recordings were, for the most part, considered disappointing regressions to past styles or mediocre pop songs designed to be commercially successful. He will be remembered, though, as an innovative trumpeter who made a lasting impression on the world of jazz and rock and roll music. **Sources:** *Entertainment Weekly*, October 11, 1991; *New York*

Times, September 29, 1991, October 6, 1991; *People*, October 14, 1991; *Times* (London), September 30, 1991; *Washington Post*, September 29, 1991.

Colleen Dewhurst

Born June 3, 1924, in Montreal, Quebec, Canada; died of cancer, August 22, 1991, in South Salem, NY. Actress. Acclaimed actress Colleen Dewhurst played Murphy's mother on the television series *Murphy Brown*, served as president of the Actor's Guild for two terms, and, most notably, changed the way Broadway theatergoers perceived playwright Eugene O'Neill. A strong and influential woman, Dewhurst did not resemble the tormented O'Neill heroines she played on stage. After weathering three stormy marriages—two to actor George C. Scott—she found happiness in her last 16 years with Broadway producer Ken Marsolais on their South Salem, New York, farm. Though best known for her theater performances, for which she won two Obies and two Tonys, Dewhurst earned three Emmys for her television roles.

The versatile actress did not always take on the most challenging roles, but as *Los Angeles Times* critic Sheila Benson put it, "We have too few women like [Dewhurst] in films. Regrettably, there is not much call for them." Dewhurst captivated critics and fans with her throaty, rumbling voice and striking, self-assured expression. As with most adulated actors, she infused each character with a charisma that yielded unforgettable portrayals. But to her friends, Dewhurst was a gentle woman. "She's like an earth mother," her friend Maureen Stapleton was quoted as saying in the *New York Times*, "but in real life she's not to be let out without a keeper .... She's the madonna of the birds with the broken wings."

The daughter of a hockey and football player, Dewhurst moved with her family from their native Montreal to Boston, later relocating to Milwaukee after her parents' divorce. As a young woman Dewhurst attended Milwaukee-Downer College, where she decided to become an actress. For many years before her career on Broadway, she worked in summer stock while supporting herself with odd jobs. Dewhurst once spoke of her growing interest in acting, as quoted by the *New York Times*: "When I started acting—just a kid—it was, 'I like theater.' Then it was 'I love theater.' Now it's more than that." The actress's first role was an omen: she was chosen to play a dancing villager in a 1952 production of

O'Neill's *Desire Under the Elms*, for which she would play the lead role in 1963.

Dewhurst's big break came in 1956 when Joseph Papp, the famous Broadway producer, cast her into *The Taming of the Shrew*, one production in his burgeoning Shakespeare-in-the-Park project. The late Papp once mourned Dewhurst in *People*: "We have suffered the loss of a true spirit, a woman of rare talent and unsurpassed enthusiasm for life and the living. Colleen will be remembered as long as joy is remembered." Dewhurst's success on stage coincided with her first partnership with George C. Scott in 1958's *Children of Darkness*, which was performed at Circle in the Square in New York City. After starring with Scott in *Antony and Cleopatra*, the two began a tumultuous personal relationship. "I always said we got along much better during the divorces," Dewhurst said of her two marriages to Scott in *People*. "We make a better brother and sister."

Dewhurst's portrayals in O'Neill plays—as Christine Mannon in *Mourning Becomes Electra*, Abbie Putnam in *Desire Under the Elms*, and Essie Miller in *Ah, Wilderness!*—were praised as authentic and touching. The London *Times* observed that "Dewhurst's Mary [of *Long Day's Journey into Night*] was no sentimentalised drug addict but a woman shockingly close to [critic] Kenneth Tynan's description of the part as an 'emotional vampire.'" The actress once noted in the *Washington Post*, "I always say that I am not an O'Neill expert. I feel all I really know are his women .... O'Neill's women have great passion, a passion for life. Nothing is done halfway. It's not little tiny things that happen to them. These plays are not about the day you cracked up the car and didn't know how to explain it."

Passionate characters were the hallmark of Dewhurst's non-O'Neill stage repertoire as well, including her roles in *A Ballad of the Sad Cafe* and *Who's Afraid of Virginia Woolf?* Active in theater-related causes, she was a member of the Board of the Actors, Fund of America, and the American Council for the Arts, among others. In addition, she served as vice-chair of Save the Theaters, a group that unsuccessfully tried to preserve several historical New York City theaters. Strong-willed and articulate, Dewhurst was outspoken in promoting Asian actor organizations, which protested the casting of a British actor in an Asian role in the musical *Miss Saigon*. The actress is survived by her two sons, Campbell and Alexander R. Scott, both of whom are active in the show business industry. **Sources:** *Chicago Tribune*, August 24, 1991; *Globe and Mail* (Toronto), August 24, 1991; *Los Angeles Times*, August 24, 1991; *New York Times*,

August 24, 1991; *People*, September 9, 1991; *Times* (London), August 26, 1991; *Washington Post*, August 24, 1991.

Leo Durocher

Born Leo Ernest Durocher, July 27, 1905, in Springfield, MA; died October 7, 1991, in Palm Springs, CA. Baseball manager. Leo "the Lip" Durocher, like embattled fellow manager Billy Martin, did not believe in mixing etiquette and baseball. Durocher managed several teams throughout his career—including the Brooklyn Dodgers, New York Giants, Chicago Cubs, and Houston Astros—with a fanatic pursuit of victory: he amassed three National League Pennants and one World Series win. Durocher often had conflicts with team owners, however, and he "estimated that he was fired and rehired informally at least 60 times by [Brooklyn's] Larry MacPhail, the general manager, before Branch Rickey took over during World War I," according to the *New York Times*. Many baseball fans elevated Durocher to folk hero status because of his antics on and off the field, which included kicking dirt on umpires and making such classic statements as "nice guys finish last."

Psychological and physical intimidation were fair play in Durocher's book, but his controversial tactics cost him many a fine and suspension. Commissioner A. B. (Happy) Chandler handed him a one-year suspension in 1947 because of what was referred to as "an accumulation of unpleasant incidents detrimental to baseball," including consorting with alleged gambling figures, the London *Times* noted. At times showing his more beneficent side, though, the manager once persuaded Willie Mays to stay with the Giants through a difficult period; Mays "told me it was too fast for him, that he couldn't play up here, and asked me to send him back to Minneapolis," Durocher once recalled, as quoted by the *Detroit Free Press*. "I put my arm around him and told him, 'Not as long as I have the Giants on my uniform. I brought you up here to play center field, and that's where you're going to play.'" Durocher himself played 17 seasons as a shortstop with such teams as the Yankees, the Cincinnati Reds, the Brooklyn Dodgers, and the St. Louis Cardinals and earned a fine fielding and hustling reputation. A member of the Cardinals in the mid-1930s, Durocher played alongside Dizzy and Paul Dean, Pepper Martin, Frankie Risch, and Joe Medwick, a group of personalities known as the Gas House Gang. A *New York Times* reporter observed that Durocher's "taste for all-out combat on the field and merry hi-jinks off it blended nicely with the rough and ready style of the Cardinals."

Durocher outlined his dog-eat-dog philosophy of baseball in his 1975 autobiography, *Nice Guys Finish Last*, and in Gilbert Millstein's 1951 *Fireside Book of Baseball*. In the latter book, as excerpted in the *Los Angeles Times*, Durocher is quoted as saying, "Look, I'm playing third base. My mother's on second. The ball's hit out to short center. As my mother goes by me on my way to third, I'll accidently trip her. I'll help her up, brush her off and tell her I'm sorry, but she doesn't go to third."

Though Durocher quit playing to become a manager in 1938, his baseball creed never changed. He turned a Dodgers team known for what the *Washington Post* termed its "daffy futility" into a winning ball club and later transformed the Giants in the same way, guiding them to a 1954 World Series victory. Soon after, he embarked on a five-year sabbatical, working for the National Broadcasting Corporation (NBC) as a commentator, but eventually returned to his baseball career. Feuds with players and management of the Houston Astros, however, prompted his retirement in 1973.

The ever-colorful Durocher, married to actress Larraine Day, apparently socialized with Frank Sinatra and, like the singer, was believed to have ties with the mafia. Accusatory headlines were in part responsible for a suspension from baseball and no doubt contributed to his ostracism from the Baseball Hall of Fame. Nevertheless, Los Angeles Dodgers manager Tommy LaSorda took the number two for his uniform out of his great respect and admiration for Durocher. The *Chicago Tribune* cited *Baseball's Greatest Managers*, in which Edwin Pope states, "Benefactor or blackguard, genius or jerk, paragon or prodigal, Leo Durocher was one of the most beguiling figures to walk through baseball." **Sources:** *Chicago Tribune*, October 8, 1991; *Detroit Free Press*, October 8, 1991; *Los Angeles Times*, October 8, 1991; *New York Times*, October 8, 1991; *Times* (London), October 15, 1991; *Washington Post*, October 8, 1991.

Tennessee Ernie Ford

Born Ernest Jennings Ford, February 13, 1919, in Bristol, TN; died of a liver disease, October 17, 1991, in Reston, VA. Singer, entertainer. Without a doubt, Tennessee Ernie Ford stayed true to his country background throughout his career, and his talent and sincerity earned him the devotion of millions of record-buying fans. His appearances on radio and television were equally popular, as folks would tune in to hear Ford coin such classic expressions as "bless your pea-pickin' heart" and "I was as nervous as a long-tailed cat in a room full of rockin' chairs" in a way that was genuine and friendly. Imitators have failed to duplicate the Ford warmth without seeming phony or patronizing, and country and gospel music lovers everywhere recognize the entertainer as a legend.

From his breakthrough with Cliffie Stone's *Hometown Jamboree*, a radio show broadcast from California, to "Sixteen Tons," the astonishingly popular folk-blues song co-written with Merle Travis, Ford never struck a wrong note, even when he sang gospel tunes in glitzy Las Vegas. "When I'd work the big rooms in Reno and Las Vegas, the first question guests would ask is, 'You're going to sing gospel, aren't you?'" Ford remarked in *People*. "So many entertainers are afraid to sing that kind of music and sing it like it ought to be done. If the audience gets a little twinge from it, fine." Ford's religious roots went back to his days as a young boy singing in his family's Methodist church, and he often ended his shows with a hymn. Entertainers with genuine charisma like Tennessee Ernie Ford are rare in the 1990s; he represents an earlier and more innocent time in the United States.

The bass-baritone studied at the Cincinnati Conservatory of Music in 1937, after holding down a ten-dollar-a-week job as a disc jockey. Ford's music career was interrupted with a stint in the Air Corps during World War II, but he went on to find work at a radio station in San Bernardino, California. At first just an announcer trying out his humorous lines on the *Hometown Jamboree*, he became a regular on the show and earned a record contract in 1947. Ford's first hits included "Shotgun Boogie"—which was his own song—"Mule Train," and "Cry of the Wild Goose." His "Davy Crockett" of 1955 was chosen as the theme for the Walt Disney television show of the same title and became a favorite among both adults and children.

Ford's songs had a crossover appeal; his gospel and country tunes often appeared on the popular music charts, and his "Sixteen Tons" of 1955 sold one million copies in three weeks and topped five million in sales in the United States alone. These figures were unprecedented in the country music industry of the 1950s, and Ford is credited with opening the way for such crossover country stars as Kenny Rogers and Willie Nelson. Ford was once quoted by the London

Times as saying that "Sixteen Tons" is "an everlasting hit. It seems that young marrieds and even high school kids know it. It caught on to every working man in the world, I guess."

Ford, who is survived by two sons and his second wife, Beverly, was presented with the Presidential Medal of Freedom by President Ronald Reagan in 1984. The entertainer had won a Grammy in 1964, was nominated for seven more, and received two Emmy nominations for his television work, which included the popular *Ford Hour*, a variety show that ran from 1956 to 1961. In 1990 Ford was overwhelmed by his nomination to the Country Music Hall of Fame. Counting among his fans Queen Elizabeth of England, the singer was the first country music performer to be invited to give a concert at the London Palladium. After his television show was canceled, Ford made appearances on many other country-oriented programs and was honored in 1990 with an hour-long cable TV special, which starred the likes of Dinah Shore and the Everly Brothers. Ford leaves behind a legacy of more than 80 records, a collection that preserves his unique 50-year career for country lovers of future generations. **Sources:** *Chicago Tribune*, October 18, 1991; *Los Angeles Times*, October 18, 1991; *People*, November 4, 1991; *Times* (London), October 19, 1991; *Washington Post*, October 18, 1991.

Redd Foxx

Born John Elroy Sanford, December 9, 1922, in St. Louis, MO; died of a heart attack, October 11, 1991, in Los Angeles, CA. Actor, comedian. Before comedians Richard Pryor and Eddie Murphy there was Redd Foxx, a bowlegged comic who dished out the same brand of humor he heard on the streets and at home, making no apologies for lewd language. "That's the humor heard in the ghettos," Foxx once remarked in the *New York Times*. "They didn't pull no punches, and they didn't want to hear about Little Boy Blue and Cinderella. So I gave them what they wanted. I busted loose." Foxx had wanted to be an entertainer from childhood and after running away from home at age 13, he spent years performing on street corners or in black vaudeville. As with many other struggling entertainers, Foxx held various odd jobs to make ends meet, but when he could not, he was sometimes arrested on petty charges for sleeping in hallways or stealing a quart of milk.

Formerly John Sanford, the comedian adopted the surname of baseball player Jimmie Foxx and was nicknamed Red because of the color of his hair and his light skin. He was later called "Chicago Red," so as not to be confused with "Detroit Red," the black activist Malcolm X, who once referred to Foxx as "the funniest dishwasher on Earth," according to the *Chicago Tribune*. In the 1950s, Foxx began to develop a following with 54 so-called party records, which contained his bawdy comedy routines. Though some record stores refused to shelve them, the albums sold well and established Redd Foxx's name in show business.

In the 1960s Foxx graduated from small, black nightclubs to venues in Las Vegas, where he lived and worked for many years. He made his first forays into television with guest appearances on such programs as *Today, The Addams Family, Mr. Ed, Green Acres, I Love Lucy*, and the *Flip Wilson Show*. "No one expected me to be on television because I had a reputation from the party records as X-rated, but that's the kind of humor I liked," the comedian was quoted as saying in the *New York Times*. For three months he starred as a New York businessman in his own *Redd Foxx Show*, but his major television success came in 1972 with *Sanford and Son*. A sitcom centering on a cranky junkyard owner and his son, Lamont, *Sanford and Son* ran from 1972 to 1977 and was one of the first shows on television with a primarily black cast. The popular program inspired many imitations and helped open the medium of television to minorities; *Washington Post* critic Laurence Laurent called the show "a small step in television's progress in showing members of a racial minority with respect, warmth and affection."

Sanford and Son made Foxx a wealthy man, but he nevertheless experienced difficulties with financial management later in life. The comedian's home in Las Vegas was raided to obtain goods for an auction in 1983 by the Internal Revenue Service (IRS), who claimed the entertainer owed more than $3 million in taxes and fines. Foxx was well known for his generosity and spending habits; he spoke bitterly of this reputation in the *New York Times*: "I've been cheated more than most people because I'm gullible and I'm a target. My heart is open, and I listen to people and I believe their sob stories."

The tax problem was not the only thing to scar Foxx's image. He was charged in 1979 with pistol-whipping an executive of his cosmetics firm. In addition, during divorce proceedings, Foxx's second wife accused him of physically abusing her. Aside from these personal difficulties, Foxx was enjoying renewed popularity shortly before his death as the star of a new television series. *The Royal Family*, a CBS

sitcom, featured Foxx and Della Reese as a retired husband and wife who allow their daughter and three grandchildren to move in with them. Foxx collapsed of a heart attack while working on the show's set. Slappy White, one of Foxx's former partners, was quoted in the *New York Times* as saying, "The comedy world is going to miss him. He broke a lot of barriers." **Sources:** *Chicago Tribune*, October 13, 1991; *New York Times*, October 13, 1991; *Washington Post*, October 13, 1991.

Theodor Geisel

Born Theodor Seuss Geisel, March 2, 1904, in Springfield, MA; died of cancer, September 24, 1991, in La Jolla, CA. Author. Theodor Geisel, better known to millions of children as Dr. Seuss, brought a whimsical touch and a colorful imagination to the world of children's books. Before Geisel, juvenile books were largely pastel, predictable, and dominated by a didactic tone. Though Dr. Seuss books sometimes included morals, they sounded less like behavioral guidelines and more like, "listen to your feelings" and "take care of the environment," universal ideas that would win over the hearts of youngsters from around the world; Geisel's 47 books were translated into 20 languages and have sold more than 200 million copies. Of the ten bestselling hardcover children's books of all time, four were written by Geisel: *The Cat in the Hat, Green Eggs and Ham, One Fish, Two Fish, Red Fish, Blue Fish*, and *Hop on Pop*.

Geisel's last two books spent several months on the bestseller lists and include themes that appeal to adults as well as children. "Finally I can say that I write not for kids but for *people*," he commented in the *Los Angeles Times*. Many of his readers were surprised to learn that Geisel had no children of his own, though he had stepchildren from his second marriage to Audrey Stone Dimond; he once said, "You make 'em, I amuse 'em," as quoted in the *Chicago Tribune*. According to the *Los Angeles Times*, the author also remarked, "I don't think spending your days surrounded by kids is necessary to write the kind of books I write.... Once a writer starts talking down to kids, he's lost. Kids can pick up on that kind of thing."

When he was a child, Geisel practiced sketching at the local zoo, where his father was superintendent. He went on to graduate from Dartmouth College in 1925 and subsequently studied at the Lincoln College of Oxford University. After dropping out of Oxford, he traveled throughout Europe, mingling with emigres in Paris, including writer Ernest Hemingway. Eventually returning to New York, he spent 15 years in advertising before joining the army and making two Oscar-winning documentaries, *Hitler Lives* and *Design for Death*.

Geisel began writing the verses of his first book, *And to Think That I Saw It on Mulberry Street*, in 1936 during a rough sea passage. Published a year later, the book won much acclaim, largely because of its unique drawings. All of Geisel's books, in fact, feature crazy-looking creatures that are sometimes based on real animals, but usually consist of such bizarre combinations of objects as a centipede and a horse and a camel with a feather duster on its head. Unlike many puppeteers and cartoonists who have capitalized on their creations by selling their most familiar images to big-time toymakers, though, Dr. Seuss concentrated his efforts on creating captivating books.

Admired among fellow authors and editors for his honesty and hard work, the Pulitzer Prize-winning author, according to Ruth MacDonald in the *Chicago Tribune*, "perfected the art of telling great stories with a vocabulary as small as sometimes 52 or 53 words." "[Geisel] was not only a master of word and rhyme and an original and eccentric artist," declared Gerald Harrison, president of Random House's merchandise division, in *Publisher's Weekly*, "but down deep, I think he was basically an educator. He helped teach kids that reading was a joy and not a chore.... For those of us who worked with him, he taught us to strive for excellence in all the books we published." **Sources:** *Chicago Tribune*, September 26, 1991; *Entertainment Weekly*, October 11, 1991; *Los Angeles Times*, September 26, 1991; *People*, October 7, 1991; *Publisher's Weekly*, October 25, 1991; *Times* (London), September 27, 1991.

Bill Graham

Born Wolfgang Grajonca in 1931 in Berlin, Germany; died in a helicopter accident, October 25, 1991. Rock music promoter. Surviving an extraordinarily stormy childhood, Bill Graham overcame great odds to become one of the most influential figures in the entertainment industry. Graham's Russian Jewish parents fled Berlin when the German Nazis—who initiated a policy of exterminating Jews—were amassing power, but his father was soon killed in an accident, and his mother, left with six children, put Graham and his 13-year-old sister in an orphanage.

In 1940 a Red Cross worker tried to save the 63 children in the orphanage from the ravages of World War II by taking the children across France; only 11 children survived, not including Graham's sister. They continued their trek across northern Africa to Cuba, eventually ending up in New York City, where Graham was put in another orphanage that he once described in *People* as "a pet shop." Later landing a job, he was able to earn enough money to bring his four older sisters to the United States; his mother had died in a Nazi concentration camp.

Graham's experience as a refugee probably inspired his later fund-raising efforts for victims of famine, natural disaster, and drug-related urban blight. In 1986, for example, he organized the Conspiracy of Hope tour and two years later arranged the Human Rights Now international tour, both of which benefitted Amnesty International, a group protesting the imprisonment of political prisoners throughout the world. Graham also earned a reputation as a fiery and opinionated businessman; aside from his successful charitable work, he helped transformed the rock and roll world into a lucrative industry. Though he was sometimes criticized as a sell-out who was willing to sacrifice the rebellious aspects of rock music in order to turn a profit, there is no doubt that Graham was instrumental in helping the genre reach a larger audience. "Bill was one of them [i.e., a businessmen] and one of us," Grace Slick of the band Jefferson Starship told *People*. "It's scary not having him here anymore. He was one of those people you thought would never die."

Indeed, in addition to his harrowing experience in Nazi Germany, Graham had another brush with war after high school. Drafted into the army to serve in the Korean War, he was awarded a Bronze Star and a Purple Heart, even though his independent spirit had earned him several court martials on minor violations. When he returned to the United States, Graham took a job as a cab driver in New York City and earned a degree in business administration from the City College of New York. In the early 1960s he moved to San Francisco, working as an office manager and actor before being hired as manager of the Mime Troupe. Often in difficult financial straits, the theater group was buoyed by Graham, who became a proficient fund-raiser. Aware of the burgeoning psychedelic rock movement of the time, he hired the then-unknown Jefferson Airplane to play a benefit concert, recalling in *People*, "We held a subterranean fund-raising. A psychedelic bacchanal. November 6, 1965—the beginning of my rock life. I had never heard of the musicians Jefferson Airplane or the Mothers of Invention. It lasted until 6 a.m. and blew my mind. Everyone wanted to do it again, so I rented an old skating rink with a stage. That became the Fillmore West." Graham repeated the success of the Fillmore in New York and went on to become a major power in the music management world. Rock groups like the Grateful Dead, the Rolling Stones, and many others came to rely on his business savvy to assure successful concert tours.

One of the qualities that Graham is credited with bringing to rock concerts is safety: "Security was given to properly accredited firms and not left in the hands of Hell's Angels," noted the London *Times*. Graham was a stickler for details, even with the bands themselves; he has been described as a bundle of nerves backstage, clutching his clipboard and stop watch. His organizing efforts helped make 1985's Live Aid concert—which raised money for African famine relief—an astonishing success that reached a worldwide audience of millions with the help of satellite link-ups. The bands themselves were grateful for Graham's meticulous sound checks and they in turn were only asked to show up in time for the performance. Graham, who was private about his personal life, was divorced twice and had two sons. His death is regarded as the passing of a patriarch in the music industry. **Sources:** *Los Angeles Times*, October 27, 1991; *New York Times*, October 27, 1991; *People*, November 11, 1991; *Times* (London), October 28, 1991.

Klaus Kinski

Born Nikolaus Gunther Nakszynski in 1926, in Sopot, Danzig (now Poland); died of heart failure, November 23, 1991, in Lagunitas, CA. Actor. Though Klaus Kinski's bulging eyes, demonic expressions, and menacing gestures made him the ideal horror-film monster, he avoided being typecast with the help of director Werner Herzog, who harnessed the actor's unique qualities and cast him in drama films. Kinski had previously taken roles in such motion pictures as the *Creature with the Blue Hand* and *For a Few Dollars More* in the late 1940s and early 1950s, but it was only after a small part in *Dr. Zhivago* that he earned a role in Herzog's 1972 *Aguirre, the Wrath of God*. The relationship between the actor and the director was notoriously stormy. Kinski would go into rages on the set, "threatening to kill his director, to trample him into the mud—a not infrequent attendant hazard of Herzog locations—or to hurl him into a river full of blood-thirsty piranhas," noted the London *Times*. Still, Herzog cast

the actor into some of his best films, including *Fitzcarraldo* in 1982 and his well-known remake of *Nosferatu* in 1979.

Contentious relationships, in fact, were the rule for Kinski; even his daughter, actress Nastassja Kinski, filed a libel suit against him. After he was married in 1971 for the third time—to Vietnamese student Genevieve Minhoi—he smashed dishes in a restaurant and fought with police. He was also known for being a nasty interviewee who would sometimes verbally attack reporters, or speak only to boast about his sexual prowess. Often hot-tempered on the set, Kinski informed the director of *Crawlspace* on his first day of work, "David Lean didn't direct me [in *Dr. Zhivago*], and you aren't going to direct me," as reported by the *Los Angeles Times*. Despite these highly publicized personal shortcomings, Kinski could realistically portray a variety of people on-screen and could inject the most seemingly repulsive characters with humanity.

Kinski's outspoken and abusive nature may be partly explained by his nightmarish childhood in eastern Europe during World War II. When an economic depression settled into the small Polish town were he was born, his pharmacist father moved the family to Berlin, where they all became German citizens but remained poverty-stricken. Kinski was drafted into the German army at age 16 and saw only a few days of combat before he was captured and sent to a British prisoner-of-war camp.

Ironically, the actor's first experience performing in front of an audience was in a talent show at the camp. After his release, Kinski wandered through Europe before "spending his first post-war winter in an unheated theater in Berlin," according to the *Chicago Tribune*. Kinski described those nomadic days in his controversial autobiography, *All I Need is Love: A Memoir*. While the book is mostly a list of the actor's sexual conquests—including reports of liaisons with his mother and his daughter, Nastassja—it also sets out the excruciating details of lice-ridden starvation in post-war Germany. Acting proved to be an outlet for the extraordinary powerlessness he felt; as he told the *Washington Post*, "If I hadn't been an actor, I would have been a murderer or the victim of a murderer."

While Kinski appeared in nearly 200 films in his lifetime, many were bit parts in B-movies made in Berlin after the war. Herzog would be one of the few who would cast the actor into lead roles. *Aguirre*—which tells the story of a Spanish conquistador who goes mad as he searches for gold in the Mexican jungles—is perhaps the film for which Kinski will be best remembered. Another popular Herzog/Kinski project, *Fitzcarraldo*, was noted for its nearly impossible filming location. A tale of obsession set in 19th-century Peru, the film featured Kinski as an Irishman consumed with the idea of bringing an opera house to the steamy wilderness. Accounts of the difficult conditions for cast and crew on the set are legendary: they neatly parallel the script of the movie.

In the early 1980s, after making *Fitzcarraldo*, Kinski moved from France to the United States, noting in the London *Times*, "I would rather wash dishes in America than make films in Europe." Among his last roles was a hypnotic Israeli Intelligence agent in *The Little Drummer Girl*, based on a book by John Le Carre. Kinski also had a part in the sexually explicit, unreleased biographical film, *Paganini*, which the actor also wrote and directed. Besides Nastassja, Kinski's survivors include a daughter from his first marriage and a son from his third. **Sources:** *Chicago Tribune*, November 26, 1991; *Los Angeles Times*, November 26, 1991; *New York Times*, November 27, 1991; *Times* (London), November 27, 1991; *Washington Post*, November 27, 1991.

Fred MacMurray

Born Frederick Martin MacMurray, August 30, 1908, in Kankakee, IL; died of pneumonia, November 5, 1991, in Santa Monica, CA. Actor. A real-life nice guy who never took acting lessons, Fred MacMurray was the highest-paid actor in Hollywood in 1943—with a salary of $430,000—but maintained a modest, easygoing nature that made him a favorite among American audiences, especially fans of his Walt Disney films. MacMurray never claimed to be "a dedicated actor," according to the *New York Times*. "I'm lazy in spurts," he once said. "I'd as soon go fishing or play golf." Unlike the many high-powered self-seekers in the film business since 1970, MacMurray relied on his natural affability to win roles and he usually played likeable, down-home characters.

The actor's atypical portrayal of a sleazy insurance investigator in 1944's *Double Indemnity*, though, is considered his best. Director Billy Wilder advised him to act against his genial nature in order to shock the audience, much as director Alfred Hitchcock instructed actor Jimmy Stewart in *Vertigo*. "Whether I play a heavy or a comedian," MacMurray once told the *New York Times*, "I always start out Smiley MacMurray. If I play a heavy, there comes a point in the film when the audience realizes I'm really a heel." The lanky pipe-smoker was often praised for his light touch as a comedic actor, which was evident in his role as the father in the long-running television series, *My Three Sons*. Still, MacMurray was unwilling to accept responsibility for the program's popularity. "He would always refer to [the actors who portrayed the sons] as the success behind his show," noted one of the show's actors, Barry Livingston, in the *Chicago Tribune*. "He was always a very humble man." A family man in real life as well, MacMurray had been married since 1954 to former actress June Haver and had a son and three daughters.

MacMurray got his start in show business performing in traveling musical comedies. He attended Carroll College in Waukesha, Wisconsin, for one year and subsequently made a living as a singer and saxophonist with dance and vaudeville bands. The son of a concert pianist, MacMurray briefly played with his own three-piece band, Mac's Melody Boys. Turning to acting, he took Broadway roles in 1930's *Three's a Crowd* and *The Third Little Show* and worked as a film extra in Hollywood while visiting Los Angeles with his mother and aunt. In 1935 he won his first starring role in a motion picture, appearing in *Gilded Lily*.

MacMurray was generally thought of at the time as a comedic actor; though he was cast opposite stunning sex symbols, he was not considered a heart throb. "Sometimes scenes include people who just say 'Hi' to indicate they're in love. I play those scenes very well," the actor once commented in the *New York Times*. His sheepishness suited the family-oriented film production team at Walt Disney to a tee, and he began playing the role of the benign father in many of their movies, including *The Shaggy Dog* in 1959 and *The Happiest Millionaire*. It seemed only natural that MacMurray would be chosen to portray the dad, aerodynamics engineer Steve Douglas, on *My Three Sons*, which ran from 1960 to 1972. Along with William Frawley, who played the boys' grandfather, and William Demarest in the role of the boys' great-uncle, MacMurray exuded an unaffectedness that made the wholesome series one of network television's most successful. On the occasion of his 80th birthday, three years before his death, the actor told a *Chicago Tribune* reporter, "I was asked the other day how I'd like to be remembered. Fondly." **Sources:** *Chicago Tribune*, November 6, 1991; *New York Times*, November 6, 1991; *Washington Post*, November 6, 1991.

Robert Maxwell

Born Jan Ludwig Hoch, June 10, 1923, in Selo Slatina, Czechoslovakia; died in a drowning accident, November 5, 1991, in the waters off the Canary Islands. Publishing magnate. Flamboyant and headstrong, Robert Maxwell (see *Newsmakers 90*) ruled his kingdom of media conglomerates with an aplomb that surpassed his tycoon contemporaries of the 1980s. When his financial dealings were questioned, Maxwell would simply redirect his efforts and influence. In the much-publicized court case involving his Pergamon Press, for example, Maxwell negotiated an out-of-court settlement with Saul Steinberg, who had accused the publisher of misrepresentation. Maxwell's business savvy helped him regain power at Pergamon and subsequently sell it to a Dutch publisher, Elseviers, for a reported $770 million.

Utilizing similar tactics in the British political arena, Maxwell earned a seat in Parliament in 1964 as a member of the Labour party. Rumors of private business misconduct tarnished his reputation, though, and he was unsuccessful in his 1970 bid for re-election. Thereafter, he was able to exert political influence only via the presses he owned. When asked in 1987 if he would allow the editor of his now-defunct paper, the London *Daily News,* to run an editorial favoring conservative former Prime Minister Margaret Thatcher, Maxwell, a liberal, replied, "He would have my permission to do so. I would have him certified. But he would certainly be able to do it," as reported by the *New York Times.*

Maxwell was born into a Hasidic family in a village on the Czech-Romanian border in 1923, a perilous time to be a Jew in eastern Europe. He was known as Abraham Lajbi Hoch for a brief time, but authorities objected to the name; they evidently approved of Jan Ludvik, a more Christian appellation. After most of his immediate family was shipped off to Nazi concentration camps—where all but two sisters perished—Maxwell went to France at the age of 15 to join the Czech volunteers in anti-Nazi activities. He was awarded a Military Cross by the British in 1945 and eventually left the service with the rank of captain; for the next 20 years, he insisted on being addressed by his military title.

The formation of Maxwell's publishing empire began with his control of the Berlin democratic press for several years after the war and ended with billions of dollars in media holdings that teetered precariously on the edge of debt. Among his papers were the New York *Daily News,* the London *Daily Mirror* and *Daily Record,* and the *European.* He also owned the Macmillan publishing house in New York and the British Printing and Communications Corps, the largest media conglomerate in Great Britain. Maxwell was well known for borrowing against one company to save another. Highly secretive in his business dealings, he reportedly lost $50 million when the London *Daily News* folded; he stated in the *New York Times,* "Never again would I launch a paper and leave it in the hands of the professionals." Though he had groomed two of his four sons, Ian and Kevin, to take over after his death, even their knowledge of Maxwell's finances was limited. Both sons would resign their positions within a few months of their father's death, leaving the future of Maxwell's papers uncertain as of early 1992.

At the time of Maxwell's 1991 death, a controversy was brewing concerning an American author's accusation that Maxwell was directly connected to arms deals with the Mossad, the Israeli secret service. While he had attended the Church of England for a brief time, Maxwell "never forgot his Jewishness," his son recalled, according to the *New York Times.* Maxwell was buried in Mount of Olives of Jerusalem, the world's oldest Jewish cemetery, and Israel's president, Chaim Herzog, spoke at the burial. "Kings and nobles came to his door," eulogized Herzog, as quoted by the *New York Times.* "Many admired him. Many disliked him. But no one remained indifferent to him."

Even after his death, mystery enshrouds the publishing tycoon; the facts about his drowning, for example, are hotly disputed. Some believe he was the victim of a political assassination scheme, while others point to a possible suicide. Maxwell was last seen by the crew of his yacht, Lady Ghislaine, shortly before 4:45 the morning of November 5, 1991. He had made telephone calls the previous evening, and those to whom he spoke described him as sounding "cheerful and normal," reported the London *Times.* The boat docked at about ten o'clock in the morning, and Maxwell's disappearance was not noticed for another several hours. By six o'clock in the evening, Maxwell's unclothed body was found floating in the sea by the Spanish Air Sea Rescue. The official statement indicated that he slipped and fell overboard and was possibly knocked unconscious during the fall. The cause of death was listed as water inhalation. **Sources:** *Chicago Tribune,* November 6, 1991; *Los Angeles Times,* November 6, 1991; *New York Times,* November 6, 1991, November 11, 1991; *Times* (London), November 6, 1991; *Washington Post,* November 6, 1991.

Freddie Mercury

Born Frederick Bulsara, September 5, 1946, in Zanzibar; died of bronchopneumonia resulting from acquired immune deficiency syndrome (AIDS), November 24, 1991, in London, England. Singer. Rock and roll anthems such as "We Are the Champions" and "We Will Rock You" were not intended to be the staple songs of sports arenas, but they remain favorites of sports fans and have immortalized the sound of Queen, the innovative rock group fronted by singer Freddie Mercury. Although AIDS had been ravaging Mercury's health since 1990, Queen—which had its heyday in the 1970s—released the album *Innuendo* in 1991, and it shot to the top of the United Kingdom's pop chart. The single "The Show Must Go On" was accompanied in the music video by a composite of Queen performances, featuring Mercury's campy, fearless persona as the band's centerpiece. "Prancing down multi-layered catwalks in a sequinned, skin-tight jump suit and ballet slippers, preening his way through a myriad of costume changes, and singing in his majestic, slightly frayed tenor voice, Mercury always matched up to the demands of projecting the group's music and image to the four corners of the world's biggest auditoriums," a London *Times* reporter opined.

Mercury's private life was often only slightly less stagey: his 41st birthday party rivaled that of millionaire Malcolm Forbes. He flew his friends to the Spanish island Ibiza via a DC9 and entertained them with flamenco dancing, a fireworks display, and a 20-foot birthday cake carried by six waiters. Yet when it came to the disease that killed him, Mercury kept quiet until the day before he died. He explained that he wished to protect the privacy of his family and friends, but wanted the world to know he had AIDS and encourage the effort to find a cure. Mercury said in a statement on November 23, 1991, that "the time has now come for my friends and fans around the world to know the truth, and I hope that everyone will join with me, my doctors and all those worldwide in the fight against this terrible disease," as quoted by the *Chicago Tribune*.

Though he was born in Zanzibar (now part of Tanzania), Mercury grew up in Great Britain. There he performed with Wreckage, a 1960s blues-based band, before joining Roger Taylor and recruiting Brian May and John Deacon to form Queen, which appeared for the first time at the London College of Estate Management in February of 1971. Peppering their act with an overarching sense of fun and self-parody, Queen developed a distinctive sound comprised of overdubbed vocal harmonies, hard rock choruses, and "occasionally bombastic" lyrics, noted the *Washington Post*.

"Bohemian Rhapsody"—a "mock opera" song—and other hits, including "Killer Queen" and "Crazy Little Thing Called Love," were particularly popular in the mid-1970s, when four of the group's albums made it to Britain's Top 30. The *New York Times* noted that Queen's popularity waned in the 1980s, but explained that the band "was partially vindicated when the hook from 'Under Pressure,' its collaboration with singer David Bowie in 1982, was borrowed by the rapper Vanilla Ice for his hit single 'Ice, Ice Baby.'" While Queen's commercial success lived on a bit longer in the U.K., Mercury, for one, did not believe in anything lasting forever. "I don't expect to make old bones," Mercury once declared, as quoted in the London *Times*. "What's more I really don't care. I certainly don't have any aspirations to live to 70. It would be boring." **Sources:** *Chicago Tribune*, November 25, 1991; *Los Angeles Times*, November 25, 1991; *New York Times*, November 25, 1991; *Times* (London), November 26, 1991; *Washington Post*, November 25, 1991.

Yves Montand

Born Yvo (some sources say Ivo) Livi, October 3, 1921, In Monsummano Alto, Italy; died of a heart attack, November 10, 1991, in Senlis, France. Actor, singer. Although Yves Montand was a native Italian, he became for the world the premier example of what makes the French French. An outspoken political activist and notorious ladies' man, Montand possessed an arresting charm, whether singing and dancing on stage or acting in one of his more than 50 films. He was not an untouchable, elite movie star or a snob in any sense, but a person whose private life seemed to be the rightful property of the French public. Media coverage of his affairs with French singer Edith Piaf and American actress Marilyn Monroe, along with his left-wing political viewpoints, made him a meaty topic of discussion. He nevertheless amassed the general approval of his fellow citizens; one of Montand's fellow Parisians expressed a widely held opinion about the actor when he reflected, "I lost a good neighbor, but France has lost a great gentleman."

Montand's liberal political opinions were taken seriously by a French public "grown cynical about career politicians," reported the London *Times*. The *Times* also recounted Montand's response to a popular call to office: "[U.S. president Ronald] Reagan stood because he was a bad actor. Since I'm a good one, I won't." Instead of following a career in politics, Montand threw himself with great fervor into his acting and singing, maintaining a hectic pace to the very end of his life. "It takes a lot of energy, a reserve of energy," Montand once acknowledged of his show business profession, according to the *Washington Post*. "I came here at 4 o'clock in the afternoon for 9 o'clock tonight. Why? Because I want to be involved in what I'm doing and cut out the rest of my life—income tax, telephone, that sort of thing, even your family."

Montand grew up in a family that fled fascist Italy in 1924, and though his father wanted to immigrate to the United States, they settled in Marseilles, France. At age 11, Montand began working in a pasta factory and, throughout his young adulthood, took odd jobs as a bartender, barber, and—at age 17—amateur nightclub performer. World War II interrupted his career as a performer, but after studying singing and acting, he began working in a Parisian music hall in 1944. Montand soon came to the attention of Edith Piaf, who groomed him for the stage and screen while living with him for several years. In 1946 he appeared with her in *Star Without Light*, his first film.

Montand eventually assembled a one-man touring show that became popular around the world in the late 1950s; he sang such songs as "Les Feuilles Mortes" and the ironic Western tune titled "Dans les Plaines du Far West," which he performed while wearing a cowboy hat. Montand married actress Simone Signoret in 1951, the same year his film career took off, and subsequently spent several years in Hollywood. There he took roles in such films as *My Geisha, Sanctuary, Goodbye Again,* and *Let's Make Love,* featuring Marilyn Monroe, who was married at the time to writer Arthur Miller. Montand and Monroe had a much-publicized—but brief—affair. When cornered by an English reporter for a personal response to her husband's extramarital behavior, Signoret retorted, according to the *New York Times:* "Tell me, do you know who could resist if they took Marilyn Monroe into their arms?"

Montand recalled years later, as quoted by the *Los Angeles Times,* that "it was a wonderful answer for Simone but, for me, oh brother!" "With typical charm and style," noted a *Los Angeles Times* correspondent, "Montand . . . credited the women in his life, especially Signoret, with his success as a performer and human being." Signoret, in fact, introduced Montand to the radical leftist movement of Paris in the 1950s and 1960s. The pair were soon labeled Communists, though Montand himself never

joined the Communist party and even became a critic of Soviet leader Joseph Stalin. "Stalinism is worse than fascism," Montand opined, as quoted by the *Los Angeles Times.* When the Soviet Union invaded Czechoslovakia in 1968, both Montand and Signoret broke all ties with the Communist party.

Though he appeared in 54 films in France between 1962 and 1982, the actor remains best known in the United States for his roles in *Jean de Florette* and *Manon of the Spring,* both of which were made in 1986. Montand became a father for the first time at age 67 when his companion after Signoret's death, Carole Amiel, gave birth to a boy, Valentin, in 1988. It was another mark of France's affection for Montand that the entire country knew—through newspapers and television—when he began to walk his three-year-old to preschool. At the time of his death in 1991, the actor was at work on a film directed by Jean-Jacques Beineix and was also planning a new touring variety show. **Sources:** *Los Angeles Times,* November 10, 1991; *New York Times,* November 10, 1991; *Times* (London), November 11, 1991; *Washington Post,* November 10, 1991.

Joseph Papp

Born Yosl Papirofsky, June 22, 1921, in Brooklyn, NY; died of prostate cancer, October 31, 1991, in New York, NY. Theater producer, director. Broadway producer and director Joseph Papp is best remembered for such long-running, blockbuster musicals as *A Chorus Line*—which had more than six thousand performances—and *Hair.* Using the proceeds from his successful plays, he also produced challenging, edgy productions by new playwrights at his Public Theater as well as free performances of Shakespeare's plays in New York City's Central Park. The son of Polish Jewish immigrants whose first language was Yiddish, Papp was one of the first producers to cast minorities into Shakespeare roles and promote productions by blacks, Hispanics, and Asian-Americans. The rewards for his hard work were enormous: Papp's dramas won three Pulitzer Prizes, six New York Critics Circle awards, and 28 Tonys. Robert Falls, artistic director of the Goodman Theater of Chicago, told the *Chicago Tribune* that Papp "leaves behind him a model of what an American theater should be—in its presentation of a broad range of the classics . . . in its nurturing of contemporary playwrights, and in the passion with which everything is produced."

Papp's ideas about politically and socially vital theater were no doubt formed in part by his involvement in the Federal Theater Project of 1935-39, which funded regional theater in 40 states and sponsored new troupes in New York City, including the Negro Theater Project. Funding was "suspended" by Congress, however, because the project's plays were often critical of the government and were thought to have Communist leanings.

Papp continued his theater career by studying at the Actors Laboratory Theater in Hollywood—which included many of the participants in the Federal Theater Project—using the G.I. education provision he obtained after serving in the army in World War II. Touring the country as an assistant stage manager, Papp eventually ended up in New York City, where he took a job as a television stage manager for the CBS programs *I've Got A Secret* and *Studio One.* On the side, he produced free performances of Shakespeare in a church basement; there he cast the young Colleen Dewhurst as Kate in *The Taming of the Shrew* in 1956. Later, Papp used his own money to fund Shakespeare performances from sets carried on a flatbed truck. In 1956, the truck collapsed in Central Park, and thereafter Papp dubbed his free summer festivals Shakespeare-in-the-Park.

Bringing theater to the masses was apparently not thought of as a patriotic idea, and Papp was brought before the U.S. House Committee on un-American Activities in 1958. While he admitted that he had not been a member of the Communist party for three years, he invoked the Fifth Amendment when asked to provide the names of party sympathizers. For defying the committee, Papp was fired from his CBS job, but regained the position after litigation. According to the *New York Times*, the producer once said, "Theater is a social force, not just an entertainment" and further declared that his goal was to "radicalize the environment" of the theater.

In 1967, Papp was granted permission by the New York City council to occupy the soon-to-be-demolished Astor Library on the lower east side. He transformed the shabby locale into the Public Theater, a six-auditorium complex—the largest of its type in the United States—that would see many world premieres of dramas in Papp's lifetime. The mid-1970s proved to be a tremendously creative time for Papp; while *A Chorus Line* was in the works, he took on management of the Lincoln Center and retained his duties at the Public Theater and Shakespeare Festival. At this point, many agreed that Joseph Papp was the most important person in New York City theater. Yet the Lincoln Center resisted

Papp's magic touch, and bureaucratic difficulties pushed him to resign in his fourth season there, even though he had produced such successful plays as *The Threepenny Opera, The Cherry Orchard,* and *Agamemnon.*

Papp experienced financial troubles in the late 1980s and after *A Chorus Line* closed he had to use the Public Theater's endowment to keep the gears oiled. His announcement in 1987 that he intended to have all 36 of Shakespeare's plays performed by 1993 was met with indifference, as were many of the plays themselves, despite the fact that such movie stars as Michelle Pfeiffer and Morgan Freeman were cast in them. Though the productions were given considerable exposure by the media, reviews were often mixed.

In May of 1990, with an undisclosed illness adding to his personal woes, Papp announced a reorganization plan, which included naming JoAnne Akalaitis his successor as artistic director of the Shakespeare Festival. At Papp's funeral on November 1st of the following year, Akalaitis was joined by New York mayor David Dinkins as well as numerous playwrights and actors, including Kevin Kline, Mandy Patinkin, and Meryl Streep. They offered their tender thoughts about Papp, whose advice had helped many performers in their early careers. **Sources:** *Chicago Tribune,* November 1, 1991; *Los Angeles Times,* November 1, 1991; *New York Times,* November 2, 1991; *Times* (London), November 2, 1991; *Washington Post,* November 1, 1991.

Gene Roddenberry

Born Eugene Wesley Roddenberry, August 19, 1921, in El Paso, TX; died of a heart attack, October 24, 1991, in Los Angeles, CA. Creator of *Star Trek.* Gene Roddenberry took the concept of television Westerns, turned it inside out, and created an innovative science fiction series that amassed a huge following. Retaining its popularity in syndication in the 1990s, *Star Trek* centers around a multicultural group from a United Nations-type organization that journeys into the future, confronting such issues as imperialism, war, diplomacy, and intergalactic sexual relations. When the show—which exhibited the pioneer spirit featured in Westerns—was almost canceled in 1968, nearly one million letters from fans poured into the offices of NBC-TV, winning the series another season. While it was not originally a long-running success story, *Star Trek* has spawned dozens of fan clubs, a Saturday morning cartoon version, comic books and novelizations, six movies, and a spin-off television series, *Star Trek: The Next Generation*, whose following rivals that of the first. Another spin-off is scheduled for 1992 and will be a "prequel" to *The Next Generation*.

The man behind the *Star Trek* industry was responsible for its optimistic vision of the future: equitable, peace-loving, yet adventurous. Daniel Masden, the president of Star Trek: The Official Fan Club, told the *Los Angeles Times* that Roddenberry "exemplified everything *Star Trek* was about, his philosophy of all races, colors and creeds working together in peace in the future where technology has not taken over man but is utilized by man. And I think people loved the idea of being able to explore the universe in his vast starship." Behind this formidable entertainment legend is a warm and friendly person beloved by his coworkers. According to *People*, George Takei, who played Sulu in the original series and the Star Trek movies, said, "He was huge and he'd grab you in his big, bearlike embrace." The futuristic nature of Roddenberry's work ensures that he will never be forgotten: he will always be associated with a hopeful outlook for the human race.

Gene Roddenberry grew up in a typical, middle-class American home; his mother was a housewife, his father was a police officer, and the family regularly attended church. Roddenberry, too, became a police officer later in life, but as far as religion was concerned, he was an agnostic, as reflected in the rationalist universe of Star Trek. Before joining the police force, Roddenberry attended the University of Miami, where he interrupted his studies to join the Air Force after the Japanese attack on Pearl Harbor in 1941. He was sent on bombing missions over the South Pacific and was eventually awarded the Distinguished Flying Cross and the Air Medal. Working a short stint as a commercial pilot when he returned to the United States, Roddenberry wrote film and television scripts in his spare time during the late 1940s and early 1950s. Among his first sales were scripts for such series as *Dragnet* and *Naked City* and the pilot episode for *The Lieutenant*.

Though many of the talented performers involved in *Star Trek* wondered at its success, the series' appeal no doubt resulted from its simple premise of the popular adventure series format applied in a futuristic setting. At the time of the show's premiere, William Shatner, the brave and amorous Captain Kirk of the Starship Enterprise in the original series and successive movies, noted in the London *Times*, "We know the ingredients and we hope they will work." The crucial element of the show's success

turned out to be Roddenberry's special vision of the future, which prompted him to fight for a female in the role of second-in-command to Kirk, a battle that he ultimately lost.

Star Trek lasted for 79 episodes, and each show was made for a mere $186,000, an unheard-of figure in the television industry of the 1990s. While some viewers worry that the message of *Star Trek* will change with Roddenberry's passing, Rick Berman, the executive producer of *Star Trek: The Next Generation*, declared in the *Los Angeles Times*, "What [Roddenberry] created during his lifetime is certainly going to continue. His death is not going to in any way stop the flow of his vision." **Sources:** *Los Angeles Times*, October 26, 1991; *People*, November 11, 1991; *Times* (London), October 26, 1991.

Rob Tyner

Born Robert Derminer, c. 1945; died of a heart attack, September 17, 1991, in Royal Oak, MI. Rock singer. Rob Tyner was the lead singer for the group MC5 (originally the Motor City Five), which was formed in the late 1960s and is considered one of the inspirations for the punk rock movement of the 1970s. The MC5's music, noted the *New York Times*, was composed of "anarchic live concerts of music with a pounding beat, distorted guitars and radical exhortations delivered in Mr. Tyner's howling voice." In 1968 the band played at the Democratic National Convention in Chicago to raise money for the White Panthers, a revolutionary political group that called for total freedom and the abolition of a monetary system. The MC5's one hit, "Kick Out the Jams," released by Elektra Records, received little radio airtime because of complaints about its obscene lyrics; the group's members, in fact, were arrested on obscenity charges in 1969, and the band was subsequently dropped by Elektra. Still, *Kick Out the Jams* made it to the Top 30, and the MC5 would record for Atlantic Records before disbanding in 1972.

The MC5's leftist political leanings were strengthened by the man who became their patron and mentor, poet/musician John Sinclair. He took on the role of the band's manager when, unable to compete as hardcore rock and rollers in the heyday of the more rhythm and blues-oriented Motown music, they found themselves in dire financial straits. Although Sinclair provided the band with some professional guidance, the MC5 continued to face problems with local club owners, who frowned upon their onstage antics. The group once burned an

American flag at the Grande Ballroom, the same place they later recorded the songs for their first album, *Kick Out the Jams.* Two other LPs released in the early 1970s, *Back in the U.S.A.* and *High Time,* would fail to win the popularity of the first. Nevertheless, the band's daring, raucous music serves as an accurate rendering of the tumultuous Detroit riots of the 1960s and a bold statement against censorship.

After the MC5's 1972 breakup, vocalist Tyner worked with some local bands. He released a solo album, *Blood Brothers,* in 1990, which received little airplay but garnered some "critical praise," reported the *Chicago Tribune.* On September 17, 1991, Tyner was found unconscious in his car near his home in the Detroit suburb of Berkley and was declared dead of a heart attack 45 minutes after arriving at Beaumont Hospital. **Sources:** *Chicago Tribune,* September 20, 1991; *Los Angeles Times,* September 22, 1991; *New York Times,* September 20, 1991; *Washington Post,* September 21, 1991.

Dottie West

Born Dorothy Marie Marsh, October 11, 1932, in McMinnville, TN; died of injuries sustained in an auto accident, September 5, 1991. Singer. Country music legend Dottie West died in a car accident on her way to a performance at the Grand Ole Opry. Her car had broken down and she was picked up by a businessman who lost control of his vehicle while driving 30 miles an hour over the posted speed limit. Frantic about getting to the Opry on time, she had urged him to speed. West, in fact, had always shown such determination throughout her singing career and with her resolve, she helped clear the way for other women performers to become prominent in the country music industry. When West first began performing, there were few gigging women country singers, and she told the *Washington Post* that "it was tough, especially to work on the road. I don't think they felt girl singers sold tickets. [Booking agents] felt people only bought tickets to hear the male singers, although Kitty Wells, Jean Shepard, and Patsy Cline had been successful already . . . . They put a package [show] together . . . and they needed a skirt on the show. When I hit that stage, I went for the applause just as hard as the guys did."

In her trademark high-heeled boots, tight jeans, and low-cut blouses, West capitalized on her femininity without being raunchy. The singer, in fact, initially turned down a duet with Kris Kristofferson called "Help Me Make It Through the Night" because she thought the lyrics were too suggestive. Though sometimes criticized for her apparel by hard-core country fans who accused her of selling out, West merely replied that times were changing and she was going to change with them. Her best-known songs were duets, and in the late 1970s she recorded singles with Kenny Rogers, including "Every Time Two Fools Collide," and "What Are We Doin' in Love." The *Los Angeles Times* quoted Rogers on the occasion of West's death: "While some performers sang words, she sang emotions." Among her accomplishments, West was the first woman to win a country Grammy. Her untimely death signaled the end of a groundbreaking career that furthered the interests of women in country music.

West's personal life was stormy at times. In 1990 she encountered terrible financial difficulties and, owing more than one million dollars on her house and other holdings, she was forced to declare bankruptcy. The Internal Revenue Service auctioned off her belongings in 1991 at the annual Country Music Fan Fair. In addition, she was divorced from Bill West, the father of her four children and husband of 20 years, in 1969 and subsequently had two other unsuccessful marriages to younger men. "Older men have been chasing around young girls for years," West once observed in the *Los Angeles Times,* "so it should be OK for women to be involved with younger guys."

West grew up in a poor family and, as the oldest of 12 children, she worked in sugar cane fields and cooked for her large family to help make ends meet. From the start she was determined to be successful in show business and put herself through music school at Tennessee Technological University. Though later the demands of working on the road sometimes competed with her role as a mother, the struggle paid off with recording contracts in the late 1960s. West not only boosted the case for women country singers—Tammy Wynette told the *Chicago Tribune* that "she paved the way for so many of us"—but she also discovered singer Larry Gatlin because of a tape he sent her. West mailed him a one-way ticket to Nashville, and Gatlin believed, according to the *Chicago Tribune,* that "if it had not been for Dorothy Marie [West], Larry [Gatlin] would've probably been a bad lawyer somewhere in Houston." **Sources:** *Chicago Tribune,* September 5, 1991; *Los Angeles Times,* September 5, 1991; *New York Times,* September 5, 1991; *Washington Post,* September 5, 1991.

1992 Nationality Index

This index lists newsmakers alphabetically under their respective nationalities. Indexes in soft-bound issues allow access to the current year's entries; indexes in annual hardbound volumes are cumulative, covering the entire *Newsmakers* series.

Listee names are followed by a year and issue number; thus **1988:3** indicates that an entry on that individual appears in both 1988, Issue 3 and the 1988 cumulation. For access to news-makers appearing earlier than the current softbound issue, see the previous year's cumulation.

1992 Occupation Index

This index lists newsmakers by their occupations or fields of primary activity. Indexes in softbound issues allow access to the current year's entries; indexes in annual hardbound volumes are cumulative, covering the entire *Newsmakers* series.

Listee names are followed by a year and issue number; thus **1988**:3 indicates that an entry on that individual appears in both 1988, Issue 3 and the 1988 cumulation. For access to newsmakers appearing earlier than the current softbound issue, see the previous year's cumulation.

Perry, Harold A.
  Obituary **1992**:1

SCIENCE
  Allen, John **1992**:1
  Irwin, James
    Obituary **1992**:1
  Kessler, David **1992**:1
  Kornberg, Arthur **1992**:1
  LeVay, Simon **1992**:2

SOCIAL ISSUES
  Bradshaw, John **1992**:1
  Dees, Morris **1992**:1
  Humphry, Derek **1992**:2
  Ireland, Patricia **1992**:2
  Kozol, Jonathan **1992**:1
  LeVay, Simon **1992**:2
  Martinez, Bob **1992**:1
  Suu Kyi, Aung San **1992**:2
  Thomas, Clarence **1992**:2

SPORTS
  Bonilla, Bobby **1992**:2
  Brown, Paul
    Obituary **1992**:1
  Dravecky, Dave **1992**:1
  Durocher, Leo
    Obituary **1992**:2
  Lindros, Eric **1992**:1
  O'Neal, Shaquille **1992**:1
  Pippen, Scottie **1992**:2
  Roberts, Steven K. **1992**:1
  Sanders, Barry **1992**:1
  Shula, Don **1992**:2

TECHNOLOGY
  Fender, Leo
    Obituary **1992**:1
  Irwin, James
    Obituary **1992**:1
  Roberts, Steven K. **1992**:1

TELEVISION
  Arledge, Roone **1992**:2
  Bono, Sonny **1992**:2
  Bradshaw, John **1992**:1
  Caulfield, Joan
    Obituary **1992**:1
  Convy, Bert
    Obituary **1992**:1
  Davis, Geena **1992**:1
  Dewhurst, Colleen
    Obituary **1992**:2
  Ford, Tennessee Ernie
    Obituary **1992**:2
  Foxx, Redd
    Obituary **1992**:2
  Franciscus, James
    Obituary **1992**:1
  Gifford, Kathie Lee **1992**:2
  Graham, Billy **1992**:1
  Grant, Rodney A. **1992**:1
  Henson, Brian **1992**:1
  Landon, Michael
    Obituary **1992**:1
  Lewis, Richard **1992**:1
  MacMurray, Fred
    Obituary **1992**:2
  Mantegna, Joe **1992**:1
  Martin, Steve **1992**:2
  Matlin, Marlee **1992**:2
  Queen Latifah **1992**:2
  Reasoner, Harry
    Obituary **1992**:1
  Remick, Lee
    Obituary **1992**:1
  Roddenberry, Gene
    Obituary **1992**:2
  Stewart, Martha **1992**:1
  Streisand, Barbra **1992**:2
  Totenberg, Nina **1992**:2

THEATER
  Ashcroft, Peggy
    Obituary **1992**:1

Barry, Lynda **1992**:1
Bening, Annette **1992**:1
Branagh, Kenneth **1992**:2
Caulfield, Joan
  Obituary **1992**:1
Convy, Bert
  Obituary **1992**:1
Dewhurst, Colleen
  Obituary **1992**:2
Mantegna, Joe **1992**:1
Montand, Yves
  Obituary **1992**:2
Papp, Joseph
  Obituary **1992**:2
Penn & Teller **1992**:1
Reeves, Keanu **1992**:1
Streisand, Barbra **1992**:2

WRITING
  Barry, Lynda **1992**:1
  Bradshaw, John **1992**:1
  Branagh, Kenneth **1992**:2
  Brown, Tina **1992**:1
  Bush, Millie **1992**:1
  Dershowitz, Alan **1992**:1
  Geisel, Theodor
    Obituary **1992**:2
  Graham, Billy **1992**:1
  Humphry, Derek **1992**:2
  Kozol, Jonathan **1992**:1
  Nemerov, Howard
    Obituary **1992**:1
  Phillips, Julia **1992**:1
  Roberts, Steven K. **1992**:1
  Roddenberry, Gene
    Obituary **1992**:2
  Singer, Isaac Bashevis
    Obituary **1992**:1
  Stewart, Martha **1992**:1
  Thompson, Hunter S. **1992**:1
  Totenberg, Nina **1992**:2

1992 Subject Index

This index lists newsmakers by subjects, company names, products, organizations, issues, awards, and professional specialties. Indexes in softbound issues allow access to the current year's entries; indexes in annual hardbound volumes are cumulative, covering the entire *Newsmakers* series.

Listee names are followed by a year and issue number; thus **1988**:3 indicates that an entry on that individual appears in both 1988, Issue 3 and the 1988 cumulation. For access to newsmakers appearing earlier than the current softbound issue, see the previous year's cumulation.

Cumulative Newsmakers Index

This index lists all entries included in the *Newsmakers* series.

Listee names are followed by a year and issue number; thus **1988**:3 indicates that an entry appears in both 1988, Issue 3 and the 1988 cumulation.